DOSTOEVSKY'S UNDERGROUND MAN
IN RUSSIAN LITERATURE

SLAVISTISCHE DRUKKEN EN HERDRUKKEN

UITGEGEVEN DOOR

C. H. VAN SCHOONEVELD

HOOGLERAAR TE LEIDEN

XV

DOSTOEVSKY'S UNDERGROUND MAN IN RUSSIAN LITERATURE

BY

ROBERT LOUIS JACKSON

MOUTON & CO · 1958 · 'S-GRAVENHAGE

SLAVISTIC PRINTINGS AND REPRINTINGS

EDITED BY

C. H. VAN SCHOONEVELD

LEIDEN UNIVERSITY

XV

PRINTED IN THE NETHERLANDS BY
MOUTON & CO, PRINTERS, THE HAGUE

"El sueño de la razón produce monstruos."

Francisco Goya y Lucientes
Capricho No. 43.

PREFATORY NOTE

This book analyzes the impact of Dostoevsky's *Notes from the Underground* (1864) and its protagonist, the Underground Man, upon Russian literature. It is concerned with the different ways in which Russian writers responded to *Notes from the Underground*, with the whole complex of "underground" psychology, philosophy, imagery, variously combined and modified, that makes it possible to speak of a body of prose works as literature of the "underground". A group of prose works drawn from three general periods in Russian literature — the 1880's, 1900-1917, 1917-1936 — graphically illustrates the continuous life in Russian literature of the basic image of the Underground Man and of the themes and motifs of *Notes from the Underground*. The direction of this study has been intensive, rather than extensive; no attempt has been made to provide an exhaustive survey of every manifestation and ramification of the "underground" in Russian literature. The first three chapters, devoted to *Notes from the Underground*, provide a background for this study.

The basic assumption of this work is that the great impact of Dostoevsky on Russian literature was due not alone to the great power of his art, but to the continuing urgency of the problems he posed in his works. These problems, centering on the relations between the individual and society, have lost none of their relevance today, not only in Russia but also in the West.

It is for Russia, however, that *Notes from the Underground* has special significance. It is not accidental that the "underground" portrait of man as morally and spiritually crippled, as irrational, as distorted in his craving for freedom, nihilistic in his rebellion, should have been produced in a country which traditionally denied to the individual the right even to recognition. The cause of the wild, chaotic, often criminal outbursts of the convict in prison, Dostoevsky wrote in *Notes from the House of the Dead* (1862), is perhaps the anguished, hysterical manifestation of individuality, the instinctive yearning to be oneself, the desire to express oneself, one's humiliated personality, a desire which suddenly takes shape and reaches the pitch of malice, of madness, of the eclipse of reason, of fits, of convulsions. Thus, perhaps, a person buried alive in a coffin and awakening in it, would thrust at the cover and try to throw it off, although, of course, reason might convince him that all his efforts were in vain. But the whole point here is that this is not a question of reason: it is a question of convulsions.

The idea expressed here is the dynamic for "underground" rebellion in *Notes from the Underground* and in the literature of the "underground". Society — indeed life itself — is a prison; it is in this conception that *Notes from the Underground* and the literature of the "underground" seeks its justification. Vyacheslav Ivanov in his study on Dostoevsky has called *Notes from the Underground* "a devastating criticism of present-day social relations . . .". The literature of the "underground" in both pre-revolutionary and post-revolutionary periods constitutes an equally devastating criticism. Sometimes the criticism is direct; an implicit but perhaps more terrible indictment is contained in the whole gallery of anguished human beings, cripples, derelicts and even monstrosities that appear in the literature of the "underground".

"¡Quien lo creyera!" ("Who would have believed it!") exclaims Goya in the title to his Capricho No. 62, depicting two monsters of depravity locked in struggle, the air around them filled with demons. As credible, and as incredible, is the world of *Notes from the Underground* and the literature that falls under its shadow. Yet Dostoevsky, who disclosed the "underground" of the soul, also helped inspire many thinkers and writers with a religious faith and an impassioned messianism. But it is Dostoevsky's "paradoxicalist", the Underground Man, rather than his saintly epileptic Prince Myshkin who is the hero of these times. This book is an inquiry into the nature of this hero as he presents himself in Russian literature.

In an earlier version, "Dostoevsky's Underground Man in Russian Literature" was a dissertation presented at the University of California, Berkeley. I would like to express my warm thanks to Professor Wacław Lednicki, Chairman of the Department of Slavic Languages and Literatures there, for his creative interest in this study and for his advice; Professors Gleb Struve and Oleg A. Maslenikov, of the University of California, for their reading of the original study and for suggestions; Professors René Wellek and Richard Burgi, of Yale University, for reading the manuscript and for their comments. I am grateful to Dr. Joshua Kunitz for his generous interest in this study. I also wish to thank the American Council of Learned Societies for a fellowship under which I began work on this book; Mr. R. Gordon Wasson, the chairman, and the members of the Committee for the Promotion of Advanced Slavic Cultural Studies, who made possible its publication. Finally, I wish to thank my wife for her keen interest in, and patience with, the "underground".

A transliteration system is used for the formal references to Russian names and works in the footnotes and bibliography. For the text and for the body of the footnotes, a transcription system based on transliteration is used, except in quotations from an English translation.

Yale University, 1957   ROBERT LOUIS JACKSON

TABLE OF CONTENTS

INTRODUCTION

Few works in modern European literature are as absorbing, elusive and disturbing as Dostoevsky's *Notes from the Underground* (*Zapiski iz podpolya,* 1864). It is the revelation of an "underground" in man without controls of reason or ethics, a darkness where suffering becomes malignant pleasure and humiliation is transmuted into rage and hate. The Underground Man will not relinquish his agony: it is his self-laceration and self-justification, his age at the "laws of nature" which have been humiliating him more than anything else in his life.

Kierkegaard in *The Sickness Unto Death* (1849) analyzed such a rage of humiliation when he wrote of the "despairer" who, offended by inescapable pain and humiliation, takes occasion to be offended at the whole of existence and "rages most of all at the thought that eternity might get it into its head to take his misery from him!" Not surprisingly does Kierkegaard remark that "this sort of despair is seldom seen in the world, such figures generally are met with only in the works of poets, that is to say, of real poets who always lend their characters this 'demonaic ideality' (taking this word in the purely Greek sense)". Such a "poet", of course, is Dostoevsky, the creator of the Underground Man. In this living image of solitude and despair, Dostoevsky reaffirms the absolute value and integrity of the single, separate individual; in the pathos of suffering, doubt and despair Dostoevsky finds the essence of man's identity.

This reaffirmation of the intrinsic worth of the individual is one of the major links between Dostoevsky and Kierkegaard: both, in essence, stand with what Hegel termed the "Unhappy Consciousness". The Underground Man's attack against "twice two is four" ("Twice two is four is no longer life, gentlemen, but the beginning of death") is an attack against a rationalistic metaphysics which seeks the salvation of the individual through his subordination to, and integration with, an all-embracive social or world order.

The appearance of *Notes from the Underground* marks the birth of the self-conscious anti-hero in Russian literature. In the figure of the Underground Man, alienated consciousness becomes aware of its alienation and adopts a consciously belligerent posture. The revolt of the Underground Man's entire life is one continuous attempt to make impotence, against an overpowering and humiliating reality. The Underground Man's entire life is one continuous attempt to make contact with the world and with himself; isolated, unable to act, he is a social zero. Society and its reformers and philosophers have already negated him. He is the negation of the negation. He is an anti-hero. "In a novel a hero is necessary," remarks the Underground Man at the conclusion of his "notes", "whereas here all the features for the anti-hero have been *deliberately* gathered, and mainly, all this is certain to produce an exceedingly unpleasant impression, because we are all divorced from life, all crippled, each of us, more or less". In the appearance of the anti-hero Dostoevsky announces the assault on society of malignant individualism; in the despairing self-defense of alienated consciousness Dostoevsky recognizes the disfiguration and final disintegration of that consciousness.

Notes from the Underground belongs to the modern European atmosphere. In its irrationalist spirit, its critique of reason, science and utopian socialism, its scepticism over man and history, its offended idealism, its nihilistic defense of the individual and despairing confession of impotence and error, its anxieties and indecisions, *Notes from the Underground* is a work of modern consciousness. The catastrophe of two world wars, the nightmare of concentration camps, political conformity and violent economic distress, the increasing sense of alienation that the individual experiences in mass culture, the threat of atomic annihilation have shaken the very foundations of a rational view of the world. The affirmers and believers are on the defensive. "In a word, you can say anything you like about world history, anything that could enter the head of the most disordered imagination. Only one thing you cannot possibly say," remarks the Underground Man, "that it is sensible. You would choke on the first word."

"Nihilism stands at the door: whence comes this uncanniest of all quests?" asks Nietzsche in *The Will to power (Der Wille zur Macht,* 1888). "Scepticism towards morality is what is decisive. The downfall of the moral interpretation of the world . . . leads to nihilism. 'Everything is without meaning.'" *Notes from the Underground* takes its place along with Nietzsche's *The Will to Power* as one of the ominous portents in the

19th century of that "advent of nihilism" which Nietzsche predicted would undermine the foundations of Western culture. "Scepticism and the sceptical view are killing everything, even the very view itself in the final analysis . . .", Dostoevsky wrote in a subscription prospectus to his journal *Time* (*Vremya*) 1862. "Where are my primary causes on which I could rest, where are my foundations?" the Underground Man asks as he is rendered impotent by the *perpetuum mobile* of his thinking. "There are no *foundations* to our society, no principles to live out their efficacy, because there has been no life even," Dostoevsky wrote a decade later in some notes on his novel *Raw Youth* (*Podrostok*, 1876). "A colossal eruption and everything is cracking, falling, being negated as though it had not existed. And not only externally, as in the West, but internally, morally."

Notes from the Underground exposes this calamity; but it is even more a manifestation of it. To experience *Notes from the Underground* is to experience the mad vertigo of "all is permissible", the sudden collapse of all foundations brought about by the destruction of reason, the questioning of all values, the unseating of moral absolutes, the discrediting of idealism. If there is any work which leaves man boundless freedom of choice, and imposes a tremendous responsibility for that choice, it is *Notes from the Underground*.

Yet it is in this very confrontation of man with his terrifying freedom that much of modern existentialism finds the stark reality of human experience and the only possible point of departure for a responsible and creative orientation to life. Sartre in *L'existentialisme est un humanisme* (1946) cites the view of Ivan Karamazov — if God doesn't exist, all is permissible — and remarks: „C'est là le point de départ de l'existentialisme."

Especially when he is seen as a prototype for a modern existentialist hero, the Underground Man acquires a tragically heroic and symbolic status. Alone in his solitude, an outcast, rejecting the blind commonplace "man of action", the Underground Man faces the "last wall"; he is no longer seduced by idealistic, romantic or humanistic faith in man, reason or socialism; he is painfully conscious of the senselessness of history and of the unreasonable nature of the world for man. Yet he maintains a rebellious posture before the "stone wall" and the "laws of nature"; he transforms his humiliation into "perpetual malice", the crisis of his existence into a permanent crisis. He is in permanent rebellion. This is his tragic status — his metaphysical misery and his metaphysical freedom.

It is but a step from the Underground Man with his despairing lucidity to the "absurd" man of Albert Camus' *Myth of Sisyphus* (*Le mythe de Sisyphe*, 1942). A comparison of *Myth of Sisyphus* and *Notes from the Underground* shows how remarkably Dostoevsky foreshadowed some of the developments in modern existentialist thought.

The Underground Man is a protean type. In his extraordinary moral and psychological complexity, the Underground Man could prefigure Kafka's anonymous, anxiety-ridden hero, desperately rushing about the "burrow" of his existence in search of security; Gide's rebellious Adam, Michel (*L'Immoraliste*, 1902) who overthrows all restraints only in the end to struggle with his "objectless liberty"; Hermann Hesse's "outsider" (*Der Steppenwolf*, 1927), half savage yet with a "longing for goodness", who rages against the "toneless, flat, normal and sterile life" and whose worst nightmare is "confinement in barracks"; the hero of Georges Duhamel's Salavin cycle; Sartre's estranged, morosely self-loving and savagely impotent destroyer, Paul Hilbert ("Erostrate", 1947), who for 33 years has been beating his head resentfully against closed doors on which are written: "No entrance if not a humanist." The Underground Man makes a strange reappearance in W.N.T. Barbellion, that pitiful and mediocre hero of his own "confession" (*The Diary of a Disappointed Man*, 1919), a "ridiculous coxcomb", a "little, skulking, sharp-witted ferret" in whom "colossal egotism is driven underground", a man who has always felt "an alien in this life, a refugee by reason of some prenatal extradition".

The Underground Man, with his psychological complexity, his blinding paradoxes, his self-accusations and penetrating ironies, seems to loom behind the figure of Camus' Jean-Baptiste Clamence in *The Fall* (*La Chute*, 1956). This egotist and philosopher-immoralist would like to "change lives" but cannot; in consequence he tastes the "double enjoyment" of his nature and of his "charming repentance"; but in his extraordinary lucidity Jean-Baptiste Clamence, like the Underground Man, makes an acute analysis of his time. The final pages of *The Fall* disclose the hero's dialectic; these pages might well serve as an introduction to the complex intentions of Dostoevsky in *Notes from the Underground*.

Notes from the Underground and its protagonist the Underground Man played an important role in Russian literature in the half century following Dostoevsky's death (1881). This role cannot, of course, be entirely separated from that of Dostoevsky's works as a whole. The major problems posed in *Notes from the Underground*, its themes and motifs are elaborated upon in Dostoevsky's great novels; the Underground Man himself is a prototype for many of Dostoevsky's later heroes.

Nevertheless, *Notes from the Underground* occupies a special position in Dostoevsky's works. It is, perhaps, the most starkly frank confession of Dostoevsky — a confession of his tragic vision of man, of his despair before that vision. Never again does despair so master Dostoevsky. In later novels a powerful positive moral-religious force counters the evil Dostoevsky finds in man. But in *Notes from the Underground* this force does not find direct expression.

It was, in part, the mood of discord, anxiety and despair that pervades *Notes from the Underground* which attracted many writers. They, too, were dealing with the individual at the edge of an abyss. The themes and motifs of *Notes from the Underground,* the personality and ideas of its protagonist, find echoes throughout the late 19th and 20th centuries in works centered on the problems of the alienated individual, desperately seeking a pivot within himself, desperately trying to formulate a social and philosophical outlook that would buttress his position in a hostile world. The irrationalist resolution of these problems in *Notes from the Underground* is prophetic of the manner in which the crisis of the individual in society would be formulated.

The manner in which Russian writers apprehended *Notes from the Underground* varied according to the moods of the period. Writers like M. N. Albov (1851-1911) and V. M. Garshin (1855-1888) — two popular writers of the 1880's — found in *Notes from the Underground* echoes of their own disillusionment and distress over the moral disintegration, opportunism and philistinism that characterized much of the 1880's. But their orientation to life, though pessimistic, is not dominated by the nihilistic spirit of "underground" rebellion.

Albov and Garshin are far from such writers of the pre-revolutionary period as L. Andreev (1871-1919), F. Sologub (1863-1927) and M. P. Artsybashev (1879-1927) who in many of their works were attracted by the cynicism and nihilism of the "underground". A minor critic, A. Zakrzhevsky, strikes the keynote of much of this literature in his book *The Underground (Podpole,* 1911):

The underground! How much that is understandable, intimate, contemporary is concealed in that word! Whose soul has not experienced the torment of the underground and its joy! Whose life under the crushing burden of a cross, under the yoke of gnawing, intoxicating laceration has not sunk into those dark cellars of grey anguish and dumb malice and incoherent, violent curses?! The underground! It is in us;

it has grown many times into our soul and entangled it with a sticky spider's web of nightmarish loneliness and dry, burning sobbing.

This "underground" that Zakrzhevsky so melodramatically glorifies is the same "underground" that enchanted more sensitive critics and philosophers like V. Rozanov and Lev Shestov.

After the revolution of 1917, writers responded with a different emphasis to *Notes from the Underground*. Many writers, sensitive to the fate of the individual in the new period, variously utilize the anti-rationalist and anti-socialist themes and motifs of *Notes from the Under-ground* to defend the individual and to express their alarm over trends towards conformity. The non-conformist irrational "underground" man becomes the medium of the author's protest.

At the same time, the "underground" man does not lose his complex and ambiguous character. Writers in this period recognize in him a dangerous ally. The egotistical hero of the "underground", however much he lends himself to the role of social critic, in the end stands only for himself. It is Maksim Gorky (1868-1936) who most sharply condemns the "underground" type and who strongly influence the official Soviet view on Dostoevsky as well as that of a number of writers.

The role of *Notes from the Underground* in Russian literature is as complex and many-sided as its meanings. The literature of the "underground" is a commentary not only upon some of the darker sides of Russian life, but upon *Notes from the Underground* itself, a work which, like the enchanted portrait of Gogol's story, continues to exercise a strange power of fascination.

CHAPTER I

NOTES FROM THE UNDERGROUND: ORIGINS

> Inertia! Oh, nature! People are alone on earth—this
> is the misfortune! "Is there a living man in the field"
> cries the legendary Russian hero. I also, not a hero,
> cry out and no one answers. They say the sun brings
> life to the universe. The sun will rise and—look at
> it, is it not dead? Everything is dead and corpses
> are everywhere. People are alone, and around them
> silence—this is the earth! "People, love one another!"
> Who said that? Whose commandment is that?
>
> The hero of Dostoevsky's *A Meek One*

Notes from the Underground was first published in Dostoevsky's journal
Epoch (Epokha) in 1864. The immediate conditions surrounding the
writing of *Notes from the Underground* were particularly difficult for
Dostoevsky and undoubtedly intensified the nervous, exacerbated tone
of his work. His consumptive wife was dying. Marya Dmitrievna, he
writes V. D. Konstant on January 10, 1864, "has death on her mind
every minute: she grieves and despairs. . . . Her chest is bad and she
has dried up like a match. Horror! It is painful and difficult to watch."[1]
A month later Dostoevsky writes his brother Mikhail that he has nothing
ready for the first issue of *Epoch,* but that he will try to get something in.
He has been "ill" for two weeks "and lately it has been getting worse".
He has had "two attacks" and is suffering from hemorrhoids which have
"attacked the bladder". He can neither "stand nor sit."[2] Part I of *Notes
from the Underground,* "The Underground", was published in *Epoch*
at the end of March, and opens with the lines: "I am a sick man*** I
am a spiteful man. I am a repellent man."

Part II of *Notes from the Underground,* "A Novelette—Apropos of
Wet Snow", was written under increasingly difficult conditions. "Life
is gloomy, my health is weaker, my wife is really dying . . . my nerves

---

[1] Dostoevskij, *Pis'ma,* ed. A. S. Dolinin (Moscow-Leningrad, 1928-1934), I, No.
185, p. 345.
[2] *Ibid.,* I, No. 188, p. 347.

are unstrung," he writes his brother April 5. "I need air, motion, but there is no time or place to walk (filth)." [3]

A few days later he writes his brother concerning *Notes from the Underground*:

... I don't know what will come of it; perhaps it will be trash, but personally I place great hopes on it. It will be a strong and frank piece; it will be truth. Although it may be poor I dare say, still it will have an impact. I am sure. But perhaps it will come out very fine. [4]

Notes from the Underground has the character of a diary or confession. As a literary form, it stands somewhere between the conversational-feuilleton style of Dostoevsky's early journalism ("Petersburg Chronicle", 1847), his journalism of the 1860's, his *Diary of a Writer* (*Dnevnik pisatelya*) which he began in the 1870's, and those of his novels and stories which are told in the first person, for example, "White Nights" ("Belye Nochi," 1848) and *Raw Youth* (*Podrostok*, 1875). The Underground Man analyzes his feelings and thoughts, and polemicizes with his interlocutors in a long monologue — Part I, and sets down his reminiscences in Part II, where he directly addresses his readers from time to time. "But I am writing for myself alone," the Underground Man insists, "and once and for all I declare that even if I write as though addressing readers, this is solely for show, because it is easier for me to write in this manner. This is only a form, only an empty form ..." [5]

The Underground Man—short and emaciated—is a retired civil servant of minor rank who, on inheriting 6,000 rubles from a distant relative, has settled permanently in his "corner", a "filthy, disgusting" room on the outskirts of Petersburg. He knows that the Petersburg climate is injurious to his health and that it is very expensive for a man of his small means to live in Petersburg, but he stubbornly and maliciously refuses to leave; and then again, he knows it "really makes absolutely no difference" whether he leaves or not.

He is alone in his "underground" and is writing down his recollections; they weigh upon him; and perhaps, he thinks, by writing them down he will "really obtain relief". But he is writing, in the last analysis, because, he is simply "bored" from not having anything to do, and "writing things down is really, after all, a kind of work". [6]

[3] *Ibid.*, I, No. 195, p. 357.
[4] *Ibid.*, I, No. 196, p. 362.
[5] Dostoevskij, *Zapiski iz podpol'ja, Polnoe sobranie khudožestvennykh proizvedenij* (Moscow-Leningrad, 1926-1930), IV, 134.
[6] *Ibid.*, IV, 135.

"I am forty now," the Underground Man observes at the beginning of *Notes from the Underground* — 1864; in his reminiscences in Part II the Underground Man emerges as a lonely "dreamer" of the 1840's divorced from real life. He had moods when he wished to embrace "all mankind", and he used to "seek salvation", he observes, "in all that was 'beautiful and lofty', in my dreams, of course. I was constantly dreaming . . ." [7] Dostoevsky writes in his prefatory note to *Notes from the Underground*:

Both the author of the notes and the "Notes" themselves are, of course, fictitious. Nevertheless, such persons as the author of these notes not only can, but even must exist in our society, considering those circumstances which have in general led to the formation of our society. I wanted to bring before the public, more conspicuously than is usually the case, one of the characters of the recent past. This is one of the representatives of a generation that is still with us. [8]

The period embraced by the Underground Man's "notes" (the 1840's to the 1860's) is a most dramatic one for Dostoevsky. It is the period in which he himself moves from the position of a "dreamer" to a critical attitude towards that same effusive idealism and sentimentalism he had embraced as a youth. Dostoevsky himself had experienced an early infatuation with Schiller and a romantic cult of friendship. The dizzying success of his first novel *Poor Folk* (*Bednye lyudi*, 1846) followed by the poor reception of "The Double" ("Dvoynik", 1846) and Dostoevsky's resulting depression, as well as his alienation from the critic V. Belinsky's circle (Nekrasov, Panaev and others grouped around the journal *Contemporary*) — all were events of the forties.

Dostoevsky soberly described the "dreamer" in one of his feuilletons "Petersburg Chronicle" ("Peterburgskaya letopis", 1847) as "a Petersburg nightmare . . . tragedy, silent, mysterious, gloomy, wild", [9] but he

---

[7] *Ibid.*, IV, 145. The phrase "beautiful and lofty" was current in Russian criticism in the 1830's and 1840's and is used sarcastically by the Underground Man as a reference to the lofty idealism of that time. A. I. Gertsen (1812-1870) describes an aspect of the intellectual atmosphere of the 1840's in his memoirs: "Our young philosophers spoiled for themselves not only sentences, but understanding as well; the attitude towards life, towards reality became academic, bookish . . . Everything that was *really* direct, every simple feeling was elevated to an abstract category and returned therefrom without a drop of living blood, like a pale algebraic shadow. In all this there was a kind of naiveté, because all this was absolutely sincere." (A. I. Gercen, *Byloe i dumy, Polnoe sobranie sočinenij i pisem* [Petersburg, 1919], XIII, 13.)

[8] Dostoevskij, *Zapiski iz podpol'ja, op. cit.*, IV, 109.

[9] Dostoevskij, "Peterburgskaja letopis'," *Stat'i, Polnoe sobranie khudožestvennykh proizvedenij, op. cit.*, XIII, 30.

had not yet broken with liberalism. He became a member of the Petrashevsky Circle—a discussion group especially interested in the social theories of Proudhon, Fourier, and other utopian socialists—and joined a smaller conspiratorial group (the Durov Circle). These activities led to his arrest and exile to Siberia in 1849.

Dostoevsky's life in prison—which he describes in a letter to N. D. Fon-Vizina in 1854 as a kind of "compulsory communism"[10]—led to a re-evaluation of his former convictions. The change in his convictions is expressed gradually in his writings. In his novel *Insulted and Injured* (*Unizhennye i oskorblennye*, 1861)—a prologue in many respects to *Notes from the Underground*—the romantic "dreamer" is parodied in the figure of the writer Ivan Petrovich, and Schiller, the idol of Dostoevsky's youth, is ridiculed.

"And what is more precious than money for a convict?" Dostoevsky asks in *Notes from the House of the Dead* (*Zapiski iz Mertvogo Doma,* 1862). "Freedom or some dream of freedom. . . . The word 'convict' means nothing else but man without a will; and by spending money, he acts according to *his own will.*"[11] The conception of freedom and free will as man's most precious possession—a dominant idea of *Notes from the Underground*—is a leitmotif of *Notes from the House of the Dead.* This conception was expressed directly by Dostoevsky in some additional pages written for, but not introduced into, the final edition of the latter work. He writes in these pages:

What is bread! People eat bread in order to live, but this is not life! Go ahead now, build a palace. Outfit it with marble, pictures, gold, heavenly birds, hanging gardens, whatever you can think of . . . and enter it. Indeed, perhaps you would never want to leave it! Perhaps in fact you really would not leave it! Everything is here! What more could you ask for! But then, a trifle: your palace is encircled by a fence and you are told—it's all yours, enjoy yourself! Only you must not move a step from here! Well, you may rest assured that at this moment you will want to abandon your heaven and vault over the fence. What is more, all this luxury, all this comfort only serves to increase your suffering. You even grow offended over just this luxury.[12]

A "palace" becomes a prison when encircled by a fence. Man prefers to live, as the Underground Man observes, "according to his own foolish

10 Dostoevskij, *Pis'ma, op. cit.,* I, No. 61, p. 143.
11 Dostoevskij, *Zapiski iz mertvogo doma, Polnoe sobranie khudožestvennykh proizvedenij, op. cit.,* III, 371.
12 A. S. Dolinin, "Nenapečatannye stranicy iz 'Zapisok iz mertvogo doma'. Tekst, istorija otryvka i počemu on ne byl napečatan." *Dostoevskij: stat'i i materialy,* ed. A. S. Dolinin (St. Petersburg, 1922), I, 365-366.

will". But Dostoevsky is prepared to admit that a "palace" could have a very strong appeal to suffering mankind. This thought is expressed in *Winter Notes on Summer Impressions* (*Zimnie zametki o letnikh vpechatleniyakh*, 1863), in the section devoted to Dostoevsky's visit to London's Universal Exhibition of 1862 with its famed "crystal palace" on Sydenham Hill. Dostoevsky is frightened and oppressed at this Universal Exhibition by the impression of finality, profound triumph, the impression of a "complete truth" that permits no argument. "Is this, indeed, the final ideal — you think; is the end here?" Millions are coming from all over the world to pay obeisance to this "Baal", this glorification of civilization, and they are "quietly, stubbornly and silently crowding into this colossal palace ... This is some kind of Biblical picture." Much "unremitting spiritual resistance and negation", Dostoevsky observes, would be necessary to avoid surrending to this impression, to avoid deifying "Baal", "that is, not to accept the existing for one's ideal".[13]

Dostoevsky rejects the "crystal palace" for its aloofness from the millions of suffering people, for its implicit ignoring of suffering. It is Dostoevsky's Underground Man who will manifest that "unremitting spiritual resistance and negation", who will reject the "crystal palace" as an ideal. Suffering is "unthinkable in the crystal palace: suffering is doubt, negation, and what kind of a crystal palace would there be if one could have any doubts about it?"[14] Dostoevsky prefigures "underground" rebellion in *Winter Notes on Summer Impressions*. Here Dostoevsky affirms that man will reject the Fourierist utopia with its guarantees of food, drink, work and everything, if he is required in exchange to give even

a tiny drop of his personal freedom for the common welfare. No, man does not want to live even on these conditions, even a little drop is too much. He keeps on thinking, foolishly, that this is a prison, that it is better to be independent, because there is complete [free] will. And even if in his freedom he is beaten, unemployed, starving and without any [free] will, the queer fellow still feels that his own will is better. Of course, the socialist will have to spit and say to him that he is a fool, has not grown up, not matured and does not understand his own self-interest; that an ant, any old inarticulate, insignificant ant is cleverer than he is because in the ant hill everything is so good, everything so ordered, everyone is replete, happy, each knows his own task, in a word:

---

[13] Dostoevskij, *Zimnie zametki o letnikh vpečatlenijakh, Polnoe sobranie khudožestvennykh proizvedenij, op. cit.,* IV, 76.
[14] Dostoevskij, *Zapiski iz podpol'ja, op. cit.,* IV, 131.

man has a long way to go before he can measure up to the ant hill![15]

In *Winter Notes on Summer Impressions* Dostoevsky criticizes the utopian socialist ideal in his own name. In *Notes from the Underground* it is the Underground Man who conducts this polemic.

Notes from the Underground (1864) is Dostoevsky's first attack in *belles-lettres* upon ethical rationalist, utilitarian and utopian socialist thought — an attitude he retained unaltered in basic content in his subsequent work.

In Part I, "The Underground", the Underground Man, on the basis of an analysis of his own personality, deduces the absolute irrationality of human behavior; then, generalizing upon his own experience, which he finds mirrored in the life of mankind, the Underground Man develops a powerful critique of reason, rationalist-utilitarian ethics and utopian socialism. Chapters VII-X (Part I) are a sharp parody of ideas expressed in the radical democrat N. G. Chernyshevsky's political-philosophical novel *What is to be Done?* subtitled *From Stories of the New Man* (*Chto delat?* 1863), a frankly didactic work which aimed at creating a new morality. Chernyshevsky's heroes are guided by this new morality in which self-interest is identical with the common good. They are rational egotists. Chernyshevsky's Fourierist vision of the future includes a "huge building", such as has never been seen before; "no, there has been one hint of it; the palace which stands on Sydenham Hill: iron and glass, iron and glass." [16]

Dostoevsky ridicules in *Notes from the Underground* Chernyshevsky's highly moralistic and rationalistic philosophy of happiness and well-being, his emphasis upon self-interest as the determining factor of human behavior, his portrait of the "new man", his utopian dreams, as an absurd simplification of human nature. To the "new man", the self-confident, monolithic, morally superior and rational *hero* of Chernyshevsky (Rakhmetov, for example, in *What is to be Done?*) Dostoevsky opposes the doubting, ambivalent, delinquent and irrational *anti-hero*. The attack on Chernyshevsky was also a blow at the sentimental humanism of the 1840's with its fervent faith in the goodness of man. The catastrophe of the "underground" dreamer in Part II of *Notes from the Underground* (the affair with the prostitute Liza, in particular) is a crushing blow directed at the ecstatic idealism of the 1840's.

The tragedy of the "underground" dreamer, in Dostoevsky's con-

---

[15] Dostoevskij, *Zimnie zametki o letnikh vpečatlenijakh, op. cit.,* IV, 88.
[16] N. G. Černyševskij, *Čto delat', Polnoe sobranie sočinenij* (St. Petersburg, 1906), IX, 258-259.

ception, is linked with the tragedy of the Russian educated class. In his journals *Time* and *Epoch* Dostoevsky speaks of the historical divorce of the Russian educated class from the people, the "soil"; he calls attention to moral and intellectual instability which he considers the consequence of that divorce. "We even love our *Russian* land in a kind of conditional, bookish way," he writes in a subscription prospectus to *Time* 1862.[17] "Scepticism and the sceptical view are killing everything, even the very view itself in the final analysis . . ." [18] "We [the editors] have said straight out and we say now that morally it is necessary to unite with the people as thoroughly and firmly as possible," reads a subscription prospectus to *Time* 1863.[19] "In our times . . . all is in confusion . . . everywhere people are quarreling over foundations, principles." [20] "Who among us in all honesty knows what is *evil* and what is *good*?" Dostoevsky asks in his subscription prospectus to *Epoch* 1865.[21]

Many of the ideas expressed in Dostoevsky's journalistic writings in the early 1860's find expression in *Notes from the Underground*. The Underground Man for Dostoevsky, first of all, symbolizes the divorce of the Russian Europeanized educated class from the life of the people. The Underground Man is a bookish man living in "abstract" Petersburg who prides himself upon being "an educated and cultivated man of our times".[22] He is a "dreamer" who has lived idly and alone in his "underground" in "moral corruption" and "divorced from life". But "we are all divorced from life, all crippled, each of us, more or less".[23]

The theme of the individual "divorced from life" — from the life of the people, the soil, the national element — is central in Dostoevsky's works. It is through this theme that the Underground Man and other heroes of Dostoevsky may be linked historically with the "superfluous man" in Russian literature. Dostoevsky points to Pushkin as the writer who first depicted a man divorced from the life of the people. Pushkin, Dostoevsky writes in his *Diary of a Writer* (*Dnevnik pisatelya*) in an explanatory note to his famous Pushkin address (1880), was the first to note the "chief phenomenon — and a pathological one — of our educated society, historically divorced from the soil, aloof from the people". He

---

17 Dostoevskij, *Stat'i, op. cit.*, XIII, 504.
18 *Ibid.*, XIII, 506.
19 *Ibid.*, XIII, 509.
20 *Ibid.*, XIII, 511.
21 *Ibid.*, XIII, 518-519.
22 Dostoevskij, *Zapiski iz podpol'ja, op. cit.*, IV, 180.
23 *Ibid.*, IV, 194.

set before us "our negative type, a troubled and unreconciled man, without faith in the native soil and in its native forces, in the last analysis negating Russia and himself . . ."[24] "Aleko and Onegin then engendered a multitude of people in our literature like themselves . . . the Pechorins, Chichikovs, Rudins and Lavretskys, the Bolkonskys . . . and many others . . ."[25]

"These homeless wanderers," Dostoevsky observes in his Pushkin address in connection with the "Aleko type", "are continuing to this very day their wandering . . ." They no longer visit gypsy camps in search of their "world ideals"; they are the ones who now "eagerly throw themselves into socialism which did not exist in Aleko's time, they come with a new faith in another pasture and work on it zealously, believing, like Aleko, that in their fantastic doings they will achieve their goals and happiness not only for themselves, but for all mankind".[26]

From Aleko to the Underground Man, from that "historical Russian sufferer" divorced from the people[27] to the "underground" sufferer and dreamer in Notes from the Underground runs a straight line — but it is a line which leads the romantic, individualistic and "superfluous" hero into the "underground".

In this descent into the "underground" the hero of Turgenev's "Hamlet of Shchigrovskogo District" ("Gamlet Shchigrovskogo uezda," 1849) and, in particular, Chulkaturin in Turgenev's "Diary of a Superfluous Man" ("Dnevnik lishnego cheloveka," 1850) appear as transitional types.[28]

The Underground Man, however, while historically linked with the "superfluous man", is a different social type. He is the first, fully conscious representative of a line of little men, clerks, dreamers, poor folk, who appear in Russian literature. Their thwarted lives, their injured souls are first disclosed in Pushkin's "Station Master" ("Stantsionny smotritel", 1830 — Samson Vyrin; in his poem The Bronze Horseman (Medny vsadnik, 1833) — Evgeny; in Gogol's "Cloak" ("Shinel," 1842) — Akaky Akakievich; and in great detail in Dostoevsky's early works, such as Poor Folk (Bednye lyudi, 1846) — Devushkin.

---

[24] Dostoevskij, Dnevnik pisatelja za 1877, 1880 i 1881 gody, Polnoe sobranie khudožestvennykh proizvedenij, op. cit., XII, 369.
[25] Ibid., XII, 370.
[26] Ibid., XII, 378.
[27] Ibid., XII, 378.
[28] Wacław Lednicki analyzes the relation of Turgenev's two stories to Notes from the Underground in his book Russia, Poland and the West (London, 1954), pp. 181-213.

But it is only in *Notes from the Underground* that Dostoevsky discloses the full implications — for both individual and society — of the little man's tragic clash with reality. "Look out! I'll get back at you!" shouts the crazed and rebellious Evgeny (*The Bronze Horseman*) at the equestrian statue of Peter the Great. *Notes from the Underground* is the epilogue to this challenge.

The Underground Man plays a complex role in the ideological design of *Notes from the Underground.* In argument, he exposes the rationalists' naive and mechanistic conceptions of human behavior; at the same time he is himself exposed in his amoral, asocial role as anti-hero. It is the living example of the Underground Man — irrational and uncontrollable — that constitutes the most devastating argument in *Notes from the Underground* against the conception of man as a rational being. And it is in his role as anti-hero that he emerges before the reader as an indictment of the educated intelligentsia "divorced from life".

The problem of Dostoevsky's attitude towards his hero — when, where and to what degree he stands with or against his hero — is a difficult one. The Underground Man's uncontrolled egotism and destructive individualism, his demand for independent will "whatever this independence costs and wherever it may lead",[29] is for Dostoevsky a tragedy of human will that must bring down upon both individual and society catastrophe. From the recognition of this tragedy comes Dostoevsky's insistence upon the voluntary renunciation by society of its tyranny over the individual and by the individual of his demands upon society,[30] upon the acceptance of Christ as the only path out of the "underground".[31]

---

[29]   Dostoevskij, *Zapiski iz podpol'ja, op. cit.,* IV, 124.
[30]   This view is stated clearly in *Winter Notes on Summer Impressions.* Dostoevsky observes here that the voluntary self-sacrifice of the individual in favor of everyone is, "in my opinion, the mark of the highest development of the individual, of his greatest power, his highest degree of self-determination, his greatest freedom of his own will." (Dostoevskij, *Zimnie zametki o letnikh vpečatlenijakh, op. cit.,* IV, 86.)
[31]   This idea, it appears, was expressed by Dostoevsky in the original manuscript of *Notes from the Underground.* He wrote his brother Mikhail on March 26, 1864, complaining about "horrible" excisions by the censor: "... It really would have been better not to have printed the penultimate chapter (the main one where the very idea is expressed) [chapter x in Part I] than to have printed it as it is, that is, with sentences thrown together and contradicting each other. But what is to be done! The swinish censors let pass those places where I ridiculed everything and blasphemed *for show,* but where I deduce from all this the need for faith and Christ—this is forbidden. Just who are these censors, are they in conspiracy against

This interpretation of Dostoevsky's attitude towards the Underground Man, however, is incomplete.[32] Dostoevsky does not wish to follow the Underground Man beyond the point at which his demand for independence and self-determination passes into destructive self-will and non-acceptance of the world. But as an artist he is too deeply committed to his hero's suffering, despairing rebellion. The irrational force that Dostoevsky calls forth in the Underground Man to challenge the concepts of rationalistic humanism acquires an uncontrolled dynamic of its own. The contradiction between Dostoevsky's religious conception of the brotherhood of man and his aesthetic commitment to his hero is never resolved in *Notes from the Underground*. It is not surprising that Dostoevsky, a decade after he wrote *Notes from the Underground*, remarks of this work: "It is really too gloomy. Es ist schon ein überwundener Standpunkt. Nowadays I can write in a brighter, more conciliatory vein."[33]

The landscape for the tragedy of the "underground" is Russian reality. Dostoevsky has no doubts about the reality of the "underground". Accused of "keeping the reader in the stinking atmosphere of the 'underground'", of a "complete lack of knowledge of real life",[34] Dostoevsky remarks in his notebook:

I am proud that I was the first to depict the real man of the Russian majority and the first to expose his disfigured and tragic side. The tragedy consists in the consciousness of disfigurement ... I alone depicted the tragedy of the underground, consisting in suffering, self-punishment, the consciousness of something better and the impossibility of achieving that something, and chiefly consisting in the clear conviction of these unhappy ones that it is like this with everyone and therefore it is not even worth while trying to reform. What is there to sustain those who are trying to reform? A reward, faith? There are rewards from no

---

the government or something?" (Dostoevskij, *Pis'ma, op. cit.*, I, No. 193, p. 353.) Dostoevsky, however, never replaced those censored words and sentences in later editions.

[32]   A. Skaftymov in his article *"Zapiski iz podpol'ja* sredi publicistiki Dostoevskogo," *Slavia* VIII (1929-1930), 101-117, 312-339, brings out clearly Dostoevsky's intentions in *Notes from the Underground* by viewing this work in the context of Dostoevsky's journalism of the period. But he does not meet the most difficult problem of *Notes from the Underground*: the divergence between intention and result.

[33]   O. Počinkovskaja, "God raboty s znamenitym pisatelem." *Istoričeskij vestnik*, XCV (1904), 533.

[34]   V. G. Avseenko, "Očerki tekuščej literatury," *Russkij mir*, Nos. 27, 55, (1875). Quoted by A. S. Dolinin in *V tvorčeskoj laboratorii Dostoevskogo* (Leningrad, 1947), p. 143.

one, there is faith in no one. But another step from here, and one comes
upon extreme depravity, crime (murder). Mystery.[35]

The experience of the "Russian majority" is the living reality of the
tragedy of the underground. The "underground" holds its victims in
pitiless darkness. It is the inescapable suffering of man that is the
foundation for the conception of the "underground".

Petersburg is the scene of the tragedy of the "underground". It is a
"misfortune" to live in Petersburg, declares the Underground Man, "the
most abstract and fabricated city in the whole world".[36] It is here at
night — the Underground Man tells the prostitute Liza — when the
dead arise, that she will knock at the lid of her coffin and cry: "Let me
out, kind people, to live in the light of day! I lived but I did not see life,
my life was used up for a rag; it was drunk away at a pothouse on the
Hay Market; let me out, kind people, once more to live in the light of
day."[37] Petersburg is a silent grave.

It is Petersburg with its fantastic white nights and labyrinthine horrors
of human existence that symbolizes for Dostoevsky the death of social
man. It separates man from man and drives him into himself; it over-
whelms him with suffering, humiliates him, perverts his ideals, transforms
his strivings from those of a constructive member of society into those
of a plunderer of bodies and souls.

The "underground" in which the Underground Man finds himself is
not only the real world of Petersburg. It is also his fantastic, withdrawn,
lonely and troubled inner world of consciousness. There is no clear
perception of the world from this "underground", no clear self-under-
standing; there is only exaggeration, rationalization, illusion. Dostoevsky
discusses the psychological consequences of a loss of equilibrium between the individual and reality in an early letter (1847) to his brother
Mikhail. Dostoevsky writes:

Of course, terrible is the dissonance, terrible the imbalance which society
creates in us. External and internal things should be in equilibrium.
For, lacking external experiences, those of the inward life gain the upper
hand, and that is most dangerous. The nerves and fantasy then take up
too much room in one's consciousness. Every external happening, from
want of habit, seems colossal and is somehow frightening. We begin to
fear life.[38]

---

[35] Quoted by Dolinin, *ibid.*, p. 148.
[36] Dostoevskij, *Zapiski iz podpol'ja, op. cit.*, IV, 112.
[37] *Ibid.*, IV, 176.
[38] Dostoevskij, *Pis'ma, op. cit.*, I, No. 44, p. 106.

The "underground" is man's inner life which has gained the upper hand. To escape from this "underground", the Underground Man would have to re-establish a working relationship with the real world he fears. Yet just this real world has driven him "underground"; there was nothing in his surroundings that he could "respect".[39] But if there were a decent life to which he could return, he would first have to leave behind him his warped personality, his deformed aspirations, his craving for power; he would have to become another man. But the Underground Man has "reached the last wall" at which you are conscious

. . . that you will never become another man; that even if there remained some time and faith to be remade into something else, you yourself probably would not want to be remade; and if you wanted to, you still would not do anything, because, indeed, there was perhaps nothing into which you could be made.[40]

This is the tragedy of the "underground;" it is symbolized by the "last wall", that blank and stark reminder that there is nothing to which one can return and nothing beyond but mystery.

Freedom from the "underground" is not only freedom from the depressing world of Petersburg and an oppressive state of loneliness and alienation; it is also freedom from the reality of the "normal" man — from the dictates of reason, the dominion of science and mathematics, from the necessity of choosing according to self-interest, from the conformist social systems of the utopian socialist, from the very "laws of nature" which "have always and more than anything else been offending" the Underground Man all his life.[41] The Underground Man rejects a reality which to him is completely ruled by logic, a reality which tyrannizes over him. His attitude towards the logic-ruled world of the "normal" man is summed up in his words: ". . . twice two is four is no longer life, gentlemen, but the beginning of death."[42] The "underground" from which the Underground Man would escape therefore, turns out to be all of reality, that is, everything which is reasonable and logical to the "normal" man but which is insupportable to the Underground Man.

The conception of all of reality as an "underground" — as a prison of reason and logic — lies at the basis of *Notes from the Underground*. The individual is sentenced to oblivion by the very laws of nature. The Underground Man is a symbol both of this human alienation and of desperate rebellion against it.

[39] Dostoevskij, *Zapiski iz podpol'ja, op. cit.*, IV, 140.
[40] *Ibid.*, IV, 113.
[41] *Ibid.*, IV, 118.
[42] *Ibid.*, IV, 130.

CHAPTER II

NOTES FROM THE UNDERGROUND: ANALYSIS

> About what can a decent man speak with the greatest
> satisfaction? Answer: about himself. Well then, I'll
> talk about myself.
>
> The Underground Man

This is a confession, a continuous stream of self-revelation and self-analysis in the form of "notes" — the most natural means of expression for a man alone with himself. Essentially, this is an internal drama and the actors are the fragments of personality. These "notes", like a stream of consciousness, have no beginning and no end. "The 'notes' of this paradoxicalist do not end here," Dostoevsky observes at the conclusion of *Notes from the Underground*. "He could not restrain himself and went on writing."[1] Every thought, feeling, experience of the Underground Man seems a repetition and redevelopment of his basic personality, his warring, contradictory nature. This repetitiveness is the very essence of the Underground Man's existence. For the tragedy of the Underground Man, in a psychological sense, is the tragedy of hopeless neurotic deadlock.

Ruthless egotism — the incessant drum beat of "I" — morbid preoccupation with self, quivering sensitivity before the reader, throbbing negations, the interplay of opposites, all introduce the Underground Man in the very first lines of this remarkable work.

I am a sick man***. I am a spiteful man. I am a repellent man. I think that I have a liver ailment. But then I don't know the first thing about my disease and I don't know for sure what ails me. I am not under medical care and never was, although I respect medicine and doctors. Furthermore, I am superstitious to an extreme, well, at least enough to respect medicine. (I am sufficiently educated not to be superstitious, but I am superstitious.) No, I do not wish to take medical treatment — out of malice. Well, now, most likely you don't care to understand this. Well, but I understand it. I, of course, am unable to explain to you just

[1] Dostoevskij, *Zapiski iz podpol'ja, op. cit.,* IV, 195.

whom I am spiting by my malice in this instance; I know very well that
I can in no way "affront" the doctors by not letting them treat me; I
know better than anyone that by all this I harm only myself and no one
else. But all the same, if I do not wish to get treated it is out of malice.
My liver ails me; well then, let it go on ailing me and get worse.[2]

This is a man at the edge of hysteria, an individual suffering from an
unbearable sense of oppression, whose sensibilities have been outraged,
whose every moment is an anguished anticipation of new insult and
injury. His gnawing dissatisfaction with himself and his hatred of the
world are expressed in his "malice", in a combination of vicious self-
punishment and a frenzied desire to affront, offend, spite the reality
pressing at the outer layer of his consciousness. He is aware of the
impotence of his malice and this awareness is a torment which makes
him double his self-punishment. He is indeed a "sick man": miserable,
self-pitying, but exacting and tyrannical.

"I have been living a long time like this," the Underground Man
declares at the end of his opening tirade, "for about twenty years."[3]

An irascible, malignant, strained voice breathlessly weaves a net-
work of words, thoughts, sophistries, paradoxes in *Notes from the
Underground*. The Underground Man seems drunk with language,
obsessed with dialectic, and the very style of his speech discloses the
fractured structure of his soul — an "hysterical craving for contradiction, contrasts".[4] Part I of *Notes from the Underground* is a monologue in which the inner conflicts of the Underground Man's personality
are projected into a dramatic plane of argument. The Underground
Man addresses his unseen interlocutors — now in an effort to justify
himself, now in apparent scorn of their opinions, as it were expressing
his desire to be free of their evaluation. But in his constant self-
justification and qualification, fear lest he be misunderstood, he discloses
his profound dependence upon them.[5]

This is a man completely lacking in self-respect, and fanatically vain;
as a government clerk he imagines that he is regarded with loathing,
although it is perfectly clear to him that out of "unlimited vanity" he
"mentally ascribed" his own self-dissatisfaction to everyone. He is
tormented by the feeling that "nobody was like me, and I was not like

[2]   *Ibid.,* IV. 109.
[3]   *Ibid.,* IV, 109.
[4]   *Ibid.,* IV, 140.
[5]   For an analysis of the internal dialectic of the Underground Man's monologue,
see M. M. Bakhtin, *Problemy tvorčestva Dostoevskogo* (Leningrad, 1929), pp. 173-
188.

anybody. I am one, while they are *everybody* . . ." [6] Consciousness in
him is the awareness of singleness, the awareness of alienation from his
fellow man. Hence his feeling of vulnerability before a world peopled
with enemies and strangers. He is suspicious and touchy and forever
ready to take offense, sometimes simply on purpose, for nothing. Solitary and brooding, he lives in that atmosphere of confusion and distortion in which feelings of persecution thrive.

The Underground Man is man-alone. His entire life, from the "terrible
penal years" of his "hated childhood" to the moment he pens his memoirs
is spent in the brooding atmosphere of loneliness, a life, at twenty-four,
already "gloomy, disorderly and solitary to the point of wildness".[7]
Spiritual loneliness in a wilderness of social relations — this is the matrix
of the deformation of the Underground Man's personality, his desires
and strivings.

At school, this orphan, already silent and crushed by reproaches,
hating his school fellows from the outset, shuts himself away from them
"in wounded and disproportionate pride". He is repelled by their
coarseness, their stupid faces, the pettiness of their thoughts, the stupidity
of their pursuits. He cannot help considering them inferior to him.

It was not wounded vanity that drove me to this, and for God's sake,
don't thrust upon me your hackneyed remarks, repeated *ad nauseam,*
"that I was only a dreamer, whereas even then they understood real
life." They understood nothing, they had no idea of real life . . .[8]

Here is a picture of the corruption of the individual by a senseless and
corrupt environment. There is no love or brotherhood in the environment of the Underground Man's school, only a lust for gain, rank and
success; there is no compassion for the poor. "Everything that was just
but humiliated and oppressed, they laughed at heartlessly and shame-
lessly." [9] The Underground Man demands of his single friend "a haughty
and decisive break with this environment";[10] he rebels against its cruelty
and stupidity, its smug indifference and fantastic assumption of superiority. But in his rebellion he bears the mark of what he is negating; he
is defaced and left nameless; tormented, he seeks to torment; humiliated,
he seeks the humiliation of others.

They were monstrously depraved. . . . I hated them horribly, although,

[6] Dostoevskij, *Zapiski iz podpol'ja, op. cit.,* IV, 138.
[7] *Ibid.,* IV, 136.
[8] *Ibid.,* IV, 153.
[9] *Ibid.,* IV, 153.
[10] *Ibid.,* IV, 153.

I dare say, I was worse than even they. They repaid me in the same coin and did not conceal their aversion for me. But I no longer wished their love; on the contrary, I thirsted for their humiliation.[11]

The Underground Man cannot face the world in any other role except that of the humiliated "fly", or the "despot". Human relations for him are a matter of struggle. Love is a struggle which begins with hate and ends with moral subjugation.

Thus, humiliation, horrible and insistent, deforms personality, transforming the soul of a fly into a spider's soul. The degradation of personality by constant humiliation and oppression, and the corresponding distention and deformation of ego in an effort to defend self is the characteristic psychological portrait of the Underground Man. Endless alternation between these elements mark the Underground Man's relations with other people.

Ambivalence defines the Underground Man's relation to his milieu; on the one hand, outer submission, on the other, inner revolt. As a government clerk, he "slavishly worshipped routine in everything external" out of a sickly dread of appearing ridiculous; he "loved to fall into the common rut and had a wholehearted terror of any kind of eccentricity" in himself.[12] But he takes to the common rut in a role that characteristically only increases his sense of wounded pride. He rationalizes that every decent person of his time must be a coward and a slave. He is "morbidly sensitive as a cultivated man of our age must be. But they were all stupid, and as like one another as sheep in a herd."[13]

The Underground Man, of course, is also a "sheep", but his subjective refusal to accept hated reality with all its degrading consequences is the very essence of his defense of his personality. This refusal is at the heart of the psychology of malice.

Malice is the "underground" protest of the humiliated individual against ineluctable abasement; it consists not in an attempt to avoid abasement (this is impossible), but in deliberate and malicious self-abasement, in order in this way passively and perversely to resist the offense to his personality. Real protest aimed at the relief of one's misery is replaced by a self-destructive "underground" resistence. Malice is no more than a last despairing effort of the individual to reject the consequences of his tragic position.

Such is the position of the man-with-toothache, a man whose malignant

---

[11]   *Ibid.,* IV, 153.
[12]   *Ibid.,* IV, 137.
[13]   *Ibid.,* IV, 137.

and disgusting groans express the "whole humiliating aimlessness" of his pain, the "whole binding force of nature at which you, of course, spit, but from which you nevertheless suffer whereas she does not". These groans express the consciousness that "your enemy is not there, but that there is pain . . .".[14]

The voluptuous pleasure which the man-with-toothache finds in his groans and in the disgusting atmosphere he creates around him, is akin to that pleasure of despair that the Underground Man experiences, that pleasure which comes from the "too intense consciousness of one's own degradation", from the feeling that you have "reached the last wall, that it was dreadful but it could not be otherwise: there was no longer any escape for you . . .".[15]

Malice is impotent; of this the Underground Man is painfully aware; it is accompanied by a rush of opposite elements which disarm and shame him so that he will confess: "I am not only not malicious, but cannot even become anything: neither malicious, nor good, neither a scoundrel, nor honorable, neither a hero nor an insect."[16]

"I swear to you, gentlemen," says the Underground Man "that to be too acutely conscious is a disease, a real, thorough-going disease."[17] Consciousness in the Underground Man is pain, the disabling feeling of impotence and humiliation; it is the element which subjects everything to chemical disintegration, thereby inhibiting action. The Underground Man cannot act because he can find no permanent primary causes, no foundation to rest upon.

I exercise myself in thought and consequently with me every primary cause immediately draws after it another still more primary one, and so on *ad infinitum*. Such is the essence of all consciousness and thought. It is a case of the laws of nature again.[18]

Malice itself might serve as a foundation, but malice, also, "as a result of these accursed laws of consciousness is subjected to chemical disintegration".[19] To serve as a basis for action, malice would have to be accompanied in the Underground Man by a firm belief in his right to be malicious, and just this conviction is lacking in him.

The Underground Man is a victim of a "logical tangle" of his own making, and though he knows that reasoning is impotent, yet he is

---

[14]   *Ibid.*, IV, 117.
[15]   *Ibid.*, IV, 113.
[16]   *Ibid.*, IV, 110.
[17]   *Ibid.*, IV, 111.
[18]   *Ibid.*, IV, 119.
[19]   *Ibid.*, IV, 119.

engaged in nothing else but deadly exercise in thought. The Underground Man — while an ideological enemy of rationalism — is himself in its fatal grip. His intellection is without moral pivot; it is subjectivized and formalized; it is part of the whole *perpetuum mobile* of his personality, a part of a distinct pattern of constant affirmation and negation of the same feelings, concepts and ideas. The direct fruit of such consciousness, as the Underground Man himself observes, is "inertia, that is, the conscious sitting with one's hands folded".[20]

The Underground Man lives in "conscious inertia", divorced from the "living life", in constant fear of reality. Yet at the same time his hungry ego craves contact with reality. When he can no longer stand solitude he rushes out into the Petersburg streets to find some means of restoring his lost sense of being.

His desire to be manhandled in the tavern, his bumping duel with the officer on Nevsky Prospect (in order to achieve social equality with him), his humiliating meeting with his old school comrades at the *Hôtel de Paris,* his "game" with the prostitute Liza in the bordello — each episode is an experiment which aims at testing his ego, at recognition of the self by the other, and therefore at self-recognition. The search of the Underground Man in the real world is a search for inner content, for a feeling of solidity and self-respect and for a true knowledge of himself. This search is disclosed in these psychological experiments.[21] The experiment is not life; it is an attempt at life, not for the sake of the goal, but in order to determine what one is and whether one is able to achieve the goal. The experiment is essentially a subjective drama; the incidental background — the stage — is reality.

But contact with reality is always painful, and sometimes tragic, and the Underground Man always returns to his "underground", to his "den", his "box" where he hides from mankind. Here in the "underground" he takes refuge from humiliating reality and seeks satisfaction for his wounded ego in self-adulating and self-glorifying dreams, in fantasy and flights into the "beautiful and lofty".

Intoxication with the "beautiful and lofty", the desire to embrace mankind, is mocked in the personality of the Underground Man: the "beautiful and lofty" is identified with the tragedy of ambivalent consciousness and with the moral chaos of the individual in the "under-

---

[20]   *Ibid.,* IV, 118.
[21]   For a discussion of the significance of the psychological experiment in Dostoevsky's works, see Georg Lukacs' essay on Dostoevsky in his book *Der russische Realismus in der Weltliteratur* (Berlin, 1949), pp. 174-194.

ground"; it is associated with the Underground Man's self-adulation and sentimentality, and with his need to escape from sordid reality. "Indeed," asks the Underground Man, "could I have resigned myself to the simple, vulgar, plain, nasty little clerk-like debauchery, and reconciled myself to all that filth!?" [22]

The tragedy of the sentimental-romantic "dreamer", the tragic impact on others of the psychological experiment, the terrible havoc wrought by humiliated consciousness in its egotism of suffering is brought out in the final episode of *Notes from the Underground* — the Underground Man's meeting with the prostitute Liza.

Here in the bordello the miserable fly reveals his spider's soul; the "dreamer", the "hero", intoxicated with his "cherished ideas" on the "beautiful and lofty", zestfully torments the prostitute Liza. This is a "game" for the Underground Man. "It was the game that attracted me most." [23] But it is not only a game: he insists he speaks sincerely and with real feeling. And indeed, it is true, for there are at least three "underground" men here: one cynically plays a "game" (the "hero" testing his ego); another sympathizes with the agony of Liza ("You see, Liza, I am talking about myself!"),[24] and a third sits and watches the other two: "I swear she really did interest me. Besides, I was somewhat weakened and agitated. And indeed, guile so easily goes hand in hand with feeling." [25]

In his efforts to make Liza suffer for his humiliations, the Underground Man exposes his mortally sick soul. The fantastic extremes of his personality explode — shame, self-abasement and despotism igniting one another. The Underground Man lacerates himself as a "disgusting person ... the most odious, most ridiculous, most petty, most stupid, most envious of worms on earth".[26] He jeers at Liza for her naiveté, confesses that he wanted to humiliate her, that "without power and tyrannizing over someone I cannot really live".[27] Love, for the Underground Man, means to show his moral superiority, but when this moral superiority is exposed, when the "hero" is unmasked in an unbearably humiliating way, he dissolves in a frenzy of malice and tramples upon all the feelings of sentiment, pity and good which as a hero he had

[22] Dostoevskij, *Zapiski iz podpol'ja, op. cit.,* IV, 146.
[23] *Ibid.,* IV, 170.
[24] *Ibid.,* IV, 171.
[25] *Ibid.,* IV, 170.
[26] *Ibid.,* IV, 190.
[27] *Ibid.,* IV, 191.

formerly embraced. And in his egotism of suffering the Underground Man announces that he would "sell the whole world for a penny in order to be left in peace. . . . I say the whole world can go to hell so long as I can always have my tea." [28]

The Liza scene is a catastrophe of idealism, a confession of the absolute failure of the individual to be good or to respond to goodness in another. The individual is disclosed as helpless before the irrational, without any inner moral controls, and the "beautiful and the lofty", far from appearing as a positive instrumentality in human relations, emerges as an adjunct to vileness.

"Liza, reviled and crushed by me," observes the Underground Man, "understood far more than I imagined. She understood . . . that I myself was unhappy." [29] Yet though he is unhappy, though indeed he suffers miserably in the continual debauch of his emotions, he will not give up the "underground", he will not give up his suffering. "Suffering — why . . . this is the sole cause of consciousness. . . . Consciousness . . . is infinitely superior to twice two is four." [30] The Underground Man does not wish to exchange places with the "normal man" — the rational man. "No, no! the underground is in any case more advantageous!" [31]

The Underground Man is a fanatical anti-rationalist. He embraces the irrational suffering of the "underground" the more firmly because of his fear and hatred of rationalist well-being and categorical necessity. The "underground" is a defense for an individual who feels himself vulnerable before a hostile, rectilinear reality. The object of the Underground Man's most vigorous attack is the embodiment of this reality — the "direct people and men of action", the "normal man". [32]

The Underground Man rationalizes his inability to become anything with the

useless consolation that an intelligent man cannot become anything serious, and it is only the fool who becomes anything. Yes, a man of the nineteenth century must and is morally obliged to be chiefly a characterless being; whereas a man with character, a man of action, is chiefly a limited being. [33]

The "man of action" is not only an abstract symbol for the Underground

[28]   *Ibid.*, IV, 189.
[29]   *Ibid.*, IV, 190.
[30]   *Ibid.*, IV, 131.
[31]   *Ibid.*, IV, 132.
[32]   *Ibid.*, IV, 114.
[33]   *Ibid.*, IV, 110.

Man; he is, first of all, the successful, vulgar hero of his times. Such a hero of his time is the Underground man's former classmate, the officer Zverkov, a person "vulgar in the extreme" before whom everybody grovels because he is a man "favored by the gifts of nature" and, more-

over, an "authority on smartness and good manners".
This last point especially used to infuriate me. I hated the abrupt self-confident tone of his voice, the adulation of his own witticisms which always turned out awfully stupid, although he was daring in his language; I hated his attractive, but rather stupid face (for which, however, I would have gladly exchanged my *clever* face) and the free and easy officer mannerisms of the "forties." I hated the fact that he used to speak of his future successes with women . . . and how he constantly would be fighting duels.[34]

The Underground Man's feelings towards Zverkov are complex and characteristically ambivalent. On the one hand, Zverkov represents everything he scorns and despises, everything insensitive, everything opportunistic and sham in society. On the other hand, Zverkov is success, self-confidence and self-mastery: everything the Underground Man craves and from the lack of which he suffers. Hence the feeling of envy before the normal "man of action" typified by Zverkov — a feeling accompanied, of course, by resentment and scorn, and the consoling rationalization that, of course, only fools and limited people are able to become something. It is the essence of the Underground Man's tragedy that in his rebellion against the Zverkovs and against his degrading environment, he should remain a prisoner psychologically of the very social ideals and strivings he loathes.

The "man of action", as he is developed in *Notes from the Under-ground*, is a symbolic type, an abstraction representing everything hostile and antithetical to the psychology and philosophy of the Underground Man. The men of action humble themselves before the impossible, before the "stone wall", that is, the "laws of nature, the deductions of natural sciences, mathematics". Once it is proved to you that you are descended from a monkey, you just have to accept it:

Please, they will cry out to you, it's impossible to object; this is twice two is four. Nature is not asking your permission; she is not concerned with your desires and with whether you like her laws or don't like them. You are obliged to accept her just as she is, and consequently all her results. A wall, you see, is a wall, etc. etc.[35]

[34] *Ibid.,* IV, 149.
[35] *Ibid.,* IV, 116.

The men of action clearly are linked in mind and spirit with the rationalistic interlocutors of the Underground Man; the latter are men whose
lives know no complexities or deviations; they are men whose philosophy
is summed up in the formula "twice two is four". They stand in obeisance
before the "laws of nature" — laws which are not concerned with the
individual's will or desires. Yet these "laws of nature", observes the
Underground Man, "always and more than anything have been offending
me all my life".[36]

In *Notes from the Underground* the "laws of nature", as a concept,
form a bridge linking the personal rebellion of the Underground Man
against ineluctable pain and humiliation with his philosophical rebellion
against the rationalists and their doctrine of necessity. These laws
symbolize for him the binding force of nature, pain and humiliation, the
whole inescapable logic of his degradation against which he rebels with
malice. With his reason the Underground Man knows that his position
is hopeless, his degradation inevitable; he is "guilty without guilt and, so
to speak, through the laws of nature".[37] But the will irrationally rejects
the evidence of reason, refuses to accept the verdict of the "laws of
nature" which is death to individuality; pain and humiliation are re-
doubled. The result is only a deeper awareness on the part of the
Underground Man of his enslavement to the "laws of nature", and
therefore fresh suffering. But suffering is the "sole cause of consciousness", and in suffering, at least, the Underground Man finds a guarantee
of his own individuality.

The Underground Man, inwardly devastated by rationalism, naturally
finds in the rationalists' obeisance to the "laws of nature", "twice two is
four", the "stone wall", an insult and threat to his personality. Against
the rationalists' philosophical attack, against the threat of their doctrine
of necessity, the Underground Man has only one recourse: just as in his
struggle for personal spiritual survival he meets all degrading situations
with irrational malice, so in his philosophical struggle with the rationalists he adopts a philosophy of malice. It is impossible to argue with
the rationalists: reason is on their side. All that remains is irrationally
to negate reason:

Good lord, what have I got to do with the laws of nature and arithmetic
when for some reason these laws and twice two don't please me? It goes
without saying I shall not break through such a wall with my forehead,

36   *Ibid.,* IV, 118.
37   *Ibid.,* IV, 113.

if I am really lacking in the strength to do it, but at the same time I am
not going to reconcile myself with it just because it is a stone wall and
I am lacking in strength.[38]

In the end of ends, the Underground Man will have neither peace nor
war; he will rather sink back into inertia and impotent malice; he will
rather choose suffering than submit to an inhuman doctrine of necessity.

    The Underground Man rebels with his whole being against rationalism
— against reason, and advances in its stead an irrational will-philosophy
of his own.

You see, gentlemen, reason is a fine thing, that is unquestionable, but
reason is only reason and satisfies only the reasoning side of man, whereas volition is a manifestation of the whole of life, I mean, of the whole
of human life, including reason and all its headscratchings.[39]

Man is irrational, *Notes from the Underground* essentially asserts, and
reason can neither comprehend nor satisfy the human spirit; on the
contrary, reason alone would destroy the human spirit, reason alone is
"twice two is four".

. . . Twice two is four is no longer life, gentlemen, but the beginning of
death. At least man always seems to have feared this twice two is four,
and I fear it now. Twice two is four is a dandy who stands right across
your path with arms akimbo and spits. I agree that twice two is four is
a magnificent thing, but when everything is said and done, twice two is
five is sometimes an exceedingly pleasant thing.[40]

The Underground Man's attack on the rationalists is more than an
attempt to discredit a social-philosophical outlook which oversimplifies
human nature; it is also a struggle to enthrone irrationalism and to
assert the necessary supremacy of "twice two is five" in human behavior
and affairs over the formula "twice two is four". The practical opposition
of reason and will in human nature and the dominance of irrational will
— established by "underground" self-analysis — is the fundamental
proposition of the Underground Man in his full-scale offensive against
the rationalists, against reason, the negation of free will and the doctrines
of utopian socialism.

    The Underground Man asks:

[38]   *Ibid.,* IV, 116.
[39]   *Ibid.,* IV, 126.
[40]   *Ibid.,* IV, 130.

Oh, tell me, who was it first declared that man does nasty things only because he does not know his true interests; but that if he were enlightened, if his eyes were opened to his true, normal interests, then man would immediately cease doing nasty things, immediately become good and generous, because, being enlightened and understanding his real interests, he would see his own advantage in good, and it is known that not a single man will act knowingly against his own interests and therefore he would, as it were, of necessity do good? Oh, the babe, oh the pure innocent child![41]

The Underground Man himself is the most powerful refutation of this theory of enlightened self-interest. "They won't let me — I cannot be good," the Underground Man confesses to Liza in despair.[42] The very essence of his personality is that he is knowingly irrational, that he does "nasty things" despite the clamour of opposite elements in him. "And what if it happens that *sometimes* man's advantage not only can, but even must in *some circumstances* consist in his desiring something that is harmful and not advantageous to himself?"[43]

The psychology of malice, the irrational yet conscious choice (contrary to self-interest) of greater suffering and humiliation is the foundation for the Underground Man's insistence upon completely free will.

"One's own free and unconstrained will, one's own caprice, albeit the wildest, one's own fancy, goaded sometimes perhaps even to madness" — this is man's interest of interests, according to the Underground Man.[44] For this interest man, "if necessary, is ready to go against all laws, that is, against reason, honor, tranquillity, prosperity . . .". This interest "destroys all our classifications and continually smashes all systems composed by lovers of the human race for the happiness of the human race. In a word, it interferes with everything."[45] At certain times man's

---

[41] *Ibid.,* IV, 120-121. The Underground Man is clearly referring to N. G. Chernyshevsky and the heroes of his novel *What is to be Done?* who expound a theory of rational egotism. Chernyshevsky, an enlightened egotist (one who recognizes his real interests and sees his advantage in good) mentally addresses an unenlightened egotist, Marya Aleksevna Rozalskaya: ". . . Now you are occupied with bad affairs because your circumstances demand this of you, but if you should be given different circumstances, you would with pleasure become harmless, even useful, because without pecuniary calculation you would not want to do evil, and if there were to be advantage in it for you, then you might do what you pleased— you might, therefore, act honorably and generously, if it should be necessary." (N. G. Černyševskij, *Čto delat', op. cit.,* p. 100.)
[42] Dostoevskij, *Zapiski iz podpol'ja, op. cit.,* IV, 191.
[43] *Ibid.,* IV, 121.
[44] *Ibid.,* IV, 124.
[45] *Ibid.,* IV, 122.

caprice may prove more advantageous than anything else, even when it harms him and contradicts what reason tells him is to his self-interest, because "it preserves for us the most important and precious thing, that is, our personality and our individuality".[46]

The Underground Man argues with his unseen interlocutors — the men who espouse the theory of enlightened self-interest, the rationalists, utilitarians and utopian socialists. The Underground Man voices the views of his interlocutors. They envisage a time when reason, common sense and science will re-educate and guide human nature.

Even more: then, you say, science itself will teach man (though in my opinion it's really superfluous) that in fact he possesses neither will nor caprice, and never did, and that he himself is no more than something in the nature of a piano key or an organ stop; and that, moreover, there are still laws of nature in the world; so that everything he does is done not at all according to his volition, but of itself, according to the laws of nature. Therefore, these laws of nature have only to be discovered and man will no longer be accountable for his actions and will find life exceedingly easy. All human actions, it goes without saying, will then be computed according to these laws, mathematically, in the form of a table of logarithms, up to 108,000 and put in calendar form; or, even better, there will appear certain virtuous works resembling modern encyclopedic lexicons in which everything will be so precisely calculated and designated that there will no longer be any more personal actions or adventures in the world. Then—all this you are saying—new economic relations will take shape, all quite ready made, and also calculated with mathematical exactitude, so that in a trice all possible questions will disappear for the simple reason that there will be answers for all of them. Then the crystal palace will be built. Then — well, in a word, the Golden Age will dawn.[47]

But such a society, in the view of the Underground Man, might become terribly boring. He would not be surprised if suddenly in this future society based on common sense some reactionary-looking gentleman were to propose kicking over all that common sense so as to enable man once again to live according to "his own foolish will". And such a person would find followers, "precisely because man always and everywhere, whoever he be, likes to act as he wishes and not at all as reason and self-interest dictate."[48]

Nothing, the Underground Man firmly believes, would ever make

[46] *Ibid.*, IV, 126.
[47] *Ibid.*, IV, 123-124.
[48] *Ibid.*, IV, 124.

man give up his free will. Even if it were proved to him by the natural
sciences and mathematics that he was a piano key, he would deliberately
do something "out of ungratefulness just in order to insist on his own".
And if he had no means at his disposal, he would invent destruction and
chaos, he would let loose a curse on the world; and if all this could be
calculated, he would "deliberately go mad . . . in order not to have reason
and to insist on his own!".[49]

The Underground Man envisages socialist utopia as the triumph of
the "laws of nature", the very forces which have offended him all his
life. These "laws of nature" lead to moral chaos; for they have "only
to be discovered and man will no longer be accountable for his actions".[50]
If there is absolute determinism — and therefore no free will — there
can be no moral accountability for one's acts. This is, in fact,
the internal condition of the Underground Man. He rationalizes his
degradation and the pleasure he obtains from it, declaring that as a result
of the "laws of heightened consciousness" and the inertia stemming from
these laws, he cannot help himself; it isn't his fault if he's a wretch.[51]
The Underground Man externalizes his feelings of oppression in the
"laws of nature" in relation to which he see himself a rebellious, but
helpless satellite. However he looks at the matter, it still turns out that
he is always guilty in everything and, "what is even more insulting, guilty
without guilt and, so to speak, through the laws of nature".[52]

Not without reason, therefore, does the Underground Man regard the
triumph of the deterministic "laws of nature" as the path to moral
chaos: he is himself an example of the moral chaos of an individual who
is completely lacking in self-mastery and constantly rationalizing his
behavior. In his complete awareness of the inner rationale of his
behavior, and in his impotence in this knowledge, in the *perpetuum
mobile* of his thinking and in his lack of any firm foundations, principles,
values, the Underground Man is an example of the bankruptcy of
rationalistic mind functioning within its own self-contained world.

The Underground Man's attack on the rationalists is the attack of
an embittered man on his former teachers for the misery they have
brought down upon him. He has himself paid the penalty of the
"dreamer", the lover of the "beautiful and lofty"; he mocks the "lovers
of humanity" for expecting new economic relations to arise "all quite

49   *Ibid.*, IV, 128.
50   *Ibid.*, IV, 123.
51   *Ibid.*, IV, 113.
52   *Ibid.*, IV, 113.

ready made".[53] Here is the echo of his own flights into the "beautiful and lofty", his dreams of "suitable activity, beneficent, beautiful and, above all, *ready made . . .*".[54]

"Of course, what won't one invent out of boredom!" exclaims the Underground Man. "After all, golden pins, too, are stuck into people out of boredom."[55] The vision of boredom overtaking rationalist utopia, and man's irrational response to it, is not an abstraction to the Underground Man, but a vision permeated with his own experience. Boredom is a daily experience of the Underground Man in both the humdrum bureaucratic ant hill and in his "underground". The Underground Man does not stick golden pins into people (at least he does not confess to this diversion), but his inventions of life out of boredom, his hysterical outbursts and plunges into filth and debauchery, are examples of his equally fantastic attempts to escape the boredom and break through the rationalistic rhythms of his life.

The Underground Man's view of history and the experience of mankind, like his view of utopia, is closely linked with his own experience. The idea of regeneration of mankind by means of a system of self-interest is absurd, according to the Underground Man, not only in its rationalistic formulation but because man has not proved himself capable of living sensibly and morally. Endless fighting, according to the Underground Man, marks history. What civilization has done is to "cultivate in man the many-sidedness of his sensations" and through this man is reaching the stage of finding "pleasure in bloodshed".[56]

The Underground Man's picture of history mirrors the tragedy of his own soul. Civilization has done for mankind what life has done for the Underground Man: provided it with an excess of consciousness, a sick consciousness which has come to find pleasure in its moral fall. Man is an ungrateful biped, says the Underground Man, but his "chief failing is his constant lack of moral sense. . . . Lack of moral sense and, consequently, a lack of common sense also."[57] The tragedy of the "underground" is here disclosed as a universal tragedy.

"Whether for good or ill, it is nevertheless sometimes very pleasant to smash something,"[58] observes the Underground Man. Men are not

---

[53]   *Ibid.,* IV, 124.
[54]   *Ibid.,* IV, 145.
[55]   *Ibid.,* IV, 124.
[56]   *Ibid.,* IV, 123.
[57]   *Ibid.,* IV, 127.
[58]   *Ibid.,* IV, 130.

like ants whose cherished goal is the eternally indestructible ant hill. Perhaps, the Underground Man feels, man loves destruction and chaos because he "instinctively fears reaching his goal and completing the building he is erecting".[59] A workman gets wages and goes to a tavern. "But" — asks the Underground Man — "where can man go?"[60]

The crystal palace, therefore, is not for man. Suffering is not permitted in the crystal palace, for "suffering is doubt, negation, and what kind of a crystal palace would there be if one could have any doubts about it? And yet I am convinced that man will never renounce real suffering, that is, destruction and chaos."[61] The Underground Man compares the social utopia of the rationalists to an ant hill; the crystal palace turns out to be no more than a chicken coop which the Underground Man will not mistake for a crystal palace. He will not accept as the crown of his desires an "apartment house with flats for poor lodgers leased out for a thousand years. . . . Destroy my desires, eradicate my ideals, show me something better, and I will follow you."[62]

In the meanwhile, this "underground", offended idealist, forced to choose between an unattractive socialist utopia and his still living ideal, will rather retire to his "underground" and remain there in conscious inertia and suffering. But nothing is permanent in the Underground Man's thinking; everything is subjected to chemical disintegration by the laws of consciousness. In the end, he is prepared to abandon even his insistence on suffering:

Here, after all, I don't really stand either for suffering or for well-being. I stand for my own caprice, and for its being guaranteed to me whenever I want it.[63]

It is useless to argue with the Underground Man that he is inconsistent. He will agree. The only consistent, predictable thing that can be said of his ideas is that they pivot around his suffering ego; in the words of Prince Valkhovsky in *The Insulted and Injured* (*Unizhennye i oskorblennye*, 1861): "What isn't nonsense is personality — myself. Everything is for me, the whole world is created for me."[64]

Reason is the unseen antagonist of the Underground Man. It destroys

---

[59]   *Ibid.*, IV, 129.
[60]   *Ibid.*, IV, 130.
[61]   *Ibid.*, IV, 131.
[62]   *Ibid.*, IV, 132.
[63]   *Ibid.*, IV, 130-131.
[64]   Dostoevskij, *Unižennye i oskorblennye, Polnoe sobranie khudožestvennykh proizvedenij, op. cit.*, III, 215.

him from within and without. What distinguishes his philosophy of irrationalism — his philosophy of malice — is that it is the philosophical counterpart of a personal irrationalism. The Underground Man seeks through a philosophy of irrationalism to assert, justify and defend the rights of the humiliated and alienated individual, just as in his day-to-day existence and experimentation he pursues the same goal on a personal plane. This total, integrated portrait of a man discloses the close link between the crisis of reason and the crisis of the individual. *Notes from the Underground* heralds the modern revolt against the concept that reason is an ally of the individual in his search for freedom; it also anticipates the modern use of philosophy in defense of irrationalism. Hegel unsympathetically but with great insight analyzed the alliance between philosophy and the alienated individual:

If we ... look at the level which the self-conscious mind at present occupies, we shall find that self-consciousness has got beyond the substantial fullness of life, which it used to carry on in the element of thought—beyond the state of immediacy of belief, beyond the satisfaction and security arising from the assurance which consciousness possessed of being reconciled with the ultimate reality and with its all-pervading presence, within as well as without. Self-conscious mind has not merely passed beyond that to the opposite extreme of insubstantial reflection of self into self, but beyond this too. It has not merely lost its essential and concrete life, it is also conscious of this loss and of the transitory finitude characteristic of its content. Turning away from the husks it has to feed on, and confessing that it lies in wickedness and sin, it reviles itself for so doing, and now desires from philosophy not so much to bring it to a knowledge of what it is, as to obtain once again through philosophy the restoration of that sense of solidity and substantiality of existence it has lost. Philosophy is thus expected not so much to meet this want by opening up the compact solidity of substantial existence, and bringing this to the light and level of self-consciousness—is not so much to bring chaotic conscious life back to the orderly ways of thought, and the simplicity of the notion, as to run together what thought has divided asunder, suppress the notion with its distinctions, and restore the *feeling* of existence. What it wants from philosophy is not so much insight as edification.[65]

The restoration of the "feeling of existence" is the psychological goal of "underground" rebellion. Yet freedom of will in the "underground" is a problem in metaphysics: its total meaning is that of saying "no" to the converging forces against which the individual is in fact impotent.

[65] G. W. F. Hegel, *The Phenomenology of Mind*, Trans. J. B. Baillie (2d ed., revised; New York, 1931), pp. 71-72.

The Underground Man is not defending his freedom, but protesting his enslavement, his permanent condition of abasement. But through sustained protest, through "malice", his refusal to recognize the right of the forces humiliating him, he gains the illusion of freedom — a negative victory that is, indeed, the difference between self-recognition and moral extinction.

The Underground Man's rebellious self-assertion recalls that of the convicts in Dostoevsky's *Notes from the House of the Dead* who in various ways seek to manifest a will of their own. The convict, Dostoevsky's writes, is very fond of playing the bully and braggart,

that is, of pretending to his comrades and convincing even himself, *if only for a while*, that he has a freedom and power incomparably greater than it appears; in a word, he can carouse, storm about, crushingly insult somebody and prove to him that he *can* do all this, that all this is in "our hands," that is, he can convince himself of something of which it is out of the question for the poor fellow even to dream. ... Finally, in all this blustering about there is a risk, which means that all this has at least the semblance of life, at least a distant semblance of freedom. And what will one not give for freedom? [66]

A pitiful, despairing protest rises from the pages of *Notes from the Underground,* a protest that touches on the deepest sources of humanity in man; yet it is continually being deformed by the pain which has called it forth. The Underground Man is the helpless little man, the hero as victim desperately seeking a way out of the "underground"; but in his search he is anti-hero, destroying himself and prepared to plunge the world into chaos in the name of unrestrained and blind self-will. "Man needs one thing," declares the Underground Man, "independent will, whatever this independence costs and wherever it may lead. But really, the devil only knows***."[67]

"Man was created a rebel," insists the Grand Inquisitor in Dostoevsky's "The Legend of the Grand Inquisitor"; "and can rebels be happy?"[68] "... Nothing has ever been more insupportable for man and human society than freedom." [69] *Notes from the Underground,* though it is directed against everything that the Grand Inquisitor stands for, is nevertheless a sombre illustration of his thesis.

[66]   Dostoevskij, *Zapiski iz mertvogo doma, op. cit.,* III, 371-372.
[67]   Dostoevskij, *Zapiski iz podpol'ja, op. cit.,* IV, 124.
[68]   Dostoevskij, *Brat'ja karamazovy, Polnoe sobranie khudožestvennykh proizvedenij, op. cit.,* IX, 249.
[69]   *Ibid.,* IX, 250.

CHAPTER III

NOTES FROM THE UNDERGROUND:
A PIVOTAL WORK

> The underground, the underground, the poet of the
> underground! The feuilleton writers repeat this as
> though there were something degrading in it for me.
> Fools, this is *my glory, because truth is here.*
>
> From the notebooks of Dostoevsky

The role of *Notes from the Underground* in Dostoevsky's works is
complex; its ramifications extend throughout his writings. *Notes from
the Underground* is a key work in which Dostoevsky develops the main
themes of his great novels. These themes may be broadly stated as
criticism of the idea that society can be reorganized on a permanently
happy basis by means of reason, and criticism of the educated Russian
man, morally and intellectually divorced from the people and poisoned
by a rationalistic ethic. The theme of freedom — the search for a way
out of the "underground", the exploration of these paths and the dangers
confronting man in this quest — is really begun in *Notes from the
Underground*.

The Underground Man occupies a transitional position in Dostoevsky's
works: he represents in part the culmination of Dostoevsky's study and
defense of the "little man", and he represents as well the beginning of
Dostoevsky's critical examination of the anti-hero and social apostate.
It is in the Underground Man that the timid rebellion of Devushkin
takes on the destructive character that Dostoevsky will condemn in
Raskolnikov.

When Chernyshevsky in his novel *What is to be Done?* contrasted
the enlightened rational egotism of the "new man" (Lopukhov, Kirsanov,
Rakhmetov) with the unenlightened egotism of the petty, stupid egotist,[1]

---

[1] Such a petty stupid egotist is the mother of Vera Pavlovna (heroine of *What
is to be Done?*)—the narrow and grasping Marya Aleksevna Rozalskaya. Her
actions, like those of Chernyshevsky's heroes, are also based on self-interest, on
"advantage," but because of her circumstances she is an unenlightened egotist
doing bad things. Chernyshevsky gently and condescendingly analyzes her in
an imaginary conversation. He observes, however, that "of all the people whom

he invited the malicious and hysterical rage of Dostoevsky's "little man". The latter in his misery and suffering was very far indeed from the lofty idealism and self-confident philosophy of the rationalists. But this "little man", as he rebels in *Notes from the Underground* is more than a rebellious Devushkin: he is conceived as one of Russian society's negative types, a former adherent of the rationalists, crippled by rationalism and by the deleterious influence of the "beautiful and lofty".

Thus, the theme of defense of the "little man" is interwoven with Dostoevsky's attack on rationalism. It is the synthesis of these themes which explains the complex ideological dialectic of *Notes from the Underground.*

In *Crime and Punishment* (*Prestuplenie i nakazanie*, 1866) and subsequent works the theme of anti-hero and social apostate is separated from the theme of the "little man". Dostoevsky turns from his earlier concentration on the "little man" to embrace a wider circle of imagery, including types which more realistically belong to the stratum of the educated Russian man of the nineteenth century.

In *Crime and Punishment* Dostoevsky, as though recoiling from his complicity with "underground" rebellion, does not use the Underground Man's philosophy of negation and rebellion as a means of attacking rationalist and utilitarian doctrines. The basic polarity in this work — as in later works — is love, self-sacrifice, religious reconciliation with reality as opposed to rationalist rebellion. This polarity is present in *Notes from the Underground,* but it is subordinated to the struggle of the Underground Man against rationalism — the most dynamic ideological tension in the work. Dostoevsky's essentially supports his rebellious Underground Man in this struggle. In *Crime and Punishment,* however, he joins rebel and rationalist in the figure of Raskolnikov and,

---

I do not like and with whom I would not wish to have anything to do, I would nevertheless more readily do business with you. Of course, you are merciless where this is necessary to your advantage. But if you should find no advantage in doing anybody harm, you would not do it out of some stupid, nasty desires..." Chernyshevsky goes on to complement Marya Aleksevna for acquiescing in the end to the marriage of her daughter Vera Pavlovna and Lopukhov. "...And indeed this is a great virtue, Marya Aleksevna, to be able to recognize the impossible!" "You had the good sense and courage to bow to the impossible without vainly doing harm to yourself and others." (Černyševskij, *Čto delat'*, *op. cit.*, p. 100.) Dostoevsky's Underground Man, of course, belongs to the group of egotists who presumably do not know their true interests. But unlike Marya Aleksevna he is a militant egotist, he resents condescending remarks, he staunchly defends petty and selfish egotism. He does not bow down to the "impossible," the "stone wall," and, obviously, is one of those egotists who, in Chernyshevsky's words, is ready to do harm "out of some stupid, nasty desires."

continuing his attack on the rationalists, in effect withdraws his support from the rebel.

The central fact of rationalism, as it is presented in *Notes from the Underground,* is its inevitable violation of the individual. This idea, expressed by Razumikhin in *Crime and Punishment* [2] is illustrated by the whole tragic drama of Raskolnikov. Raskolnikov's crime is, in part, a rationalistic distortion, arrived at through utilitarian humanism, ratiocination and self-isolation. The Underground Man's "game" with Liza, his testing of ego, is paralleled in *Crime and Punishment* by Raskolnikov's experiment. It is the voice of the Underground Man that is heard in Raskolnikov's cry: "Freedom and power, but chiefly power! Over every trembling creature and over the whole ant hill! That is the goal! Remember that!" [3]

Raskolnikov's apocalyptic vision of the destruction of society on earth (in the Epilogue of *Crime and Punishment*) symbolizes his own tragedy. "Spirits endowed with reason and will" introduce moral chaos and destruction into society, just as "reason" helped lead Raskolnikov to moral chaos and disaster. Reason alone provides no foundation for moral behavior. This idea is first developed in *Notes from the Underground.*

The theme of evil "spirits endowed with intellect and will" introducing destruction and chaos into the life of society is developed in Dostoevsky's novel *The Devils* (*Besy,* 1871). Shatov gives direct voice to the anti-rationalist theme. [4] The "beautiful dreams" of the "lovers of humanity"

[2] Razumikhin observes: "That is why they [the socialists] dislike so much the *living* process of life: there is no need for a *living soul!* The living soul demands life, the living soul does not obey mechanics, the living soul is suspicious, the living soul is retrograde! But the sort of soul they want though it smells of carrion, though it may be made of rubber, still it is not alive, still it is without will, still it is slavish and will not rebel! And the result is that everything is reduced to the laying of bricks and the planning of corridors and rooms in the phalanstery! The phalanstery may be ready, but human nature is still not ready for the phalanstery, it wants life, the living process has not yet reached completion, it is too soon for the cemetery!" (Dostoevskij, *Prestuplenie i nakazanie, Polnoe sobranie khudožestvennykh proizvedenij, op. cit.,* V, 209.)

[3] *Ibid.,* V, 269.

[4] Shatov observes: "Reason and science in the life of peoples always, from the beginning of time to the present, have played only a secondary and auxiliary role ... Peoples are formed and moved by a different force ... This force is that of an unquenchable desire to go on to the end and at the same time to deny the existence of an end ... Reason has never been able to define good and evil, or even to separate good from evil, even approximately; is has always shamefully and pitifully mixed them up; the solutions moreover have been those of brute force." (Dostoevskij, *Besy, Polnoe sobranie khudožestvennykh proizvedenij, op. cit.,* VII, 206.)

in *Notes from the Underground* have degenerated in *The Devils* into
the nightmare of Shigalevism. The division of humanity into superior
"underground" men and the stupid "herd" (*Notes from the Underground*), into those with the right to transgress and those who "like to be
obedient" [5] (*Crime and Punishment*) is now reincarnated in Shigalev's
system of earthly paradise — a paradise "based on the facts of nature
and very logical".[6] Shigalev is a "fanatical lover of humanity". Stepan
Verkhovensky in *The Devils* is disclosed as the spiritual link between
the idealism of the 1840's and Shigalevism.

The monstrous program of Shigalev and Petr Verkhovensky is no
more than a codification of the despotic strivings of the Underground
Man. "Starting from unlimited freedom I arrive at unlimited despotism,"
Shigalev remarks.[7] This idea, in its psychological content, is born in the
"underground" where freedom for the individual is freedom to tyrannize,
to subjugate, to debauch, to expand.

There can be no other social paradise on earth except a Shigalevian
one — Shigalev emphasizes. "He is perhaps much nearer to realism
than anyone," observes the lame teacher, "and his earthly paradise is
almost the real one, the very one for the loss of which mankind is sighing,
indeed if it ever existed." [8] The theme of man's inability to bear freedom
is expressed by Murin in "The Landlady" ("Khozyaika", 1847). "Give
a weak man freedom and he will bind it himself and return it to you." [9]
The Underground Man, at the conclusion of his "notes", expresses a
similar pessimistic thought. "Well, just try, just give us, for example, a
little more independence, untie the hands of any of us, broaden the
sphere of our activity, relax the control and we — yes, I assure you —

---

[5]   Dostoevskij, *Prestuplenie i nakazanie, op. cit.*, V, 212.
[6]   The lame teacher in *The Devils* outlines the nature of Shigalev's social organization for the earthly paradise of the future: "He proposes as a final solution of
the problem to divide humanity into two unequal parts. One-tenth will receive
individual freedom and unlimited power over the remaining nine-tenths. The
latter must give up their individuality and be transformed into something like a
herd and by their boundless obedience achieve through a series of regenerations
a state of primeval innocence, something like a primitive paradise, although,
however, they will have to work. The measures proposed by the author for de-
priving nine-tenths of humanity of their will and the measures for transforming
them into a herd by means of a re-education of whole generations, are quite
remarkable, based on the facts of nature and very logical." (Dostoevskij, *Besy,
op. cit.*, VII, 330-331.)
[7]   *Ibid.*, VII, 329.
[8]   *Ibid.*, VII, 331.
[9]   Dostoevskij, "Khozjajka," *Polnoe sobranie khudožestvennykh proizvedenij, op.
cit.*, I, 352.

immediately should beg to be under control again." [10]   This thought, too, lies at the basis of the conception of "The Legend of the Grand Inquisitor". Man is "weak and vile", [11] the Grand Inquisitor declares. Man cannot support the burden of freedom of choice. Happiness and rest for his tormented, suffering soul will only come when man renounces freedom and hands over his burden to those who will voluntarily assume his sufferings. This is a central idea of "The Legend of the Grand Inquisitor". It is antithetical to the rebellious spirit of the Underground Man, but it is rooted in the deep despair of *Notes from the Underground*.

"The Legend of the Grand Inquisitor" is the intellectual fruit of Dostoevsky's greatest rationalist and sceptic, Ivan Karamazov; in the last of Dostoevsky's great anti-heroes, the "disease of consciousness" attains its highest development. Ivan is dominated by the pride of intellect, the pride of reason. ". . . Ivan doesn't love anybody," Fedor Karamazov keenly observed. [12] Yet the egotism of Ivan, like the egotism of the Underground Man, has not crushed a passionate idealism.

The Underground Man's rejection of the rationalists' "crystal palace" world harmony is related to Ivan's rejection of God's world, of the possibility of world harmony. The Underground Man rejects the world harmony of the rationalists because it is based on an ignoring and negation of suffering, of contradiction, of the irrational element in life. Ivan with his "Euclidian reason" cannot accept a world harmony that is based upon the tears and suffering of children, upon tears and suffering that are unatoned for. He cannot accept a world that is not justified by reason. Here the "reason" of Ivan is not restrictive and negative, but positive. "I do not want harmony, out of love for humanity I do not want it." [13]

Thus, both the anti-rationalist Underground Man and the rationalist Ivan arrive at the same conclusion — the conclusion of uncompromising idealists — namely, that a harmony which does not cope with the problem of suffering, the problem of the irrational, is unacceptable. The Underground Man does not reject the ideal of the crystal palace: it is, after all, an ideal for him, too; he rejects only the chicken coop which is, he feels, what the crystal palace of the rationalists amounts to. "Destroy my desires, eradicate my ideals, show me something better and I will follow you." [14] Ivan essentially could say the same thing.

[10]   Dostoevskij, *Zapiski iz podpol'ja, op. cit.,* IV, 195.
[11]   Dostoevskij, *Brat'ja karamazovy, op. cit.,* IX, 254.
[12]   *Ibid.,* IX, 173.
[13]   *Ibid.,* IX, 243.
[14]   Dostoevskij, *Zapiski iz podpol'ja, op. cit.,* IV, 132.

Ivan does not reject God (the highest incarnation of the ideal), he rejects an imperfect "God's world".

While the Underground Man's insistence on the absolute fulfillment of the ideal is supported by Dostoevsky, Ivan's uncompromising idealism is viewed by Dostoevsky as ultimately destructive and negative (although Dostoevsky shares Ivan's pain and despair over suffering). Dostoevsky seems ready in *The Brothers Karamazov* to accept less than the whole ideal; he reveals in "The Legend of the Grand Inquisitor" what Rozanov has described as a certain "weariness".[15] Pessimism and despair about the fate of man unite the Underground Man and Ivan; but the despair that leads the Underground Man to the idea of the never-ending rebellion of the individual against any and all encroachment on his freedom evokes in Ivan "The Legend of the Grand Inquisitor".

Dostoevsky's negative attitude towards Ivan's rationalistic insistence on the absolute ideal reflects a more realistic approach to suffering and evil: in *The Brothers Karamazov* Dostoevsky clearly and powerfully challenges the dreamer and idealist who — like the Underground Man — demands everything "ready made". The "dreaming kind of love", Zosima observes, "thirsts for quick heroism rapidly performed and in the sight of all. . . . Active love, on the other hand, is work and endurance. . . ."[16]

The elder Zosima has a keen understanding of "underground" psychology. He observes:

The man who lies to himself and who listens to his own lies comes to

---

[15]   V. Rozanov in *The Legend of the Grand Inquisitor* (1890) calls attention to a "radical change" in Dostoevsky's attitude towards freedom which took place between the writing of *Notes from the Underground* and "The Legend of the Grand Inquisitor." In *Notes from the Underground,* Rozanov believes, freedom is regarded as man's most precious possession. Since that time, however, much changed in Dostoevsky's views: "Weariness and sorrow replaced his former confidence, and a thirst for tranquility is disclosed most strongly of all in 'The Legend'. The lofty gifts of freedom, truth, moral valor—all this is set aside as burdensome, superfluous for man; and one thing is called for: *some kind* of happiness, *some kind* of rest for the 'petty rebel,' who is at the same time a tormented, suffering creature, sympathy for whom chokes out everything else in [Dostoevsky's] heart, every impulse towards the divine and nobly human. To a certain extent 'The Legend of the Grand Inquisitor' may be regarded as the idea of the final ordering of man's lot, an idea which was unconditionally rejected in *Notes from the Underground.* But this difference must be borne in mind: whereas in *Notes from the Underground* the question was one of a *rational* ordering based upon a careful and detailed study of the laws of physical nature and social relations, in 'The Legend' the question was of a *religious* ordering which takes its starting point from a profound penetration into the *psychic structure of man.*" (V. Rozanov, *Legenda o velikom inkvisitore* [Berlin, 1924], pp. 135-136.)

[16]   Dostoevskij, *Brat'ja karamazovy, op. cit.,* IX, 60.

such a pass that he is no longer able to distinguish any truth either in himself or in his surroundings and, therefore, loses all respect for himself and for others. And having no respect for anyone, he ceases to love, and lacking love, in order to occupy and distract himself he gives way to passions and coarse pleasures and sinks to bestiality in his vices, and all from continual lying both to people and to himself. The man who lies to himself can be offended more easily than anyone. You know it is sometimes very pleasant to take offense, isn't it? And a man may know that nobody has insulted him, and that he himself has invented the insult and lied for show, exaggerated in order to make it picturesque, in a word, has made a mountain out of a mole hill—he knows that himself, but still he will be the first to take offense, and will revel in his resentment until he feels great pleasure in it, and so pass to genuine vindictiveness.[17]

Zosima's words seem directed at the Underground Man himself. And, significantly, they are directed at Fedor Karamazov — spiritual brother of the Underground Man. In Fedor Karamazov may be found the same self-deception, the same tortured posturing, the same cynical and shameless behavior that is characteristic of the Underground Man. He delights in his shamelessness and in his moral fall. In Fedor Karamazov, as in the Underground man, shamelessness, deliberate malice, is the distorted expression of humiliation.

Self-humiliation is a source of pleasure to many of Dostoevsky's heroes. These "underground" feelings are experienced, for example, by Stavrogin in *The Devils*. Stavrogin writes in his "confession":

Every exceedingly disgraceful, immeasurably humiliating, vile and, above all, ridiculous situation in which I have happened to be in my life, always aroused in me, alongside of an immeasurable anger, an incredible delight. It was just the same in moments of crime and in moments when my life was in danger. If I were stealing something, I would feel, while committing the theft, an ecstasy from the consciousness of the depths of my vileness. It was not the vileness that I loved (here my reason was usually quite intact), but I enjoyed the ecstasy that came from the tormenting consciousness of my debased action.[18]

The Underground Man has identical feelings. He relates that he would return to his den after a night of debauchery and experience "a secret, abnormal, vile pleasure" in the consciousness that "today I committed

---

[17]   *Ibid.,* IX, 46.
[18]   Dostoevskij, *Besy, op. cit.,* VII, 594. Stavrogin's observations appear in Dostoevsky's first redaction of Stavrogin's "confession," excerpts from which are given by the Soviet editors at the conclusion of Vol. VII. See also, Dostoevskij, "Ispoved' Stavrogina," *Dokumenty po istorii literatury i obščestvennosti* (Moscow, 1922), p. 17.

another disgusting deed. . . ." ". . . The pleasure here came precisely from a too vivid consciousness of one's degradation." [19] Stavrogin's pleasure in being slapped recalls the tormenting pleasure of the Underground Man at this form of humiliation. "When I have been slapped," Stavrogin observes, "(and I have been slapped twice in my life) that [feeling] was even here, in spite of a terrible anger. But if one can restrain one's anger in such circumstances, the pleasure will exceed all expectations." [20]

Stavrogin is perhaps Dostoevsky's most sinister embodiment of the anti-hero. Divorce from the people and the "living life", idleness and boredom, love of oneself and of one's own psychologizing, cold, formalized intellect, the confusion of moral criteria, delight in self-humiliation — these features unite the Underground Man and Stavrogin: but the dialectic of internal struggle, so intense and ever-present in the Underground Man, is felt feebly in Stavrogin. The features of his personality have become frozen like the features of his face.

The theme of the coexistence of lofty feeling and sentimentality with "underground" filth and vileness is one which preoccupies Dostoevsky in his works. Dostoevsky's "Eternal Husband" ("Vechny muzh", 1870) is a remarkable study of this phenomenon. Pavel Trusotsky (a betrayed romantic like the Underground Man) is a living "Schiller in the image of a Quasimodo".[21] The eternal husband, Trusotsky, loved the former lover of his wife, Velchaninov, with malice. He came "in order to knife me, but thought that he was coming to 'embrace and weep'," [22] Velchaninov observed, adding: "The most monstrous monster is the monster with noble feelings . . ." [23] Velchaninov recognizes in Trusotsky "underground filth", as he later recognizes in himself an "underground man". In Trusotsky Dostoevsky created a psychological type extremely close to the Underground Man.

"Eternal Husband," Dostoevsky wrote N. N. Strakhov March 18, 1869, was written in response to a request that he write in the manner of *Notes from the Underground*. "But this is not *Notes from the Underground*, it is something quite different in form, although the essence is the same, my eternal essence . . ." [24]

[19]   Dostoevskij, *Zapiski iz podpol'ja, op. cit.*, IV, 112-113.
[20]   Dostoevskij, *Besy, op. cit.*, VII, 594-595.
[21]   Dostoevskij, "Večnyj muž," *Polnoe sobranie khudožestvennykh proizvedenij, op. cit.*, IV, 460.
[22]   *Ibid.*, IV, 460.
[23]   *Ibid.*, IV, 461.
[24]   Dostoevskij, *Pis'ma, op. cit.*, II, No. 325, p. 183.

A study in ambivalent consciousness, many of Dostoevsky's heroes, like Trusotsky, love — in their hatred and malice — and hate — in their loving. "Yes, he loved me *out of malice*," Velchaninov remarks of Trusotsky; "this is the strongest kind of love."[25] The same ambivalence seems to have lent a special intensity to Dostoevsky's feelings towards the romanticism of the 1840's. The furious malice of *Notes from the Underground* is not explained alone by the simplicities of the rationalists; it suggests also a man who is trampling something that is hateful because it was extremely dear.

Many pages from *Raw Youth* (*Podrostok*, 1876) recall *Notes from the Underground*. As in *Notes from the Underground*, the writer of these "notes" is the hero of his own story. The hero, Arkady Dolgoruki, cannot "restrain" himself from writing; yet, he insists, he will never write his autobiography. "One has to be too disgustingly in love with oneself in order to write without shame about oneself." He considers it "indecent and vile" to display one's inner soul on the literary market place, yet with vexation he foresees that it will be impossible to "get along completely without a description of feelings, without reflections (perhaps even vulgar ones): such is the corrupting influence any literary enterprise has on a man, even though it is undertaken only for himself."[26] He is writing for himself, but he is continually addressing the "reader".

. . . The reader, perhaps, will be horrified by the frankness of my confession [a reference to his "idea" of becoming a Rothschild], and will in all simplicity ask himself: how is it that the author does not blush? I answer: I am not writing for publication . . . And therefore, if in these notes I sometimes address the reader, that is only a device. My reader is an imaginary person.[27]

Raw Youth is broader in scope than *Notes from the Underground*. There is a complex drama and a complex web of themes. But in the person of Arkady Dolgoruki, Dostoevsky presents a variation of the Underground Man. Arkady reveals the same "underground" pattern of behavior:

Was there malice in me? I don't know, perhaps there was. Strange to say, I always had, perhaps from my earliest childhood, the following characteristic: if I was maltreated, oppressed, insulted to the last degree, I always manifested an insatiable desire passively to submit to insult

---

[25] Dostoevskij, "Večnyj muž," *op. cit.*, IV, 46.
[26] Dostoevskij, *Podrostok, Polnoe sobranie khudožestvennykh proizvedenij, op. cit.*, VIII, 5.
[27] *Ibid.*, VIII, 73.

and even to increase my humiliations beyond the desires of my offender. "All right, you have humiliated me, well, I will humiliate myself even more; go ahead, look and enjoy it!" Touchard beat me and wanted to show that I was a lackey and not a Senator's son, and so I at once entered into the role of a lackey at that time . . . I could have kept up a passive hatred and underground malice in this way for years.[28]

In Arkady, Dostoevsky explores the formative years of the "underground" individual — a theme briefly but intensely developed in *Notes from the Underground*. The retreat of the humiliated youth into brooding isolation, the striving for power (as a purely subjective need), the preoccupation in this connection with the psychological experiment, the "underground" faculty of "cherishing in one's soul the loftiest ideal side by side with the most extreme vileness, and all this absolutely sincerely",[29] the ambivalence of rebellious lackeyism, the growing "spider's soul" — characterize Arkady Dolgoruki.

Arkady challenges his socialist-minded companions, and his words seem to come right out of *Notes from the Underground*:

Nothing is clear in our society, gentlemen. Indeed, you deny God, you deny heroic feats; but just what deaf, blind, dull inertia could compel me to act in one way, if it is more advantageous to me to act in another way? You say: "a rational attitude towards humanity is all to my advantage." But what if I find all these rational notions, all these barracks and phalansteries irrationel? What the devil do I care for them, for the future when I only live once in the world! Permit me to decide myself what is to my own advantage: it is more enjoyable. How is it my affair what happens in a thousand years with all your humanity if for all this, according to your code, I am to get neither love, nor future life, nor recognition for my efforts? No, indeed, if that's how it is then I'd rather live for myself in the most ignorant way, and it would be a good thing if they all went to perdition![30]

If Pavel Trusotsky and Arkady Dolgoruki are close to the Underground Man, the same may be said of Liputin in *The Devils* — a vain, malicious minor official, a punctilious little man and petty despot — and of the dying consumptive Ippolit Terentiev in *The Idiot* (*Idiot*, 1868). "Après moi le déluge"[31] is the title Terentiev affixes to his "confession", a

---

[28]	*Ibid.*, VIII, 279.
[29]	*Ibid.*, VIII, 321.
[30]	*Ibid.*, VIII, 49.
[31]	The prosecutor at the trial of Dmitry Karamazov remarks of Fedor Karamazov: "All the moral principles of the old man turn on 'Après moi le déluge'; everything that is the reverse of the concept of the citizen, the most complete, indeed hostile separation from society: 'let the whole world go up in flames, so long as I am all right.' " (Dostoevskij, *Brat'ja karamazovy, op. cit.*, X, 359.) The

profoundly "underground" document. He regards himself as sentenced to death by dark, deaf and insolent forces of nature — and he rebels. His last decision is to commit suicide, the only thing he still has time to begin and end of his own free will. He writes:

Let me tell you that there is a limit to disgrace in the consciousness of one's own insignificance and powerlessness beyond which a man cannot go, and after which he begins to feel a tremendous pleasure in his own disgrace.[32]

Pleasure in one's own disgrace, a pleasure that is intensified by rebellion against that very disgrace, is the essence of "underground" being.

Two heroes of Dostoevsky who seem almost to re-embody the Underground Man are the hero of the brief sketch "The Verdict" ("Prigovor", October, 1876, *Diary of a Writer*) and the hero of "A Meek One" ("Krotkaya", November, 1876, *Diary of a Writer*).

Dostoevsky is discussing the problem of suicide. In "The Verdict" he offers to the reader the "deliberation of a suicide *out of boredom* — of course, a materialist".[33] Dostoevsky discloses, in the words of his "materialist", a sequence of logical thought leading the hero to self-destruction. The monologue of the "materialist" is an example of the complete formalization of the thinking processes:

To be conscious means to suffer: but I do not wish to suffer—because why should I consent to suffer? Nature through my consciousness tells me about some kind of harmony of the whole. . . . It tells me that I—although I know quite well that I cannot and never will participate in the "harmony of the whole," and that, indeed, I will never even know what it means—it tells me that nevertheless I must submit to this message, humble myself, accept suffering in the form of the harmony of the whole and agree to live. . . . But my consciousness is not harmony, but on the contrary disharmony: because I am unhappy with it. Look, who is happy in this world and what kind of people *consent* to live? Precisely those who are like animals and come nearest to their type by virtue of the low development of their consciousness.[34]

Underground Man's outlook, also, is noted for its egotistic nihilism. He is prepared to "sell the whole world for a penny in order to be left in peace . . . I say the whole world can go to hell so long as I can always have my tea." (Dostoevskij, *Zapiski iz podpol'ja, op. cit.*, IV, 189.)

[32] Dostoevskij, *Idiot, Polnoe sobranie khudožestvennykh proizvedenij, op. cit.*, VI, 365.

[33] Dostoevskij, *Dnevnik pisatelja za 1873 i 1876 gody, Polnoe sobranie khudožestvennykh proizvedenij, op. cit.*, XI, 425.

[34] *Ibid.*, XI, 425-426.

One immediately recognizes the Underground Man in this "materialist"
— the lonely, suffering, egotistical, rationalizing man divorced from the
"living life". Like the Underground Man, he is tormented by the
"harmony of the whole", by an oppressive Euclidian reality, by a feeling
of the senselessness of suffering in which "there is no guilty one".[35]

Like Arkady Dolgoruki, this materialist cannot be happy "even in
the face of the most lofty and *immediate* happiness of love for neighbor
and for mankind", since he knows that "tomorrow all this will perish:
and I, and all this happiness, and all this love, and all humanity will be
transformed into nothing, into former chaos". He "will not and cannot
be happy on condition of being threatened by tomorrow's zero".[36]

The hero of "The Verdict" contains elements of both the Underground
Man and Ivan Karamazov. Even accepting the possibility of a rational
and scientific organization of life on earth, of man's future happiness,
Dostoevsky's "materialist" believes, the mere thought that "because of
some inert laws nature found it necessary to torture man for thousands
of years before bringing him to this happiness is unbearably out-
rageous".[37] This same thought, of course, underlies Ivan's rejection of
a future harmony. Further, contemplating the sad thought that man
may have been placed on earth for an "insolent experiment", Dostoevsky's "materialist" observes:

The sadness of this thought consists chiefly in the fact that once again
there is no guilty one; nobody conducted the experiment; there is nobody
to curse, since everything simply happened according to the dead laws
of nature which I simply do not understand, with which my consciousness
can in no way reconcile itself.[38]

Indignation against senseless suffering in which "there is no guilty one",
rebellion against the "laws of nature" which symbolize this suffering is,
of course, the heart of *Notes from the Underground*. The Underground
Man, rebelling, rebels in the name of his own personal suffering; Ivan,
rebelling against God's world, rebels in the name of suffering mankind.

Dostoevsky's "materialist", unable to reconcile himself with the "dead
laws of nature", sentences nature — which has brought him into existence
for suffering — to annihilation, together with himself. "And since I
cannot destroy nature, I am destroying only myself, solely from the
boredom of enduring a tyranny in which there is no guilty one."[39]

[35]   *Ibid.*, XI, 427.
[36]   *Ibid.*, XI, 426.
[37]   *Ibid.*, XI, 426.
[38]   *Ibid.*, XI, 427.
[39]   *Ibid.*, XI, 427.

Suicide, in "The Verdict", is presented as the logical end result of "underground" malice and negation. In "The Verdict" Dostoevsky discloses his clear understanding that the *perpetuum mobile* of such a type as the Underground Man inevitably must come to a halt. In "The Verdict" the "underground" type, like so many other Dostoevsky heroes, is viewed at the moment of crisis and catastrophe. "The Verdict" could be an epilogue to *Notes from the Underground*.

The hero of Dostoevsky's story "A Meek One" is one of the most terrible of Dostoevsky's heroes. One recognizes in this pawnbroker who quotes Goethe the face of the Underground Man. The hero of *Notes from the Underground* and the hero of "A Meek One" are one man.

Dostoevsky's pawnbroker describes himself as a coward and egotist, a man of difficult and ridiculous character, a dreamer, never liked in school. In this tragedy — related by the pawnbroker himself — Dostoevsky exposes the mechanism of a corrupt, rationalistic consciousness. The story is in essence a development of the Underground Man's "game" with Liza. This is the attempt of a degraded man, a spiritual despot, to play the hero, the deliverer, to make another soul pay for his spiritual injuries. The pawnbroker subjects his bride to his "system", his "idea" — the idea of meeting her enthusiasm with silence. He is proud and he wants her to discover his pride for herself. "I wanted her to be standing before me in homage for the sake of my sufferings . . ." [40] In essence, the pawnbroker wishes to fortify his ego by "conquering" his bride; and he enjoys the idea of her humiliation.

When his experiment ends in tragedy, in the suicide of his bride, he cannot help feeling that he "made some mistake here! Something went wrong here. Everything was clear, my plan was as clear as the sky." [41] Dostoevsky's pawnbroker is a man in whom moral consciousness is dead.

In "A Meek One", as in "The Verdict", Dostoevsky further analyzes the hero of *Notes from the Underground*. The heroes of these two stories closely resemble the Underground Man: it is Dostoevsky's orientation towards this "underground" type that has changed. There is no poetry or pathos in the heroes of "The Verdict" and "A Meek One" — here all is *Wahrheit*; there are no extenuating circumstances from the life of the "little man" to arouse the reader's sympathy; there are no conflicting ideological themes such as the theme of the defense of free will. A comparison of "The Verdict" and "A Meek One" with *Notes from the Underground* suggests the meaning of Dostoevsky's remark to

40   *Ibid.*, XI, 452.
41   *Ibid.*, XI, 455.

Pochinkovskaya about *Notes from the Underground* — "Es is schon ein überwundener Standpunkt."[42] What Dostoevsky had transcended was his support of the rebellious individual.

" 'People, love one another!' Who said that? Whose commandment is that?"[43] the hero of "A Meek One" asks at the end of his reminiscences. Man is alone; he is trapped in his singleness, in his egoistic self-consciousness. Only through merging of the self in the totality, in brotherhood, will man break out of the circle of his loneliness. This idea — Dostoevsky's great antithesis to the "underground" — is most vividly expressed in the last of Dostoevsky's works — *The Brothers Karamazov.*

Brotherhood, Zosima's "secret visitor" observes, will come only after man has passed through a period of human isolation.

The kind that is now prevalent everywhere, and especially in our century, but it has not yet reached its limit, and its end is not yet in sight. Because everyone is now striving to isolate his person as much as possible, wants to experience in himself the fullness of life, whereas from all his efforts there comes instead of the fullness of life only complete self-destruction, because instead of the complete self-determination of his being he falls into absolute isolation. Because everyone in our century has divided into units, each one is withdrawing into his hole, each one is holding himself aloof from the next person, is hiding, and hiding what he possesses, and ends by being repelled by other people, and repelling people from himself. He accumulates wealth in isolation and thinks: how strong I am now and how secure, but the madman does not know that the more he accumulates, the more he sinks into self-destructive impotence. Because he is accustomed to rely on himself alone and to separate himself as a unit from the whole, he has taught his soul not to believe in human help, in people and in humanity, and only trembles lest he lose his money and the privileges he has acquired through it. Everywhere these days the human mind is sneeringly refusing to understand that the true security of the individual lies not in his personal, isolated efforts, but in general social solidarity. But it will inevitably happen that an end will come to this terrible isolation . . .[44]

These observations disclose Dostoevsky's deepest insight into his epoch — "and the end is not yet in sight". The atomization of the individual in society, the atrophy of his social instincts, the separation from humane values, is a phenomenon of the 19th and 20th centuries.

[42] O. Počinkovskaja, *op. cit.,* p. 533.
[43] Dostoevskij, *Dnevnik pisatelja za 1873 i 1876 gody, op. cit.,* XI, 475.
[44] Dostoevskij, *Brat'ja karamazovy, op. cit.,* IX, 299.

Notes from the Underground is a germinal work in Dostoevsky's major period of creative work after exile. It is not surprising, therefore, that it plays a central role in the Russian literature that fell under the shadow of Dostoevsky.

CHAPTER IV

THE 1880's

The 1880's mark a turning point in the development of Russian literature. The poet Nekrasov died in 1878; Dostoevsky died in 1881; Turgenev died in 1883. Tolstoy renounced the role of pure artist in the 1880's and gave his attention to moral-religious matters. A new period of intellectual ferment and literary activity had not yet begun.

Political suppression and the collapse of social idealism provided the setting for the confusion and searching that characterized the intellectual world of the 1880's. The assassination of Alexander II in 1881 inaugurated a period of intense political reaction and repression; it was followed also by the decline of the whole spirit of opposition to the tsarist regime, centering about the Populist movement.

The turning away from political life and towards concentration upon worldly success and philistine ideals, accompanied by the doctrines of "small deeds" and reconciliation with reality — all marked the atmosphere of the 1880's. Tolstoyanism, with its emphasis on passive and peaceful means to non-political goals, was at its apogee. The popularity of such Tolstoyan aspirations as self-perfection was symbolic of the change from social idealism to a new stress on the individual.

A parallel trend carried intellectual circles into a reaction against the utilitarianism of previous decades; it was reflected in literature by a turn towards "aestheticism" — towards an interest in problems of form and a search for spiritual experiences. Later to flower in the tendency of modernism and the Symbolist school, the new spirit was groping and tentative.

More characteristic, perhaps, of the mood of the 1880's was a melancholy protest, resignation and despair. Typical representatives of this state of mind were the poet S. Y. Nadson (1862-1887) and the prose writers V. M. Garshin (1855-1888) and M. N. Albov (1851-1911). Their writings give expression to the broken hopes of a generation of idealists and dreamers swallowed up in a moral atmosphere of desolation. The "demon" that torments him — Nadson writes in a poem — is the "demon of anguish and doubt".[1] And in another poem, "Our generation knows no youth", he writes bitterly:

> Who among us has loved, forgetting the whole world?
> Who has not renounced his gods?
> Who has not fallen in spirit, slavishly losing heart,
> And thrown down his shield before the enemy?
> Almost from the cradle we grow decrepit in heart,
> We are oppressed by a lack of faith, we are gnawed by anguish,
> We are not even able to desire passionately,
> We even hate furtively![2]

It was only in a subjective and pessimistic form that writers like Nadson could express the social idealism they still retained.

The writer A. P. Chekhov (1860-1904) belonged also to the 1880's. Reaching maturity in this twilight decade, he embodied in his plays and stories much of its enclosed and humdrum atmosphere. At the same time, he belonged in spirit to a new period of scientific progress, educational advances and growth of industry. For all the new difficulties, the new gloom and oppression that accompanied these trends, they were to be background for a true literary revival.

---

[1] S. Ja. Nadson, "Iz dnevnika," *Stikhotvorenija S. Ja. Nadsona* (Petrograd, 1916), p. 207.
[2] "Naše pokolen'e junosti ne znaet," *ibid.*, p. 96.

CHAPTER V

M. N. ALBOV'S "DAY OF RECKONING"

> ...There was nothing in my surroundings at that time
> which I could respect or to which I could feel attracted.
> The Underground Man

"The name of Dostoevsky," wrote the critic A. V. Amfiteatrov, "is the threshold over which all who wish to speak about Albov must inevitably step."[1]

M. N. Albov's "Day of Reckoning: A Psychiatric Etude" ("*Den itoga: psikhiatrichesky etyud*") first appeared in 1879; it is dedicated "to the great shadow of Dostoevsky". It is difficult to believe that this work, so imitative of Dostoevsky in theme, style and device, was seriously regarded in literary circles. Yet the literary historian S. A. Vengerov declares that Albov was "not an *imitator* of Dostoevsky", but that he "only writes in the very same genre, because the spiritual world existing at the boundary of psychology and psychiatry is fully understandable to him." Albov's work, Vengerov felt, was a reflection of the "personal spiritual life of the author".[2]

Vengerov's defense of Albov is not without importance. Albov is not simply an imitator; he is also something of a Dostoevsky hero of his times. In an autobiographical note, cited by Vengerov, Albov styles himself as a "frightful dreamer" in his youth, and ascribes this fact to the solitariness in which he grew up. He was lonely and without friends, and overprotected; "after all, who knows what might come from street boys: they can pummel, insult!"[3]

Albov's self-identification with Dostoevsky's heroes not only testifies to the great power of Dostoevsky's fictional world, but also to the closeness of that world to life itself. This was an era in which the spiritual world of Dostoevsky's heroes was a common reality. But it was not yet the era that was to recognize in Dostoevsky the supreme embodiment of the fitful strivings of the modern individual.

---

[1]   A. V. Amfiteatrov, "M. N. Al'bov," *Slavnye mertvecy, Sobranie sočinenij* (St. Petersburg, 1912), XIV, 331.
[2]   S. A. Vengerov, *Kritiko-biografičeskij slovar' russkikh pisatelej i učenykh* (St. Petersburg, 1889), I, 464.
[3]   *Ibid.*, pp. 460-461.

Albov's adaptation of "underground" themes in "Day of Reckoning" is valuable as a commentary on the disillusionment and despair among the intelligentsia in the 1870's and 1880's. "Day of Reckoning" is a study of the sick consciousness of a Petersburg student of the 1870's, Petr Petrovich Glazkov, on the day of his "reckoning". Oppressed by a feeling of impotence and insignificance, Glazkov finally reaches the conclusion that the only form of heroism possible for him is suicide, because he is the "unintegrated combination of the strivings of an eagle with the sum of strength of a lady bug".[4] Isolated, introverted, he has been living a lonely life, moving from flat to flat, deliriously tramping streets or spending days in his room in self-laceration.

The experiences of Glazkov's childhood, in their psychological aspects, resemble those of the Underground Man and Arkady Dolgoruki. Glazkov was of good family, but very poor, and, filled with shame and humiliation, he always carried the "consciousness of his position with lacerating malice at the bottom of his heart".[5] He shut himself off in the pride of isolation and was always "clambering onto a pedestal", dreaming of another world where he would be "better than everyone, higher than everyone".[6] Reality is painful to Glazkov, as it is to the Underground Man, and he takes refuge from it in self-adulating dreams and fantasy. Vanity and pride, as in the Underground Man, alternate with the lacerating consciousness of inferiority, with impotent "malice" now directed against himself, now against others.

"You are a *coward,* that's the nub of the whole matter,"[7] Glazkov's "demon" tells him. Glazkov cannot declare himself to the girl he loves; vanity does not permit him to throw off "the mask of affected loftiness and enter into the competition".[8] He cannot act, his will disintegrates ("Oh, this cursed lack of will!"),[9] and he sinks into inertia and despair. He rejects the path which would "unite his crippled infected life with

---

[4] M. N. Al'bov, "Den' itoga," *Sobranie sočinenij* (St. Petersburg, 1908), I, 134. The lonely, morbidly sensitive, broken hero of his times was a type that especially interested Albov. An early variation of Glazkov may be found in Chemeritsyn, hero of Albov's unfinished story, "On an Autumn Evening" ("Osennim večerom," 1876). Chemeritsyn ruminates: "Oh, how many times precisely as now has he lain, exhausted by sleeplessness, analyzing the impressions of the day, absorbed with himself, with his speeches and actions, with all his deceit, lying and tortured posturings..." (Al'bov, "Osennim večerom." *Sobranie sočinenij, ibid.,* III, 326-327).

[5] Al'bov, "Den' itoga," *ibid,* I, 9.

[6] *Ibid.,* I, 10.

[7] *Ibid.,* I, 6.

[8] *Ibid.,* I, 65.

[9] *Ibid.,* I, 81.

alien, fresh life",[10] and so bring unhappiness to someone else. Thus, the Underground Man, as he rushed off in pursuit of Liza, asked himself: ". . . Just why am I running after her? . . . Will I not hate her, perhaps, tomorrow just because I am kissing her feet today? Could I make her happy? Did I not learn today again for the hundredth time what I am worth? Would I not torment her!"[11]

"Underground" heroes, in love, can only torment. In one scene, an obvious reflection of the Underground Man-Liza episode, Glazkov revenges himself upon the gentle seamstress, Katya Ershova, for his feeling of humiliation. He falls into a "rhapsody of malice".[12] He complains that Katya has rights over him and that "What is worse than everything in this base game, I am indeed and in real fact bound hand and foot in your power." Glazkov resents Katya's "slavish humility and devotion" as the source of her power over him. He had prepared this whole tirade quite deliberately in order to "offend" her, to "spit" on her "as savagely as possible",[13] although here, he confesses later to Katya, there was only hatred of self and self-torment. "Only understand my position," he explains; "to be conscious of myself as an insignificant nothing, to despise myself at every step — and to have to greet people. O, Lord! This is beyond my strength!"[14]

Glazkov has an outer resemblance to Raskolnikov. Yet Raskolnikov is a giant compared to Glazkov. Raskolnikov and the Underground Man do not admit defeat. They protest. Glazkov's will is broken. "Life rolls on its way," Glazkov observes with a resignation unknown to those Dostoevsky heroes, "crushing him who risks seizing it by the wheel."[15]

Albov, following Dostoevsky's method in *Notes from the Underground*, invests his hero with a dual role; Glazkov is not only a victim — the "sick son of his century",[16] as Vengerov described him — but a critic of his times. The Underground Man criticizes the utilitarian socialists and, in the background, all of educated Russian society for its romantic illusions, its rationalistic humanitarianism, its divorce from the "living life". He also criticizes philistinism and social opportunism as symbolized by Zverkov.

Glazkov's criticism is not directed against rationalism, but rather at

10   *Ibid.*, I, 89.
11   Dostoevskij, *Zapiski iz podpol'ja, op. cit.,* IV, 193-194.
12   Al'bov, "Den' itoga," *op. cit.,* I, 36.
13   *Ibid.*, I, 41.
14   *Ibid.*, I. 42.
15   *Ibid.*, I, 11.
16   Vengerov, *op. cit.,* p. 467.

a vulgar social environment in which man, love, altruism are not necessary, but "only metal is necessary";[17] at an intelligentsia whose idealism and will to act has been undermined by philistine ideals and petty interests and ambitions. His criticism is directed at the "living slime" which has engulfed all ideals and idealism.

Glazkov is a symbol of an intelligentsia which is losing its social vitality. He, too, participated at one time in the social movement, but the flame that served "past, vain dreams" went out long ago. Like the Underground Man, Glazkov is a disillusioned idealist. He withdraws into isolation with a typical "underground" contempt for the "stupid" masses chasing after insignificant goals, for those who are thriving in the "living slime".

In his impromptu address at the Rozanov send-off party (a scene based on the Zverkov send-off dinner), Glazkov gives expression to his contempt and scorn for society; his half-crazed words recall the Underground Man's pride, mortified vanity, and tortured posturings before Zverkov, Ferfichkin, Trudolyubov and Simonov:

I should like to convey what I felt when I arrived here. It was the feeling of a person who has landed in a place where he ought not to be. Everybody shunned me. And this is as it should be! Indeed, every one of you goes about with a label, each of you amuses himself with any kind of rattle—and suddenly a man appears who is quite free of all this. It's beastly to look at him! Isn't that so? I noticed this! You think that I am offended and complaining? Ah, not a bit; on the contrary, I am glad, that's just why I came here. Yes, yes, only for that reason! This seems strange to you. But if you can conceive how I despise you all, then you will understand me for sure. I came to amuse myself! Do you know that I am terribly proud? I wanted to tickle my pride. I thought: after all, this is all of Russian society in miniature, ergo—an assemblage of various types of human impotence. All this casts about, throbs in the living slime under various sobriquets, both carriers of ideals and simple pickpockets. All this swarms out of the skin in pursuit of any kind of rubbish in which each person supposes his personal happiness, and all this reduces itself to nothing but the gratification of one's vanity. Gentlemen, how petty and vulgar all this is![18]

Glazkov's demon-tormenter points out to him the distorted "underground" character of his separation from the community; he ridicules his remarks at the party for Rozanov:

You wanted to amuse yourself a little, to strike a pose before yourself, indulge in self-adulation, as though to say: now that's what I'm like;

[17]   Al'bov, "Den' itoga," *op. cit.*, p. 113.
[18]   *Ibid.*, I, 124.

you there, are crawling in your ant hill, while I am not of this world![19]

Glazkov finds a representative of the "living slime" in his old comrade Rozanov, an individual who bears much the same relation to Glazkov as Zverkov to the Underground Man. Glazkov had once idolized Rozanov as a leader of the revolutionary movement, a leader of the "stupid masses"; but now Rozanov has replaced the "red shirt" with the "formal jacket" and is setting out for an important post in the provinces.[20] "Let the rams butt each other or smash against the wall — it will be so much the worse for them, but not for the wall!" [21] This is the philosophy of Rozanov.

Rozanov — in the terminology of *Notes from the Underground* — is a man of action; he calmly accepts the change in fortunes of the radical movement. He is not going to beat his head against the "wall," that is, against reaction. In this he contrasts with the preachers of blind butting. Glazkov remarks:

Just look at Gribovsky over there. Is it really easy for him, a preacher of blind butting, among this diverse crowd? Everyone who does not beat his head against the wall is a major enemy for him. He is ready to lay down his head for this wall, to put on the martyr's crown! Let us suppose that hungry malice has a lot to do with it. Malice, I dare say, is the chief thing. Indeed, this is a disease! Indeed, this is suffering![22]

The preachers of blind butting are men of the "underground". Glazkov, disillusioned, holds aloof from both men of action like Rozanov and

[19] *Ibid.*, I, 131. Albov, while sympathizing with many of his hero's views, at the same time condemns him for his egotism. In "How the Firewood Burned," ("Kak goreli drova," 1887), Albov's criticism of egotistical rebellion against the so-called "ant hill" is brought out with particular force through a "letter from afar" written to the hero on his "night of reckoning": "Do not let these words be a voice crying in the wilderness. What is needed is not great strength, heroic exploits. We are all builders of one great building and each of us is carrying his stone for the general cause. Granted that we will not see the end of our work, granted that many of us will fall in the beginning, worn out and crushed, yet others will take our place and the building will be completed. Believe in yourself, believe in the cause and do not give yourself up to the deceit of human vulgarity and to your egotism, and if you want something you will do it, because he who wants will find the means." (Al'bov, "Kak goreli drova," *ibid.*, IV, 311.) The image of the "building" and of each individual carrying a "stone" to the great edifice is a tormenting one to the Underground Man. "And so long as I live and desire," declares the Underground Man, "may my hand wither if I carry even one brick to such an apartment house." (Dostoevskij, *Zapiski iz podpol'ja*, *op. cit.*, IV, 132).
[20] Al'bov, "Den' itoga," *op. cit.*, I, 115.
[21] *Ibid.*, I, 123.
[22] *Ibid.*, I, 123.

"underground" men of the Gribovsky kind. Like Gribovsky he, too, resists the dominion of the "wall", but his resistance has a different character; like the Underground Man he neither accepts the "wall", nor rejects it by blind butting. His malice is turned wholly within and is expressed in its ultimate form: suicide.[23] This is the "beatitude to bow to oneself"[24] — the only formula which Glazkov can find to act upon. This beatitude, characteristically, is achieved through impotence:

The greater the impotence, the more heightened the delight! ... What awakens in you scorn for yourself, turn that into your pride! ... To oppose all your being against something, something that is difficult, disgusting—it makes no difference what, only it must be absolutely the single most disgusting of all your aversions—in this there is beatitude! The whole secret is in the break. The sharper the pain of the first minute, the more tremendous the beatitude of the subsequent one.[25]

Here is "underground" malice, the delight of despair, as a formula for suicide.

Suicide — the formula of bowing to oneself — is Glazkov's means of achieving self-respect, a means of overcoming the humiliation of his cowardice and of attaining the "heroic". But like all forms of malice, it is a protest. Vengerov, who considered Glazkov typical of the generation of the 1870's, interpreted Glazkov's formula of bowing to oneself as representing a "proud striving to laugh openly in the face of the moloch of darkness and to set as one's only law one's own, Roman-strict conscience. There was a conscious ignoring of the surrounding morass and a firm resolve to give heed only to that which would place man high in his own eyes."[26]

Glazkov's "beatitude to bow to oneself", his malice, his suicide, were expressions of scorn for the social slime of his era. What was for Dostoevsky primarily a means of attack against ethical rationalism,

---

[23] The "underground" hero of Dostoevsky's sketch, "The Verdict," ("Prigovor," 1876) declares that "consciousness is not harmony, but on the contrary, disharmony ..." (Dostoevskij, *Dnevnik pisatelja za 1873 i 1876 gody*, XI, 425-426.) It is essentially this inner contradiction that leads him to suicide.. Glazkov's "demon," prodding him to suicide, declares that he (Glazkov) is going to destroy himself because he is an "anomaly," because he is the "unintegrated combination of the strivings of an eagle with the sum of strength of a lady bug ... You violate harmony! You violate the logical order of things. Just as soon as you realize this, you must correct the mistake of nature." (Al'bov, "Den' itoga," *op. cit.*, I, 134.)
[24] *Ibid.*, I, 138.
[25] *Ibid.*, I, 125.
[26] Vengerov, *op. cit.*, p. 467.

primarily a means for defending the individual against the inhuman demands of categorical necessity, was for Albov a weapon against moral-spiritual disintegration in society. It was, finally, a means of giving expression to the isolation of the individual. Characterized not only by social protest but also by destructive "underground" egotism, this isolation provided the setting where Albov's hero played out his drama of futility.

Dostoevsky's *Notes from the Underground* supplied the concept of "malice" and its position as bridge between personal rebellion and social protest. It supplied the psychology as well as many of the themes and devices for this story in which the hero is both exposer and exposed.

CHAPTER VI

V. M. GARSHIN'S "NIGHT" AND "THE INCIDENT"

> Where are my primary causes on which I can rest,
> where are my foundations? ... I exercise myself in
> thought and consequently with me every primary
> cause immediately draws after it another still more
> primary one, and so on *ad infinitum.*
>
> The Underground Man

"Have you read Albov's 'Day of Reckoning' in *The Word* (*Slovo*)?"
Garshin wrote his mother in a letter of March, 1879, "You, I know, do
not like anything except 'O. Z.' [*Fatherland Notes* (*Otechestvennye
zapiski*)], but read this. The fool Burenin says that this is Dostoevsky
played like 'Freischütz with the fingers of timid pupils', but in my opinion
this is sheer nonsense. There is, it is true, a certain awkwardness of
exposition, but in my opinion Dostoevsky did not have such clarity and
precision of analysis. It is true, I have read only Part I." [1]

Garshin knew Albov and valued him both as a fellow writer and a
friend. In the autumn of 1879 Garshin wrote his short story "Night"
("Noch", 1880), which treats the same problems raised in "Day of
Reckoning": isolation of the individual, disillusionment with self and
society, disintegration of personality, suicide.

Garshin's dislike of Dostoevsky as a person and his low evaluation of
him as a writer is known.[2] A recent critic, discussing the difference
between the creative work of Garshin and Dostoevsky, suggests that "to
the gentle, kind, sensitive nature of Garshin every form of violence was
abhorrent, as it was not to Dostoevsky".[3] While this is undoubtedly
true, Garshin's kinship with Dostoevsky seems more complex than this
judgment indicates. An analysis of Garshin's works suggests that his
conscious rejection of the "underground" elements in Dostoevsky's

---

[1] V.M. Garšin, *Pis'ma, Polnoe sobranie sočinenij*, (Moscow, 1934), III, 177.
[2] Garshin wrote his mother, January 15, 1882, that "... if Gl[eb] I[vanovich]
Uspensky] tells of loathesome things done by the late Dostoevsky, he will be
guilty only in the event that what he has told is untrue; anyway, you yourself
recently wrote me that Dostoevsky, by rumor, was a most repulsive person."
(*Ibid.*, p. 237.) Garshin wrote V.M. Latkin, in December 1883, of the first volume
of Dostoevsky's works: "If I were to write such rot, and then see it in print,
I would surely hang myself." (*Ibid.*, p. 304.)
[3] Fan Parker, *Vsevolod Garshin: A Study of Russian Conscience* (New York,
1946), p. 54.

writings may have been part of a struggle against such elements in himself. Garshin's story "Night" lends credence to this possibility. In this story Garshin describes the struggle of a man to free himself from his "underground".

"Night" is the study of a man at the "moment of reckoning" — the moment of catastrophe. Aleksey Petrovich, the hero, can find nothing in himself to respect, nothing to build upon.

I have gone over everything in my memory and it seems to me that I am right, that there is nothing to rest upon, no place to put one's foot, to make a first step forward. Forward: but whither? I do not know, but only out of this enchanted circle. In the past there is no buttress, because all is a lie, all is deceit.[4]

Like Stavrogin (*The Devils*) in his letter to Dasha,[5] Aleksey Petrovich discloses his inner sense of bankruptcy and loss of knowledge of self. "The moment of reckoning has arrived — and I am a conscious, crooked bankrupt,"[6] Aleksey Petrovich declares "with strange pleasure" on the night of his death. He is tormented with "underground" lacerations. He tramples with malicious pleasure upon his "pride" and he finds nothing but filth in his soul. Yet he would be outraged if somebody else attacked his pride as he was now doing. He scorns the vanity and dissembling of the false and vulgar world about him, its pretended love of the good. Yet he himself is a vanity-filled dissembler and his scorn for himself is therefore all the more intense. If he did anything in his life, it was "not out of a desire to do good, but out of vanity"; if he did not do any evil, it was only "out of a faint-hearted fear of people".[7] Suicide, he feels, will eliminate not only vanity, but the hated world about him.

Like the Underground Man, Aleksey Petrovich has a multiple, lacerated soul, a soul "already torn to rags". Many voices speak to him, and they all say different things, "and just which of these voices was his — his 'I' — he could not make out".[8] He wants to make contact with himself, with an honest, undissembling self, but all his life he has been

---

[4]   Garšin, "Noč'," *Polnoe sobranie sočinenij V.M. Garšina* (St. Petersburg, 1910), p. 173.
[5]   Stavrogin writes "I have tried my strength everywhere ... But to what to apply this strength—that is what I have never understood ... My desires are too weak; they cannot provide direction ... I know that I ought to kill myself, wipe myself off the earth like a vile insect ... I know it will be just another deceit, the last deceit in an endless row of deceptions." (Dostoevskij, *Besy, op. cit.*, VII, 550-551).
[6]   Garšin, "Noč'," *op. cit.*, p. 173.
[7]   *Ibid.*, p. 179.
[8]   *Ibid.*, p. 173.

playing a role in a farce, and even now he is "putting on like an actor". "In truth, do I really know what I am in reality? I am too confused to know." [9] Aleksey Petrovich raises here a central problem of the "underground": loss of knowledge of self.

Aleksey Petrovich, one critic observed, is the "Hamlet of his times, man poisoned to the marrow by scepticism".[10] Just in this scepticism he is closest to the Underground Man. Aleksey Petrovich observes:

You speak passionately, as though sincerely, but in your soul sits always a worm which gnaws and sucks. This worm is the thought which seems to say: how now, my friend, aren't you telling lies in all this? Do you really think that which you are saying? ... Are you really thinking that which you are thinking?[11]

These questions are part of a *perpetuum mobile* of consciousness. Thus the Underground Man, also, after heated arguments with his rationalistic interlocutors declares that he does not believe a single word he has written. "That is, I do believe I dare say, but at the very same time, for some unknown reason, I sense and suspect that I am lying like a shoemaker."[12]

Aleksey Petrovich can find nothing to rest on, no foundation. He feels that he cannot live with himself, with all his deception, and decides to kill himself. But the desire to commit suicide is contradicted by the thought that perhaps not everything in his life is false, perhaps something decent is possible in the future. Such is the "enchanted circle" in which Aleksey finds himself.

Aleksey Petrovich, however, differs from the Underground Man. He rejects the very thing that the Underground Man in his despair embraces: egotism. "Except ye become as little children ..." he reads in the Bible, and realizes that it means "not to place oneself first in everything". He realizes that one must make contact with real life, with the great mass of people. He must tear

from his heart this vile little god, this monster with a huge belly, this disgusting "I" which, like a tapeworm, sucks the soul and keeps on demanding for itself more and more food. But out of what shall I tear it? You have already devoured everything. All my strength, all my time was devoted to serving you. Now I fed you, nevertheless I bowed to you,

[9] *Ibid.*, p. 174.
[10] P. F. Jakubovič, "Gamlet našikh dnej," in *Polnoe sobranie sočinenij V. M. Garšina* (St. Petersburg, 1910), pp. 544-545.
[11] Garšin, "Noč'," *ibid.*, p. 185.
[12] Dostoevskij, *Zapiski iz podpol'ja, op. cit.*, IV, 133.

sacrificing to you everything good that had been given me. And thus I bowed, bowed, bowed![13]

Garshin's hero rejects the path of Glazkov who proclaimed the "beatitude to bow unto oneself". Rather, he identifies himself with a concept of moral regeneration that Dostoevsky advances in his great novels. He feels a need for active love and self-sacrifice, for salvation through real earthly suffering. Aleksey Petrovich, tortured by loneliness, by "underground" conflicts and tension, nevertheless reaches towards the vision of a Zosima.

But the "underground" does not easily release its victims. Aleksey Petrovich reaches the conclusion that it is necessary to" 'reject himself', to kill his terrible'I' ".[14] Just this disharmony with self is a permanent characteristic of "underground" man. Like the hero of "The Verdict", Aleksey Petrovich no longer finds it possible to live with this disharmony. And in a state of ecstasy, of tremendous emotional catharsis he leaps up — and perishes. The death of Aleksey Petrovich is a triumph for the "underground", a triumph for the forces of disintegration. The vision of salvation is not strong enough to re-integrate the conflicting parts of his personality, to eradicate the sick desire for self-destruction. Yet Aleksey Petrovich dies in the name of the renunciation of ego and in this respect his suicide — as a symbolical act — sharply contrasts with the suicide of Glazkov which is carried out in the name of the "beatitude to bow unto onseself".

Technically, Aleksey Petrovich does not commit suicide. His corpse lies in the room along with a "loaded weapon". His death, Garshin suggested to N. K. Mikhaylovsky, was the result of a heart attack.[15] Yet whatever the form of his death, the hero's psychological development seems to lead to suicide. The strange ending of "Night" suggests that Garshin may have been resisting the inner logic of his hero's development.

[13]   Garsin, "Noč',"op. cit., pp. 185-186.
[14]   Ibid., p. 186.
[15]   N. K. Mikhaylovsky in his first review of "Night" overlooked the fact that Aleksey Petrovich does not shoot himself. In a subsequent review, he reports that Garshin explained to him that Aleksey Petrovich "did not shoot himself but died from a tumultuous upsurge of new feeling which physically expressed itself in a heart attack." (N. K. Mikhajlovskij, "Ešče o Garšine i o drugikh," Sočinenija [St. Petersburg, 1897], p. 328.) I. I. Yasinsky writes that when he suggested to Garshin that Aleksey Petrovich had had a heart attack, Garshin responded: "I really don't know. But nevertheless you are right. And, perhaps, he remained alive in order to do something for a while." (I. I. Jasinskij, "Vsevolod Garšin," Polnoe sobranie sočinenij V. M. Garšina [St. Petersburg, 1910] p. 516.)

Aleksey Petrovich is intensely idealistic, but he lacks the strength to cope with reality; fearing life, he withdrawns into himself and directs upon himself all that moral disgust he feels for his own weakness and for the vulgar, dissembling world. In him sensitivity passes directly into "underground" laceration, self-depreciation and self-loathing.

The tragedy of Aleksey Petrovich, like that of Glazkov, is a "tragedy of the underground". This tragedy "consists in the consciousness of disfigurement . . .", Dostoevsky wrote, "in suffering, self-punishment, the consciousness of something better and the impossibility of achieving that something." [16] In both "Day of Reckoning" and "Night" the authors formulated the problem of the socially isolated intellectual in "underground" terms.

Garshin's story "The Incident" ("Proisshestvie", 1878) shows the marked influence of Dostoevsky's *Notes from the Underground*. "My story," Garshin wrote in a letter, "does not touch at all on the war, on social, political or other questions. Simply the torment of two broken souls." [17] A young clerk, Ivan Ivanych Nikitin, falls in love with the prostitute Nadezhda Nikolaevna and wishes to marry and save her. She rejects him and he commits suicide in despair. Here it is not the rescuer, Ivan Ivanych, but the prostitute Nadezhda Nikolaevna who belongs to the "underground".

The story of "The Incident" is told for the most part in the first person (Nadezhda Nikolaevna and Ivan Ivanych alternate in the role of narrator). Nadezhda Nikolaevna's narration is strikingly similar in style and mood to the Underground Man's confession. The voice of Nadezhda Nikolaevna is heard as from the "underground". For more than two years she has been living in a "disgusting room" and now, suddenly, on meeting Ivan Ivanych, she has begun to think. Yet her mood is depressed:

How boring and stupid all this is! After all, I am not going to make my way out of here anyway. I am not going to make my way out simply because I don't want to. I have been sucked into this life, I know my path.[18]

Nadezhda Nikolaevna's lonely and dissolute life recalls that of the Underground Man.

---

[16] Quoted by A. S. Dolinin, *V tvorčeskoj laboratorii Dostoevskogo, op. cit.,* p. 147.

[17] Garšin, *Pis'ma, op. cit.,* III, 154.

[18] Garšin, "Proisšestvie," *Polnoe sobranie sočinenij V. M. Garšina* (St. Petersburg, 1910, pp. 100-101.

I have again lost consciousness and again waked up. Three weeks of constant reeling about! How do I stand it! Today my head, my bones, my whole body aches. Depression, boredom, aimless and tormenting ratiocination. If only somebody would come.[19]

I went out of the house, not knowing myself where I was going. The weather was foul, the day was gloomy; a wet sleet fell on my face and hands. It would be much better for me to stay at home.[20]

As in *Notes from the Underground* and other works of Dostoevsky, falling sleet and gloomy weather form a background to the tragedy of the "underground".

Nadezhda Nikolaevna's speech, her moods, her personality — everything is marked by contradiction, negation and self-laceration. The Underground Man stands alone against "everybody". Everybody in "The Incident" is the public that despises Nadezhda Nikolaevna, the public which she, in turn, hates. She speaks out scornfully, derisively, cynically with the abandon of one who has reached what the Underground Man terms the "last wall". She declares with malice: "Yes, even I have my post! . . . Why does all this public look so scornfully upon me? What if I do carry on a filthy, disgusting business, what if I do occupy a most contemptible place; but after all, it is a place! This judge also has a place. And I think that both of us***."[21] Nadezhda Nikolaevna, like the Underground Man, embraces her misery and degradation with a kind of deliberate malice — but it is malice based on despair.

I want to stop, to hold on to something, even to a straw, but I do not have even a straw. I lie! I do have one! And not only a straw but, perhaps, something more reliable; but I have sunk so low that I do not want to extend a hand in order to reach for support.[22]

Nadezhda Nikolaevna is trapped in her "underground". There is a way out, but it is blocked by the consciousness of inner disfigurement, by the feeling that it is impossible to escape. Perhaps, Nadezhda Nikolaevna thinks, she might love Ivan Ivanych. But she quickly repels this thought. "Now he is ready to lick my hands, but later, later he will trample me with his feet and say: 'And still you resisted, despicable creature! You despised me!' Will he say this? I think he will say it."[23] For Nadezhda Nikolaevna there is no way out of her terrible life, her "nightmare".

Ivan Ivanovich Nikitin, though an extremely weak man, is not a half-

---

[19]   *Ibid.,* p. 107.
[20]   *Ibid.,* p. 109.
[21]   *Ibid.,* p. 102.
[22]   *Ibid.,* p. 103.
[23]   *Ibid.,* p. 110.

cynical half-sentimental poseur from the "underground". His function in the story is strikingly different in character from that of the Underground Man in the Liza episode of *Notes from the Underground*. Ivan Ivanych means his protestations of love. His weakness is not one of "underground" duality.

Garshin continues Dostoevsky's attack on sentimental-romanticism as a disguise for cynicism and sensuality. Nadezhda Nikolaevna rejects Ivan Ivanych in part because she fears that his fine feelings would be replaced sooner or later by despotic vileness, that is, she fears that he may be a sentimental poseur. She is already accustomed to the "preaching" of people who visit her — people who ask her her name, how old she is, and whether "one can't in some way get away from such a life".[24] It is in this spirit that the Underground Man conducts his colloquy with Liza.

There is the disgusting German with the initials of his fiancée on his arm who declares to Nadezhda Nikolaevna, "jetzt aber bist du meine Liebe, allerliebstes Liebchen," who reads verses from Heine and lauds Goethe and Schiller; there is the young man who recites by heart a whole page from some Russian philosopher who wrotes of prostitutes as the " 'safety valves of social passions.' Vile words," remarks Nadezhda Nikolaevna, "and the philosopher, probably, is foul, but worst of all was this little boy repeating those 'safety valves'."[25] The Underground Man, of course, could head the list of all these preachers.

Garshin's attack on sentimental-romanticism is focused on a society which loftily condemns, yet secretly sanctions and perpetuates vileness and corruption. Dostoevsky is more concerned with the disclosure of the irrational in man. Condemning those who veil cynical abandon with sentimental-moral preachment, Garshin does not (as Dostoevsky does in *Notes from the Underground*) cast suspicion on all altruism. "The Incident," however, is influenced strongly by *Notes from the Underground* in theme, style, and device. The tragedy of Nadezhda Nikolaevna is essentially a "tragedy of the underground". It is not surprising that Garshin himself recognized his indebtedness to Dostoevsky. "They all demand something 'sensible'," he wrote his mother February 19, 1878, "but mine ["The Incident"] is not at all sensible, but rather 'crazy', something out of dostoevshchina. It seems that I have the predisposition and ability to follow in his [Dostoevsky's] footsteps."[26]

---

[24]   *Ibid.*, p. 100.
[25]   *Ibid.*, p. 102.
[26]   Garšin, *Pis'ma, op. cit.*, III, 156.

In his story "Nadezhda Nikolaevna" (1885), in which the heroine of
"The Incident" reappears, Garshin indicates that it is possible to escape
from the "underground". Lopatin, the painter, who brings about a deep
change in Nadezhda Nikolaevna, is by no means an "underground"
man, although the manner in which he begins his "notes" (the narration
is conducted alternately through the "notes" of Lopatin and the "notebook" of the cynical Bessonov) recalls the Underground Man. Lopatin
writes:

I have long wanted to begin my notes. . . . I cannot rid myself of my
recollections, and a strange thought has entered my head. Perhaps, if
I set them forth on paper I will in this way settle accounts with them.
Perhaps they will leave me and let me die tranquilly. This is the strange
reason impelling me to take up my pen. Perhaps this notebook will be
read by somebody, perhaps not. I don't care.[27]

How far Garshin is from any "underground" parody of the romantic
hero-savior may be seen in his treatment of this theme in "Nadezhda
Nikolaevna". The egotist Bessonov, who cynically calls Lopatin a
"sentimental artist", remarks that he himself "almost took on the role
of savior which now Lopatin is magnanimously playing. But I was more
experienced then, than he is now." [28] Bessonov can only see inexperience
and sentimentality in the completely sincere feelings of Lopatin. His
cynical remarks reveal his own "underground" personality.

I am an unclean person, malicious and—depraved. . . . There are many
more depraved than I am, but I consider myself more guilty. I hate
myself because I cannot be as clean as I would like to be—as you
[Lopatin] for example.[29]

Bessonov had been intimate with Nadezhda Nikolaevna before Lopatin
met her, and it is only in the end that the "mask of indifference and
politeness" fell from this man who craved power. He realized then that
he loved Nadezhda Nikolaevna.

    In "Nadezhda Nikolaevna", clearly, Garshin identifies "underground"
sentimentality and vileness not with Lopatin who would rescue Nadezhda
from her plight, but with the depraved Bessonov. In this way Garshin
seems to combat Dostoevsky. He separates into the personalities of

[27]   Garšin, "Nadežda Nikolaevna," *Polnoe sobranie sočinenij V. M. Garšina* (St.
Petersburg, 1910), p. 294.
[28]   *Ibid.*, p. 377.
[29]   *Ibid.*, p. 301.

Bessonov and Lopatin qualities that coexist in the personality of the Underground Man.

It is apparent from these stories that even a writer who, like Garshin, disliked Dostoevsky, was not immune to the mood of an era saturated with *dostoevshchina*. Yet while they reveal similarities in style and theme, the stories are no less revealing of the differences between the two writers in inner consciousness. Aleksey Petrovich, like the Underground Man, can find no resting place on the treadmill of his thoughts; but he does not, in the end, stand only for himself, his own caprice. There is malice in him and in Nadezhda Nikolaevna, but it is not misanthropic and uncontrolled. Garshin's attack on sentimental-romanticism is an attack on social hypocrisy; the Underground Man's attack on sentimental-romanticism is an attack against idealism. But the Underground Man and Garshin's Aleksey Petrovich and Nadezhda Nikolaevna are at the center of the same crisis: that of the individual in a hostile society.

CHAPTER VII

1900 TO 1917

The early years of the twentieth century, among the most brilliant in Russian literature, were played out against a background of war, revolution and political oppression. *Mal de siècle* marked the mood of the period. Russia's defeat in war with Japan (1905) shook the autocracy; but the failure of the revolution of that year brought about a new stifling of political activity and social idealism and deepened the gloom among the intelligentsia.

With these years was associated the Symbolist movement in literature. Both aesthetic and philosophical in its orientation, the Symbolist movement was rooted in the revolt of the 1890's against social utilitarianism in the arts and philistinism in life. Inspired by the German romantics and French symbolists, it was nourished in an atmosphere of expanding industrialism in which the individual was isolated and lost. Nietzsche, with his ultra-individualism, and Dostoevsky with his "underground", his Russian nationalism and religious striving, were spiritual mentors of the epoch.

The Symbolist writers brought to Russian literature a vital concern with aesthetics in their search for new expression and development of a highly evocative, musical language. Their use of symbols, however, was not only a stylistic device, but for many of them implied a whole metaphysical outlook. The universe appeared to them literally as the "forêt de symboles" of Baudelaire's poem "Correspondances"; the poet appeared as a seer and his art as revelation of the truth.

United in their defense of individualism, the Symbolists were represented by such diverse figures as Merezhkovsky with his metaphysical preoccupations, the rhetorical V. Y. Bryusov and C. D. Balmont, strongly under Western influence, the poets Aleksandr Blok, A. Bely, and Zinaida Gippius, F. Sologub with his Manichaean philosophy and his strange cult of beauty.

A trend parallel to the Symbolist movement between 1900 and 1910 continued the great realistic tradition of the 19th century. Represented chiefly by Gorky and Andreev, it included A. A. Kuprin (1870-1938), A. I. Bunin (1870-1953), and a number of minor figures. The prevailing intellectual climate comes through clearly in the works of these writers, some responding to it with more or less open tendentiousness, others with scepticism and pessimism. The spirits of Schopenhauer, Nietzsche, and Dostoevsky saturated the works of Andreev and even appear in the writings of Gorky, who struggled against them.

Especially after 1905, much of Russian literature was marked by a tone of negation and despair; by a glorification of individualism that was likewise a glorification of egoism; by preoccupation with sexual and erotic themes and with suffering, violence, death, and suicide. By about 1910, the force of Symbolism as a literary movement was nearly spent, swallowed up in mysticism, while realism indulged in a mood of misan-thropy and self-seeking, typified by Artsybashev's student-hero, Sanin (*Sanin*, 1907), who finds the meaning of life in the satisfaction of all desire. And when desire is exhausted, Artsybashev suggests in a later novel, *At the Last Boundary* (*U posledney cherty*, 1913), there remain only self-destruction and the destruction of all humanity.

While to some writers of the turn of the century, Dostoevsky could serve as a source of spiritual-religious inspiration, others could also turn to Dostoevsky for a strain of anti-rationalism, cynical egotism and despair with humanity which finds expression in *Notes from the Under-ground*. "We all stem from Dostoevsky," wrote the critic A. Dolinin in 1913. "This is what many of our serious modern writers might have, or rather must have said about themselves."[1]

[1] A. Dolinin, "Otrešennyj (k psikhologii tvorčestva F. Sologuba), "*Zavety* No. 7 (1913), p. 68.

CHAPTER VIII

LEONID ANDREEV AND
NOTES FROM THE UNDERGROUND

> He will launch a curse upon the world and as only
> man can curse (it is his privilege, the primary dis-
> tinction between him and other animals), he may by
> his curse alone attain his object—that is, really con-
> vince himself that he is a man and not a piano key.
> The Underground Man

In his "Letter on the Theater" ("Pismo o teatre", 1912) Leonid Andreev
raised the question of whether the contemporary theater needed action
in the traditional forms of movement and activity on the stage. "To this
heretical question I take the liberty of answering: no," Andreev wrote.
Life itself, he continued, "in its most dramatic and tragic collisions is
moving ever further away from external action, is passing ever more into
the depths of the soul, into the tranquility and immobility of intellectual
experiences ... Life has passed within ..."[1]

Life has become more psychological ... a new hero has entered: intellect. Not hunger, not love, not vanity: thought, human thought in its
sufferings, joys and struggle—here you have the true hero of modern
life.[2]

Andreev sums up a spiritual event the consequences of which are analyzed in *Notes from the Underground* and in many of Dostoevsky's
other works: the separation of man from the "living life" and the
concrete world of human relations and activity, the withdrawal of man
into himself. In *The Brothers Karamazov* Dostoevsky, in the words of
Zosima's secret visitor, posits the tragedy of human isolation as the
central spiritual event of "our century, but it has not yet reached its
limit, and its end is not yet in sight".[3] Andreev's heroes are almost all
lonely men. In each of them sooner or later — as for the hero of "A
Holiday" ("Prazdnik", 1900) — the "consciousness of loneliness flared
up and like lightning illuminated the black abyss which separated
him ... from the whole world and from people".[4]

[1] L. N. Andreev, "Pis'mo o teatre," *Polnoe sobranie sočinenij* (St. Petersburg,
1913), VIII, 306-307.
[2] *Ibid.,* VIII, 308.
[3] Dostoevskij, *Brat'ja karamazovy, op. cit.,* IX, 299.
[4] Andreev, *"Prazdnik," op. cit.,* VII, 228.

The new "hero of modern life" is intellect. "Of all the amazing, inconceivable things in which life abounds," Dr. Kerzhentsev, hero of "Thought" ("Mysl", 1902), remarks, "the most amazing and inconceivable is human thought. In it there is divinity, in it lies the pledge of immortality and mighty power, knowing no limits."[5] But intellect, reason, thought betrays Dr. Kerzhentsev and shatters his mind. Intellect is disclosed as essentially impotent. "What is thought?" Andreev observed. "It is doublefaced and disgusting in its impotence."[6]

Andreev rejects reason with the bitterness of a disillusioned rationalist (in this he resembles the Underground Man). "The negation of reason," wrote the critic V. V. Vorovsky, "overthrowing it, disputing all credibility of its testimony on the grounds that it does not provide absolute truth is a *rationalistic negation* and therefore fruitless."[7] Just this kind of rationalistic negation of reason seems most characteristic of Andreev.

"Among the past Russian writers," Andreev told Leonid Grossman, "Dostoevsky is closest to me. I consider myself his direct pupil and follower."[8] This is unquestionably true. But Andreev seems more the follower of the "underground" Dostoevsky, the man of fear and despair, than the religious Dostoevsky, the man searching for faith, preaching reconciliation with reality and filled with an intense pity and compassion for suffering humanity.

The impact of *Notes from the Underground* can be felt in Andreev's stories: "The Story of Sergey Petrovich" ("Rasskaz o Sergee Petroviche", 1900), "The Wall" ("Stena", 1901), "Curse of the Beast" ("Proklyatie zverye", 1907) and "My Memoirs" ("Moi zapiski", 1908). Each of these stories treats the problem of "underground" rebellion against the "wall", against fate, against conformity and depersonalization. "Underground" rebellion in Andreev as in Dostoevsky, is related to the fate of the "little man". This is brought out particularly clearly in "The Story of Sergey Petrovich". But Andreev devoted a number of early stories to the "little man", and in many of them the problem and psychology of "underground" rebellion is explored.

In his story "Laughter" ("Smekh", 1901), Andreev metaphorically introduces a central problem of the "little man" — one raised by

[5] Andreev, "Mysl'," *op. cit.,* II, 120.
[6] Maksim Gor'kij, "Leonid Andreev," *Sobranie sočinenij* (2d ed.; Moscow, 1932-1934), XXII, 99.
[7] V. V. Vorovskij, "Leonid Andreev," *Literaturno-kritičeskie stat'i* (Moscow, 1948), p. 157.
[8] L. Grossman, *Bor'ba za stil'* (Moscow, 1927), p. 271.

Dostoevsky in *Notes from the Underground*. Every effort of the young man at a masquerade party to talk to his girl is greeted by roars of laughter evoked by his ridiculous costume and mask. "Oh, if only I had a human face even for one moment!"[9] the hero cries in despair. But there was only a mask, "a face in the abstract". Every feature of the face was in the right place, "but there was nothing human about it. . . . It expressed neither sorrow, nor cheerfulness, nor surprise — it expressed absolutely nothing!"[10]

The despair of the individual unable to communicate, isolated and threatened by a reality which would transform his individuality into something expressing "absolutely nothing", is at the heart of the rebellion of the "little man".

The little man's desperate fear of life, of a threatening unknown, and his withdrawal into isolation, is the theme of Andreev's stories "At the Window" ("U okna", 1899), "In the Basement" ("V podvale", 1901) and "The City" ("Gorod", 1902). The heroes of these stories are transitional types, little men who have not risen to the point of self-conscious protest and rebellion. Yet in many features these men are linked with the Underground Man.

"Perhaps it is because I have lost the habit," the Underground Man observes, "but all my life any external event, even the slightest, made me feel that right then and there some radical break in my life was at hand."[11] Fear of a radical break in his life causes Andrey Nikolaevich ("At the Window") to decline to marry a girl across the street. He prefers to sit by the window and look and listen.

He would have liked it always to be a holiday; then he could watch how others live and not experience that fear that accompanies life. Time froze for him in these minutes, and his yawning, transparent abyss remained immobile. Years could pass in this way and not a single feeling, or a single thought would be added to his dead soul.[12]

Andrey Nikolaevich has already entered the "underground". He feels secure from the "invasion of people" — in his room. But his thought casts him out under the sky and makes him the center of "world creation". Out in the world every "little man" must confront his antithesis, the undivided, ruthless, opportunistic, successful man of action.

---

9   Andreev, "Smekh," *op. cit.,* I, 138.
10   *Ibid.,* I, 136.
11   Dostoevskij, *Zapiski iz podpol'ja, op. cit.,* IV, 154.
12   Andreev, "U okna," *op. cit.,* I, 115.

Everywhere crude, noisy, bold people constantly are elbowing their way forward and they all want to grab a little more. Cruel, implacable, they go forward heedless of obstacles, whistling and cackling, and they trample others, weak people. One squeak comes from the trampled, but nobody wants to listen to it. It serves them right.[13]

One thing torments the Underground Man as a clerk: "I am one, while they are *everybody* . . ."[14] He is isolated in a world of strangers. The lonely bank clerk Petrov ("The City"), short and stooped, lives alone. He is not liked because he is gloomy and irritable. He fears the city's populousness and immensity in which he finds something "stubborn, unconquerable and callously cruel . . .".[15] But more terrible is the mass of human beings. "There was a multitude of them, and all of them were unknown to him, strangers." Petrov looks at these strangers, each with his own world, "with a feeling of terror and impotence".[16]

During the black rumbling nights Petrov wants to "cry out from fear and to betake himself to the deep cellar in order to be perfectly alone. There one might think only of those one knew and not feel so infinitely alone among a multitude of alien people."[17] Thus, also, the Underground Man lived in his "underground" den and hid from mankind. Fear of life is the first step in that process of estrangement which ends with the violent recoil of "underground" man from an alien world. The feelings of terror and impotence in Petrov have not yet grown into the sick strivings of the "underground" individual, yet this development does not seem very far off.

Sometimes the Petrovs voluntarily go down into the "cellar", at other times they are thrown there by life itself. Khiznyakov's is the latter fate ("In the Basement"). He is a lonely, broken man huddled up in a basement room beneath a mountain of clothes and rags.

At every sound speaking of life he seemed to himself to be huge and unveiled, and he hugged himself together all the tighter and silently groaned—neither with voice nor in thought—since he feared now his own voice and his own thoughts. He prayed to someone that the day might not come so that he might always lie under the heap of rags, without movement or thought . . .[18]

---

[13]   *Ibid.,* I, 125.
[14]   Dostoevskij, *Zapiski iz podpol'ja, op. cit.,* IV, 138.
[15]   Andreev, "Gorod," *op. cit.,* VII, 200.
[16]   *Ibid.,* VII, 201.
[17]   *Ibid.,* VII, 203.
[18]   Andreev, "V podvale," *op. cit.,* I, 154.

Andreev's "In the Basement" explores that world in which fear of life
is the beginning of death.

Andrey Nikolaevich, Petrov, Khiznyakov hardly protest against the
loneliness, misery, and terror in which they spend their lives. In the
personality of Sergey Petrovich ("The Story of Sergey Petrovich"),
Andreev depicts the tragedy of self-awakening.

When Dostoevsky's Makar Devushkin read Gogol's "Cloak" he
recognized himself, but only in an offensive caricature. He was mortified,
indignant, outraged. Out of Devushkin's feelings of indignation and
humiliation was born the stubborn and perverse rebellion of the Underground Man. When Andreev's Sergey Petrovich reads Russian novels,
however, he finds them "truthful"; they are painful to read because they
make him realize that "he was precisely one of those little people, eaten
up by life, about whom are written these fat and gloomy novels".[19]
Sergey Petrovich, one of the "little men" in nineteenth century Russian
literature, rebels; but his rebellion is marked by the fatalistic resignation
with which he views his image in Russian literature.

When Sergey Petrovich examines his life in the glaring light of the
Nietzschean vision, he sees only a "long grey and narrow corridor,
deprived of air and light. Behind — the corridor lost itself in the grey
memories of a cheerless childhood, up ahead — it sank into the gloom
of a similar future."[20] There is no exit from this gloomy corridor into
the world where living people are laughing and crying. Nietzsche has
brought Sergey Petrovich to this stage of painful self-consciousness.

Sergey Petrovich is almost a caricature of the Underground Man, a
caricature in which the principal features are helplessness and mediocrity.
He was a weak-chested, unoriginal student who had "absolutely no
living connection with people . . .",[21] a dreamer who read to drive away
boredom; in his dreams he was always the object of the applause of
his friend Novikov and others. Like the Underground Man, he is painfully conscious of unattractive features (flat nose, thick lips, low brow)
which, he feels, "wiped from his face his individuality". He contrasts
himself with his spiritual mentor Novikov who has "keen, bold eyes, a
high forehead and a correctly outlined beautiful oval of a face".[22]

Sergey Petrovich's relationship with Novikov (a "man of action" in
Nietzschean disguise) has the main elements of that complex relation-

[19]   Andreev, "Rasskaz o Sergee Petroviče," *op. cit.*, I, 64.
[20]   *Ibid.*, I, 67-68.
[21]   *Ibid.*, I, 63.
[22]   *Ibid.*, I, 61.

ship that exists between the Underground Man and "man of action" —
attraction, envy and hatred. Sergey Petrovich wanted, at first, to
submerge his "I" into the powerful "I" of Novikov but, he bitterly
learned, it was impossible. His feelings begin to alter: Novikov, whom
he formerly loved, now seems to him alien and puzzling.

But Sergey Petrovich, unlike the Underground Man, never reaches
that advanced stage of rationalization in which his own impotence is
transformed into cultural superiority. He never rejects Novikov as a
vulgar, limited man of action. For Sergey Petrovich lacks the high
intelligence necessary for such elaborate rationalization; he is himself a
"limited man". Yet even the limited consciousness of a Sergey Petrovich,
Andreev demonstrates, is prey to "underground" resentments and lacerations when that consciousness is made aware of its desires. At times it
is difficult for Sergey Petrovich to "reconcile himself with a severe fact
— life".[23] Then life goes on its torpid way when suddenly he recognizes
with horror that he is still the "same, petty, insignificant man". For
whole nights he dreams of suicide until his "spiteful and demanding
hatred of himself and his lot was replaced by a placid and gentle pity".[24]

When the brilliant Novikov introduces Sergey Petrovich to Nietzsche's
works the contradictions in his personality acquire a fatal sharpness.
Sergey Petrovich enters a period of spiritual revolt, of "rebellion against
nature and people".[25] He is taken up by the image of the superman and
of everything that Nietzsche said about the strong, free and bold in
spirit. The idea of the superman — of self-mastery, power, happiness —
appeals to the "little man" Sergey Petrovich.

Sergey Petrovich's strivings for happiness seem marked by the "underground". He, too, wants to "dominate" over life and people, and he
envies those who can do good and those who can kill, steal and commit
violence. Yet, like the Underground Man, he cannot become anything,
or do anything either good or evil.

He could neither rise high enough, nor fall low enough in order to
dominate life and people—in one case standing above their laws, and
creating them himself, and in the other, standing outside of everything
that is obligatory and terrible for people.[26]

Sergey Petrovich is alone, isolated like the Underground Man and he
faces people, the world, nature as enemies which strive to subvert his
will and dehumanize his personality. It is not surprising that Sergey

[23] *Ibid.,* I, 63.
[24] *Ibid.,* I, 65.
[25] *Ibid.,* I, 75.
[26] *Ibid.,* I, 70.

Petrovich feels that he is being used by alien forces. Angrily he recognizes himself as a man whose "usefulness lies outside his will". He is useful for the market as a "nameless 'somebody'", for statistics and history as a "nameless unit",[27] for scientists as a corpse, for the capitalists as a source of wealth, for the writer as one of the "innumerable Sergey Petrovichs" who are stepping stones to a monument, and for the reader "as an object in the exercise of good feelings".[28] Andreev carries the rebellion of the "little man" to its apogee — to a rebellion against the theme of the "little man" in Russian literature.

Sergey Petrovich is overcome by the "shame and dull anger of a man who for a long time did not understand that he was being laughed at . . .". He does not want to be dumb material for the happiness of others, but wants himself to be happy, strong and free. "And he rebelled against the nature which had deprived him of individuality, he rebelled like a slave . . ."[29] He rises up in rebellion — and collapses.

Sergey Petrovich's rebellion is too late, his spiritual and intellectual forces are too inadequate to carry on the Underground Man's kind of war against reality — a war in which the very evidences of reality are denied, negated. That is why he decides with Nietzsche that if one cannot triumph, one must die. This admission of defeat would be impossible for the Underground Man; for, though he will not beat his head against the wall, yet he is not going to reconcile himself with it just because it is a stone wall and he lacking in strength. After all, suffering is the "sole cause of consciousness", and "consciousness . . . is infinitely superior to twice two is four".[30]

All that is left for Sergey Petrovich is that paradoxical defiance of reality — suicide — which of course marks the final defeat of the individual. In suicide Sergey Petrovich seeks to attain what he failed to do in life — to break the "iron cage" of life, to triumph over the "dark forces of nature". Suicide for Sergey Petrovich, as for Glazkov, is the only form of heroism possible.

Sergey Petrovich's revolt is abortive. What is notable in "The Story of Sergey Petrovich", as a story devoted to the theme of the "little man", is its tendency to degrade the "little man". It is Novikov, the superman, the man of action who is the norm and who triumphs, in spirit, in "The Story of Sergey Petrovich". Sergey Petrovich himself is a symbol of

[27] Ibid., I, 71.
[28] Ibid., I, 72.
[29] Ibid., I, 72.
[30] Dostoevskij, Zapiski iz podpol'ja, op. cit., IV, 131.

hopeless mediocrity. The tendency to impoverish and degrade the "little man" and to exalt the idea and image of the superman gives a unique quality to Andreev's story.

In *Notes from the Underground* Dostoevsky calls for the eternal struggle of the individual for his rights. In "The Story of Sergey Petrovich" Andreev suggests the futility both of this struggle and of the "little man" himself.

The city in Andreev's work is the matrix of human tragedy. The concept of the city as an "underground" in which the individual is condemned to loneliness, the concept of the city as an embodiment of everything rational and mechanistic that oppresses the individual is the philosophical center of Andreev's story "Curse of the Beast".

Andreev's nameless hero, visiting the city, fears the "stone cages" which line the streets. "And I am afraid of the city", he declares, "of its stone walls and of its people who have small, compressed, cubic souls, who have so many doors and not a single free exit."[31] The visitor to the city rebels against a loneliness in which he is alone, yet not alone. Alone, surrounded by so many windows and doors, Andreev's hero "sensed a lie, and like every lie, it was immediately transformed into a secret threat".[32]

The horror of "underground" loneliness and isolation is joined in "Curse of the Beast" with a horror of ant hill existence. All the danger that the Underground Man envisages in the rationalistic socialist utopia of the future, Andreev's hero finds in the grey city of the present. He is first naively pleased, then horrified by the

fateful tragic sameness of things that ought to be different, this murderous necessity for everyone to creep into the very same form: to have a nose, stomach, to feel and think according to the very same textbooks of logic and psychology . . .[33]

Andreev's hero rejects city life for the same reason that Sergey Petrovich rebelled against the life of society: it undermines his sense of individuality. His "will", his "desires", he feels have lost their independence and to a great extent are subordinated to the will and desire of other people.

. . . I became terrified and agitated: it seemed to me that I had lost something and this something which I had lost was my *I*.[34]

---

[31]   Andreev, "Prokljatie zverja," *op. cit.,* VIII, 114.
[32]   *Ibid.,* VIII, 122.
[33]   *Ibid.,* VIII, 118.
[34]   *Ibid.,* VIII, 120.

The motif of "underground" rebellion against urban isolation and violation of individuality is carried in the "curse of the beast", a fierce, terrible cry of a lonely, dying beast. The cry comes from a filthy basin in the zoo. Like the Underground Man, the beast in his impotent malice and despair pours out his curses on all mankind. He is "cursing with the curse of a beast both this city, and the people, and the earth, and the sky".[35]

For Andreev the curse of the beast is only an allegorical expression of the curse of man, a curse echoing the despair of all mankind. The visitor to the city observes:

I am afraid of the curse of the beast. Why was he cursing me? Why? Am I to blame that things are so bad on earth? When I was born the earth was this way and it will remain this way when I die. Indeed, so short and impotent is my life! [36]

And in his despair Andreev's hero calls out to the beast:

We will curse together. Cry, cry out louder! Let the city, the earth, the sky hear you! Cry out louder, old creature. You do not have much longer to live, cry out about the danger, cry out about the horror of this life, cry out about death! And curse, curse, and to your curse of the beast I will join my last curse of man.[37]

The curse of the beast has all the impotent despair and enraged anarchism of a creature whose entire being has been cruelly violated. The curse of the beast is the curse of man who refuses, like the Underground Man, to be turned into a piano key. Of this man the Underground Man declared:

He will launch a curse upon the world and as only man can curse (it is his privilege, the primary distinction between him and other animals), he may by his curse alone attain his object—that is, really convince himself that he is a man and not a piano key.[38]

But "Curse of the Beast" brings out a truth which is implicit in *Notes from the Underground*: namely, that in the very act of exercising his privilege to curse — "the primary distinction between him and other animals" — man is himself transformed into an animal. Here the

[35]   *Ibid.*, VIII, 134.
[36]   *Ibid.*, VIII, 136-137.
[37]   *Ibid.*, VIII, 144.
[38]   Dostoevskij, *Zapiski iz podpol'ja, op. cit.*, IV, 128.

defense of man's humanity turns out to be its destruction. "Underground" man emerges as false prophet.

Man — the proud eagle — has fallen into degradation. Such is the idea implicit in the image of the caged eagles in the zoo: dirty, wing-clipped, their eyes express petty malice and envy.

Their hoarse, wild scream which sounds so mightily over the tops of mountains, over the great expanse of ocean, here became like drunken voices of angry, offended people, whining over the closeness, disorder and senselessness of life. I do not know their language, but clearly, with disgust, I understood their vulgar language, abominable hints, loathesome whining complaints, cynical laughter and curses.[39]

Such is the "underground" existence which Andreev generalizes for urban mankind.

Andreev is filled with horror and despair before life and death. He joins his curse to the "curse of the beast" and, although he knows it is futile, he accepts "underground" malice and despair as the only and last means of self-expression for man.

Man is surrounded everywhere by a wall of horror, and resistance to that wall, though noble and right, is nevertheless hopeless and degrading. This thought, implicit in "Curse of the Beast", is the central idea of Andreev's early story "The Wall".

The theme and symbol of the "wall" strongly suggest Dostoevsky's use of the "wall" in *Notes from the Underground*. The "stone wall" is a symbol of unavoidable humiliation to the Underground Man, of everything hostile to his craving for freedom and individuality. He will not beat his head vainly against this wall; but neither will he reconcile himself with it. It is better to sink down in impotent malice, grinding one's teeth in despair, than to submit to the wall. The Underground Man's willingness, figuratively, to beat his head vainly against the wall is Andreev's point of departure in "The Wall".

A mass of lepers are beating their heads against a gigantic wall which bisects the sky and divides the earth, lying on it like a boa-constrictor. This wall is an incarnation of cruelty and oppression, a symbol, too, undoubtedly, of the gigantic wall of tsarism stretching from one end of Russia to the other. It is a brutal, dull inhuman force crushing freedom and driving men to madness and suicide.

Against this great wall lepers throw themselves, bespattering the wall

---

[39] Andreev, "Prokljatie zverja," *op. cit.,* VIII, 132.

with their blood, crying out in despair: "kill us! kill us!" Again and again the human wave was rolled back, "until fatigue supervened and a death-like sleep and stillness".[40] One leper hears a trembling shudder run through the wall, and proposes that the battle be continued, that a mountain of corpses be built so that some shall reach the top. But his glance is met only by backs, "indifferent, fat and weary".[41]

The insane mass of lepers beating their heads against the wall express — like the "curse" of the "beast" — the suicidal malice and enraged anarchism of humanity, degraded and debauched. But even this classic "underground" means of struggle is futile, Andreev suggests. The majority of men, he indicates, are not willing to carry on the struggle for some distant goal which they will not see; the price is too high to pay; but above all, they are tired, and in their despair they are more likely to see in the wall the impossible. In discussing the work of Andreev, Ivanov-Razumnik wrote:

Although he understands by the "wall" not logical norms, but the abstract concept of destiny, fate, Moira . . . nevertheless for him it is easier to smash his head against the wall than to reconcile himself with it. And let the "wall" always remain the victor, but the irreconcilable curse of Man, objectively conquered, makes him the victor from our subjective, human point of view.[42]

The psychology of resistance that Ivanov-Razumnik ascribes to Andreev is, of course, the psychology of malice of the Underground Man. Yet an element of doubt and scepticism weakens Andreev's "underground" resistance. There is little subjective triumph in the "indifferent, fat and weary" backs of the majority of lepers, and the victory is at best ambiguous in Andreev's story "My Memoirs", in which the hero capitulates before the "walls" of his prison.

"The Wall" is a pessimistic response to the rebellious challenge of the Underground Man; "My Memoirs" is even more pessimistic. In it Andreev reaffirms the idea that struggle against the "wall" is futile. The story disputes the idea, strongly developed in *Notes from the Underground,* that man will always and everywhere choose suffering in preference to happiness without will. But the central idea which Andreev wishes to convey in "My Memoirs" is the same that Dostoevsky advances in *Notes from the Underground*: the evil and absurdity of any theory of

[40] Andreev, "Stena," *op. cit.,* I, 145.
[41] *Ibid.,* I, 146.
[42] Ivanov-Razumnik, *O smysle žizni* (St. Petersburg, 1908), p. 119.

life that is based exclusively upon reason and logic. Andreev attempts to discredit reason by a *reductio ad absurdum*.

Andreev's objective involved the creation of the strange hero of "My Memoirs" — a memoirist, an old man, now revered and honored as a philosopher, who had been imprisoned for many years. Although absolved of a hideous crime, he now resides voluntarily under self-imposed guard in a prison of his own construction. The purpose of his "modest 'Notes'," the nameless hero writes, addressing the reader, is to show how

a man, a creature of the higher order, possessing both reason and will, could find both hope and life in the most fearful conditions where it would seem that there was no room for either hope or life. I want to show how a man, *condemned to death*, with his free eyes looked out on the world through the grated window of his prison and discovered in the world a great meaning, harmony and beauty.[43]

The real hero of "My Memoirs" is not the outwardly content, condescendingly benign philosopher, but the man condemned to death, a creature without hope or life, like the caged beast or the trapped eagles in Andreev's "Curse of the Beast". The memoirist, on his confinement to prison, had the temperament of an "underground" man. He writes of himself in that period:

Here was almost a youth, twenty-seven years old . . . unrestrained, impetuous, given to abrupt deviations. A certain dreaminess, peculiar to the age; a vanity easily offended and which revolted at the most insignificant provocation; a passionate impetuosity in solving world problems; fits of melancholy, alternating with equally wild fits of merriment—all this gave the young mathematician a character of extreme instability, of woeful and sharp discordance.[44]

The hero of "My Memoirs" is indeed a candidate for the "underground." Andreev places his hero in the fearful conditions of solitary confinement in order to test his qualifications — and finds him inadequate. Yet at first the young mathematician responded to his confinement with typical "underground" malice: he cursed the world and life, beat the walls and doors with his fists, and even his head, but only caused himself a rather sharp pain. Little by little, the memoirist writes of this period, he

arrived at a complete negation of life and of its great meaning. These were really terrible days and nights when, crushed by walls, receiving

43   Andreev, "Moi zapiski," *op. cit.,* III, 190.
44   *Ibid.,* III, 191.

no answers to any of my requests, I walked back and forth in my cell endlessly, and one after another threw into a black abyss all the great values which life has endowed us with: friendship, love, reason and justice.[45]

The world of many of Andreev's heroes is a prison from which there is no exit. For Sergey Petrovich life resembled a "corridor", an "iron cage", for the hero of "Curse of the Beast" city life is a prison, for the hero of "My Memoirs" life is literally a prison consisting of solid and impregnable walls. It is not difficult to recognize in the memoirist's prison a lonely "underground". The horror of both the Underground Man's "underground" and the prison-underground of the memoirist is loneliness — the agony of so many Andreev heroes. The memoirist in his hours of despair cries out in his "Diary of a Prisoner":

What horror, what pain! My friends, you have left me alone! My friends, do you understand what you have done—that you have left me alone? Is it conceivable to leave a man *alone*? Even a snake has a comrade, even a spider has a friend—but a man you have left alone. He has been given a soul—and left alone; he has been given a heart, reason, a hand to clasp, lips to kiss—and left alone! What shall a man do when he is left alone?[46]

Both the memoirist and the Underground Man are confronted by the same question: what shall man do now that he is left alone in the "underground"? Both men want to live, but their understanding of what constitutes life is not the same. The memoirist exclaims:

How many weak people would have perished in my place, a victim of madness, despair, anguish—but I triumphed over everything! I turned the world about; I gave to my soul a form that my thought desired. In the wilderness, working alone, sick from weariness, I erected an harmonious building, in which I am living now joyfully and tranquilly— like a tsar. Destroy it—and tomorrow I will begin a new one and, sweating blood, I will build it! *Because I must live!*[47]

And the memoirist tells how he found "harmony", "beauty", and "reason" in the "sacred formula of the iron grate".[48] But the Underground Man, as though answering the memoirist, declares: ". . . Twice

---

[45] *Ibid.*, III, 192.
[46] *Ibid.*, III, 195.
[47] *Ibid.*, III, 206-207.
[48] *Ibid.*, III, 220.

two is four is no longer life, gentlemen, but the beginning of death." [49]

The formula of "twice two is four" and the Andreev formula of the "iron grate" express the same idea: the subordination of life to reason and logic. For the philosopher-memoirist this formula has positive meaning:

The iron grate . . . is only a formula, a simple, sober, honest mathematical formula. . . . The grate is the scheme in which are placed the laws guiding the universe, which do away with chaos, substituting in its place strict, iron, inviolable order, forgotten by man. [50]

This is the formula — which meant death to the Underground Man — in which the memoirist found life.

The Underground Man embraces suffering in his struggle for survival as an independent individual; the memoirist rejects suffering, in the end, in the name of reason and logic; the memoirist is crushed by suffering. The "mathematician" in him asserts itself.

Andreev explores his hero's fascination with the technical play of thought divorced from conviction or principle. Although innocent, the memoirist reasons, the "game of circumstances" was such that he could establish the truth of his innocence only by falsehood and not by the truth. And when, through a juggling of facts, he established his innocence to himself, he experienced a great feeling of astonishment that by "telling the truth I lead people into error and then deceive them, while by maintaining falsehood I lead them, on the contrary to truth and knowledge". [51] Reason and logic corrupt the memoirist.

The memoirist's prison-underground becomes his utopia in which he serves both a citizen and architect. Here all is reasonable, solid, secure; here the all-important "wall" separates him from the world where men live their false and foolish freedom. The ideal of an ordered world becomes his apologia for slavery. The strict and logical prison regulations become a positive, soothing feature in his life.

The hours for rising and going to bed, for meals and walks are arranged so rationally, in accordance with the real requirements of nature, that soon they lose the character of a certain compulsion and become natural, even dear habits. [52]

[49]   Dostoevskij, *Zapiski iz podpol'ja, op. cit.,* IV, 130.
[50]   Andreev, "Moi zapiski," *op. cit.,* III, 221-222.
[51]   *Ibid.,* III, 189.
[52]   *Ibid.,* III, 204.

The memoirist is not only citizen in his utopia, but an architect. He invents, for example, the "peephole" for every prisoner's door, "thus opening a field for wide and fruitful observations".[53] Through the peephole the guard watches, controlling the memoirist's movements, reading his thoughts, his intentions, his dreams. And in all this the memoirist finds the greatest pleasure and satisfaction, for the rigid rules of prison life free him from "those unbearable hesitations, doubts and errors with which practical life is filled".[54]

The Underground Man observed that "suffering is doubt, negation, and what kind of a crystal palace would there be if one could have any doubts about it?"[55] These lines provide the key to the memoirist's thinking and behavior. He has created, in effect, a crystal palace out of his prison. The thought that it is not perfect, that escape is possible, that one can doubt it, threatens to plunge him into his former state of suffering, and suffering is doubt, negation. It is to eliminate suffering that the memoirist feverishly accepts the "harmony" of his prison.

The suicide of the imprisoned artist K. ("I am leaving this prison of yours",[56] he writes the memoirist) plunges the memoirist into agonizing suffering — a state well described by the Underground Man as one of "half despair, half faith," a feeling of the "deeply rooted, yet, in part, not unquestioned hopelessness of one's position".[57] Old wounds are reopened. Only the thought that K. has fallen from one prison into another from which it would be impossible to escape — the prison of death — restores the old man's confidence in his rationalistic prison-utopia.

But the moment of doubt and despair is revealing. Behind the mask of smug, self-satisfied, hypocritical complacency is disclosed the lonely, mutilated, offended soul of a personality that has debased itself and is conscious of its disfigurement. Behind the mask of the philosopher is the same lonely, tormented "underground" man that beat his head vainly against the walls of his cell.

Ambivalence marks the personality of the memoirist. If the lower half of his face (in the artist K.'s portrait) expresses calm dignity, the eyes, on the other hand, express suffering and horror, the glimmer of madness, the "painful eloquence of a deep and infinitely lonely soul".

53　　*Ibid.*, III, 204.
54　　*Ibid.*, III, 205.
55　　Dostoevskij, *Zapiski iz podpol'ja, op. cit.*, IV, 131.
56　　Andreev, "Moi zapiski," *op. cit.*, III, 231.
57　　Dostoevskij, *Zapiski iz podpol'ja, op. cit.*, IV, 115.

It was a "terrible face, full of wild contradictions".[58] The artist K. captured the essence of the memoirist's personality: madness. The fact of madness is significant. Man — the Underground Man believed — would never allow his free will to be calculated out of existence, "man would deliberately go mad . . . in order not to have reason and to insist on his own!"[59]

The madness of the memoirist suggests confirmation of the Underground Man's estimate of man. The memoirist takes the path of submission, but he traverses that path only in madness. There is an outer reconciliation effected by a debauched intellect, but no inner reconciliation, no peace for the tormented soul: rent by contradictions the memoirist remains locked in his "underground" of horror and suffering.

Lev Shestov, commenting on the nature of idealism, observed:

Idealism is not at all so ideal as might be expected in view of that solemnity with which its prophets announce themselves. In the last analysis it lives by very earthly hopes, and its *a priori* and *Ding an sich* are only the high walls by which it guards itself from the more difficult demands of real life. In this sense, idealism is similar to Eastern despotism: outside all is brilliant, beautiful, eternal; inside—horrors.[60]

It is this kind of idealism that Andreev, following Dostoevsky, exposes in "My Memoirs". The "beauty" and "harmony" and "meaning" of the memoirist's prison-utopia, like the "beautiful and lofty" in *Notes from the Underground* is only an evasion of painful reality.

Andreev's "My Memoirs", like "The Story of Sergey Petrovich" and "The Wall", differs from *Notes from the Underground* in its completely pessimistic approach to man-in-revolt. The memoirist may be mad, but he is a detestable symbol of the defeat of the individual in his struggle to preserve identity. The mere creation of such a type is indicative of how hopeless Andreev considered all rebellion against the "wall".

Andreev's attitude towards the problem of rebellion recalls "The Legend of the Grand Inquisitor". "I swear that man is weaker and more vile than you ever imagined him to be,"[61] declares the Grand Inquisitor. These words could stand as an epigraph to "My Memoirs" and, indeed, to many of Andreev's works. In the image of the memoirist, Andreev

---

[58]   Andreev, "Moi zapiski," *op. cit.,* III, 216.
[59]   Dostoevskij, *Zapiski iz podpol'ja, op. cit.,* IV, 128.
[60]   Lev Šestov, *Dostoevskij i Nitše: filosofija tragedii* (Berlin, 1922), p. 58.
[61]   Dostoevskij, *Brat'ja karamazovy, op. cit.,* IX, 253.

degrades man. The Underground Man, despite the disfiguration of his personality, clings at least to the idea of human dignity. The memoirist is a mockery of that idea.

The influence of *Notes from the Underground,* among other works of Dostoevsky, may be noted in Andreev's early story "Thought". The theme of "Thought", like that of "My Memoirs", is the catastrophe of pure intellect.

Dr. Kerzhentsev, hero of "Thought", loved his obedient, punctual and swift thought. He takes pride in designing and executing a perfect murder in which he feigns insanity. But "thought", like a "drunken snake", glides into his body and soul and cries out: "You thought you had simulated, but you were insane." [62] Dr. Kerzhentsev's mind is shattered. Had he simulated insanity in order to kill? Or did he murder because he was insane? He realizes now that he is not "master of his thought, but a miserable slave, pitiful and impotent". [63]

His "I" destroyed, Dr. Kerzhentsev finds himself hurled into the "emptiness of an infinite void", into "ominous solitariness" "surrounded and suffocated by morosely silent, mysterious enemies". [64] It is in this void, in the confines of an insane asylum, that Dr. Kerzhentsev writes his notes — the story of "Thought". Dr. Kerzhentsev, always a man of hidden, solitary nature, passes into the loneliness of a permanent "underground".

Intellect divorced from moral life leads to the degeneration of personality. ". . . Without a pure heart," the Underground Man observes, "there can be no full, correct consciousness." [65] This truth is hidden to Dr. Kerzhentsev as it is hidden to the hero of "A Gentle One" (with whom Dr. Kerzhentsev has much in common). Dr. Kerzhentsev cannot evaluate his catastrophe in other than intellectual terms.

For Dr. Kerzhentsev, the Underground Man and the hero of "A Gentle One", human relations often take on the character of a game, the object of which is to bolster or test the ego. Dr. Kerzhentsev murders the husband of a woman who had rejected his offer to marry her. One of the reasons that he was put in an insane asylum, he writes, was the "absence of a motive for the crime". [66] "But is it impossible to suppose," he writes, "that by the murder of Aleksey I simply wanted to test my

[62] Andreev, "Mysl'," *op. cit.,* II, 125-126.
[63] *Ibid.,* II, 126.
[64] *Ibid.,* II, 135.
[65] Dostoevskij, *Zapiski iz podpol'ja, op. cit.,* IV, 133.
[66] Andreev, "Mysl'," *op. cit.,* II, 100.

powers?"[67] The Underground Man also wished to test his power in his "game" with Liza.

In their spiritual development, the Underground Man and Dr. Kerzhentsev reveal important differences. But both men are spiritual despots. The Underground Man as a youth repulsed his single friend just in order to "triumph" over him. Dr. Kerzhentsev liked to simulate friendship, draw a person out, and then "throw away his little soul, with the profound consciousness of my inner strength and inner freedom". "A tendency towards dissembling was always in my character," Dr. Kerzhentsev observes, "and was one of the forms in which I strove for inner freedom."[68]

The "game" and dissembling are aspects of the loss of knowledge of self. Dr. Kerzhentsev in his satanic pride thought he knew himself, but his catastrophe discloses to him the chaos of his soul. The themes of the game and dissembling are important themes of the "underground". They symbolize the disintegration of the personality of the "underground" man.

In his pride of intellect and will to power, Dr. Kerzhentsev is a spiritual brother of Raskolnikov and Stavrogin. But the problems of his personality (like those of Raskolnikov and Stavrogin) are linked with the problems of intellect and moral being raised in *Notes from the Underground*.[69]

---

[67]   *Ibid.*, II, 129.
[68]   *Ibid.*, II, 106.
[69]   Another work of Andreev that deserves mention is "Darkness" ("T'ma," 1907). In his article comparing *Notes from the Underground* and Andreev's "Darkness," Clarence A. Manning brings out various parallels between the two works. (Clarence A. Manning, "T'ma Andreeva i Zapiski iz podpol'ja Dostoevskogo," *Slavia* V [1926-1927], 850-852.) In both *Notes from the Underground* and "Darkness" the hero's actions symbolize a defeat of moral-idealism; in both cases the conception of the hero-savior is under attack. Andreev's revolutionary terrorist, ashamed of his moral loftiness before a prostitute, comes to the conclusion that he has no right to be good when others like the prostitute live in darkness. He decides to give up his life as a revolutionary in order to merge his life with those who cannot attain the height of moral loftiness.

CHAPTER IX

F. SOLOGUB'S *PETTY DEMON*

> I was tormented at that time by still another circum-
> stance: namely, that nobody was like me and I was
> not like anybody. "I am one, while they are *every-
> body*," I thought—and grew despondent.
>
> The Underground Man

The personality of the provincial school teacher Ardalion Borisych
Peredonov in *Petty Demon* (*Melky bes*, 1905) is infantile, regressive.
Peredonov is an accretion of primitive fears and terror. He is morose,
sullen, malevolent. He is morbidly suspicious and superstitious to an
extreme. He dislikes laughter and is filled with perpetual malice.
Peredonov might be a caricature of the Underground Man if he were
not so terrible, if he were not himself a perfectly distinct and symbolic
creature of the "underground".

It is difficult to convey the zoology of Peredonov. He is cowardly,
mean, and sadistically cruel; he is a liar, a hypocrite, and a born spy.
He spits at people, whips school boys, dirties walls, informs, burns
books, torments cats, and constantly sucks caramels. He is lewd, foul,
and corrupt à la Karamazov and is no more capable of love than a pig.

Peredonov is "underground" personality at the final stage of disintegration. The faculty for correct perception and evaluation is
shattered and conscious personality is lost in the rising chaos of instincts.
The individual has reached the last stage of his separation from the
world — a state of mad solitariness in an alien world. Like the Underground Man, Peredonov is alone, and the consciousness of his isolation
is tormenting.

Peredonov walked amidst the depression of these streets and houses,
under an estranged sky, upon an unclean and impotent earth and was
oppressed by vague terrors—and there was no consolation for him in
the heavens and no joys on earth, because even now, as always, he
looked on the world with dead eyes like some demon despairing with
fear and anguish in his loneliness. His feelings were dull and his consciousness was a corrupting and deadening apparatus. Everything
coming in contact with his consciousness was transformed into vileness
and filth. He would notice the imperfections in things and these imperfections pleased him. When he passed by a straight and clean pillar,
he wanted to make it crooked or filthy it up. He laughed with joy when

something was bespattered in his presence. . . .There were neither beloved objects for him nor beloved people, and therefore nature could act on his feelings only onesidedly, could only oppress them. It was the same in meetings with people. Especially with outsiders and strangers to whom one could not speak crudely. Happiness for him meant to do nothing and, shut off from the world, to gratify his belly.[1]

Peredonov's feeling of alienation is matched only by his "underground" feeling of hatred and malice for the world. The whole essence of Peredonov is a rebellion of man, "blinded by the illusions of personality and a separate existence",[2] against the humiliation and persecution of a world order he cannot understand. The anguish of the man-with-toothache in *Notes from the Underground* expressed the consciousness that "your enemy is not there, but that there is pain . . .".[3] Peredonov's anguish before the world about him could be expressed the same way. His enemy is symbolized by the tormenting image of the *nedotykomka*, a nimble, grey, featureless creature: now it is here, now there, now gone; it is elusive, disguised, protected by forces beyond human control. The grey *nedotykomka* persecutes Peredonov. It is the embodiment of his alienation.

"I am one, while they are *everybody* . . ."[4] These words of the Underground Man fully express the essence of Peredonov's relation to the world about him: his loneliness, alienation, and feeling of persecution. The story of Peredonov is that of the gradual degeneration of a paranoiac. Peredonov, in seeking the post of Inspector of Education, gradually loses himself in the maze of his own suspicions and fears. He sinks into a world of illusions.

Peredonov creates the fantastic atmosphere of hostility and persecution which bears down upon him. But he is also the victim of a certain real laughing conspiracy; a conspiracy of people quite as disgusting, spiteful, and self-seeking as he. These are the Rutilovs, Grushinas, Ershovas, and others who surround him with their laughter and sneers just as the "judges, dictators" in *Notes from the Underground,* surround, mock, and spit at the persecuted "underground" mouse.

In insane desperation, Peredonov murders his friend Volodin — a man who he feared would take his place after he (Peredonov) was poisoned by ill-wishers; he would be buried as though he were Volodin, while Volodin would become an inspector. Peredonov's fear of Volodin

[1] Fedor Sologub, *Melkij bes, Sobranie sočinenij* (St. Petersburg, 1913), VI, 112.
[2] *Ibid.*, VI, 295.
[3] Dostoevskij, *Zapiski iz podpol'ja, op. cit.*, IV, 117.
[4] *Ibid.*, IV, 138.

as a competitor grotesquely parallels Golyadkin Senior's fears of
Golyadkin Junior in Dostoevsky's "The Double" — a situation which is
reflected again in *Notes from the Underground* in the inherently com-
petitive nature of the Underground Man's relationship with Zverkov
and the successful man of action. It is perhaps not accidental that
Volodin is a person "surprisingly similar to a young ram . . . a stupid
young man".[5] Peredonov's fear of Volodin, however, is completely
groundless; as groundless as are his hopes of obtaining the position of
inspector.

With this deeply morbid and suspicious nature coexists a "twice two
is four" mentality.

"Now, you just stand at the gates," Rutilov persuasively said, "and I
will bring out any one [of the girls] you want. Now listen, I'll prove it to
you. Twice two is four, isn't it?"
    "That's so," answered Peredonov.
    "Well, then, it's twice two is four that you ought to marry one of
my sisters."
    Peredonov was thunderstruck.
    "After all it's true," he thought, "of course, twice two is four."[6]

This is the logic of the paranoiac. For the Underground Man thinking
tends to become an exercise; it already oscillates in a *perpetuum mobile*.
For Peredonov, thinking lacks even the character of an exercise: it is a
wholly integrated facet of his paranoia. Peredonov dislikes thinking.
"Twice two is four" is the measure of his thinking capacities.

Peredonov cannot articulate his feelings like the Underground Man in
ideas and imagery. He cannot analyze himself or others. Intellect in
him is insentient. But there is another kind of self-expression in which
Peredonov excels. This is his zoological "articulation": his irrational
behavior, his obscenity, his disgusting actions, his whipping, kicking,
spitting, and defiling, his love of imperfections and revelling in filth.
This is the malignant revenge of a dull-headed creature, the "curse of
the beast" against an unknown enemy that has caused it pain. The
people around Peredonov direct their malice at others. Peredonov's
malice, like that of the Underground Man, seems directed at the entire
world order.

The malice of Peredonov is symbolized, significantly, in the delight
he takes in spattering filth on walls, in spitting at them and tearing the
wall paper. The "wall" here has somewhat the same meaning it has in

---

[5]   Sologub, *op. cit.,* VI, 21.
[6]   *Ibid.,* VI, 47.

Notes from the Underground and in Andreev's "The Wall"; it symbolizes all that is hostile and alien, oppressive and painful. "We always filthy up the walls when we eat," Peredonov exclaims, "that's so we'll leave a reminder behind us!"[7] Peredonov senses that he does not belong to this world and he revenges himself upon it by leaving it in shambles.

Sologub traces to its source the instinct of destruction in Peredonov. Peredonov descends into a world of "wild illusions":

Mad horror forged in him a readiness for crime, and an unconscious, dark image of future murder, concealed in the lower strata of spiritual life, an agonizing itch to murder, a state of primitive wrath, oppressed his diseased will. Still chained—many generations lay on the ancient Cain—it found satisfaction in breaking and damaging things, in hacking with an ax, slashing with a knife, chopping down trees in the garden so as to prevent any spy from hiding behind them. And the ancient demon, the spirit of prehistoric confusion, hoary chaos, reveled in the destruction of things, while the wild eyes of the madman reflected horror, like the horror of the death agonies of some monster.[8]

Man is irrational. Man not only loves to build; he also loves destruction and chaos. These ideas are central ones in *Notes from the Underground*; they find their most complete embodiment in the figure of Peredonov.

Peredonov is the zoological expression of those forces of destruction, chaos and madness which the Underground Man predicted would be loosed upon the world by thwarted man. Sologub, like Andreev, shows that this rebellion of the "underground" in man, in its final stages, is wholly destructive.

For Sologub, Peredonovism is the deformation of the ideal, the perversion of the pure enjoyment of beauty; it is coarseness, flaccid sensuality, lewd eroticism, obscenity, and filth. It is in the cult of "beauty" that Sologub seeks an answer to Peredonovism. The episodes in the *Petty Demon* devoted to the "pagan" Lyudmila's love for the boy Sasha Pylnikov, to her attempts to introduce him to her cult of nakedness and beauty, form the spiritual-aesthetic antithesis to the Peredonov deformation of the ideal.

There is a sharp contrast between Peredonov's eroticism and Lyudmila's cult of beauty. Yet the "underground" with its sadistic-masochistic pleasure-in-pain principle is also felt in Lyudmila's refined eroticism. Lyudmila, who sometimes dreams that "He is on the cross, and on the body there are drops of blood,"[9] says to Sasha Pylnikov:

[7]   *Ibid.,* VI, 23.
[8]   *Ibid.,* VI, 332.
[9]   *Ibid.,* VI, 346.

"I love the body, strong, agile, naked, which is capable of enjoyment."
"Yes, but it can suffer also," Sasha quietly said.
"And suffer, and this is good," Lyudmila passionately whispered.
"There is sweetness also in pain, if only to feel the body, if only to see
nakedness and bodily beauty." [10]

There is sweetness also in pain — this is of the essence of "underground"
experience.

In *Notes from the Underground* Dostoevsky showed that extreme
servility, the pathological humiliation of personality, and "underground"
rebellion and despotism constitute one psychological phenomenon. The
Underground Man slavishly keeps to the "common rut", but in his
relations with petitioners and even more in his experiments with people
outside his official duties, he discloses an hysterical craving for power
and a savagery (the Liza episode) without bounds.

In Peredonov servility and savagery are at once an involuntary reflex
and a deliberate policy. He slavishly bows before his superiors, is
cowardly to an extreme, informs on others to gain favor. Yet his
servility conceals a deep cruelty and sadism. Peredonov can be merciless
with those over whom he exercises authority. "Fear of people . . . gives
. . . the right to be mercilessly savage with people," the "underground"
Makarov observes in Gorky's "The Story of a Hero", "an indisputable
right because its root is in the instinct of self-preservation." [11] Peredonov's
life is a terrorized striving for self-preservation: but he has no self
to preserve.

Peredonov is perhaps the most frightening "underground" man in
Russian literature. Morally blind and inarticulate, he is like a robot
creature, the very quintessence of all that is evil and destestable. The
Underground Man, though a man who is not in complete control of
himself, nevertheless is not an example of absolutely autonomous, destructive instinct. "Opposite elements" are at play within him and no
matter how he strives to repress them, they are there; he cannot crush
the consciousness of "good" and the desire to be "good". Just this
striving to be "good" is absent in Peredonov, although in a metaphysical
sense

even Peredonov strove for the truth, in accord with the general law of
all conscious life, and this striving oppressed him. He was himself not

[10]   *Ibid.*, VI, 344.
[11]   M. Gor'kij, "Rasskaz o geroe," *Sobranie sočinenij* (2d ed.; Moscow, 1932-1934),
XXI, 92.

conscious that just like all people he was striving for truth and that that was why his disquietude was confusing. He could not find truth for himself, and had got entangled and was perishing.[12]

The "underground" rebellion of Peredonov, like that of the Underground Man, is a rebellion against helplessness, pain and anguish that has no apparent cause or meaning. But objectively his rebellion is a manifestation of pure evil. Sologub isolates and studies the purely evil, demoniac aspects of the "underground". He himself emphasizes these aspects in his remarks on Peredonov in an introduction to the English edition of his novel.

The portrait of Peredonov is an expression of the all-human inclination towards evil, of the almost disinterested tendency of a perverse human soul to depart from the common course of universal life directed by one omnipotent Will; and, taking vengeance upon the world for its own grievous loneliness, to bring into the world evil and abomination, to mutilate the given reality and to defile the beautiful dreams of humanity. This inclination towards evil, raging in the hearts of mankind in all latitudes and longitudes, invests itself only outwardly with an appearance of selfish expedience. A soul marred by this tragic affliction, that of a morose separation from the world, is borne along by a sovereign justice, which rules worlds and hearts, upon disastrous paths, towards madness and towards death.[13]

The catastrophe that the "underground" represents for the individual and for society finds one of its most sinister embodiments in Sologub's Peredonov.

---

[12] Sologub, *op. cit.,* VI, 332-333.
[13] Sologub, Author's Introduction to the English Edition, *The Little Demon,* trans., John Cournos and Richard Aldington (London, 1916), pp. xv–xvi.

CHAPTER X

A. I. KUPRIN'S "RIVER OF LIFE"

> ...I often looked upon myself with a furious dis-
> satisfaction which verged on loathing.
>
> The Underground Man

"Depraved, filthy, infected with disease, disfigured, cowardly — they were like loathesome reptiles shut up in a narrow cage. ... Throngs of gluttons and debauched people, re-enforced by hypocrites, charlatans, thieves and thugs set one crowd of drunken slaves on another crowd of trembling idiots and lived like parasites on the rot of social disintegration. And the earth, so spacious and beautiful, was narrow for people, like a dungeon, and stifling like a vault."[1] In these words the orator in the Year 2906, in "The Toast" ("Tost", 1905), described the life of the 20th century.

The hero of "River of Life" ("Reka zhizni", 1902), a lonely student, is morally disfigured and crippled by the old world described by the orator; he commits suicide, fittingly, in a dingy, provincial hotel — The Serbia — the very essence of filth, vulgarity, and senselessness. But in his dreams he envisages that other world, spacious and beautiful, to which Kuprin's orator belongs. Sooner or later, the student muses, the "River of Life" "will wash away all strongholds that have imprisoned the free spirit. And where formerly there were shoals of triviality — there will be found the greatest depths of heroism."[2]

The hero of "River of Life" in his idealism recalls Chekhov's dreamers (Vershinin, Astrov, and others). But in the moral-spiritual deformation of his personality he belongs, like Glazkov and Aleksey Petrovich, to the "underground". It was already too late when he greeted the new and passionate ideas of his time.

...My soul was already permanently devastated, dead and disgraced. A low, neurasthenic fearfulness had worked its way into it, like a tick

---

[1] A. I. Kuprin, "Tost," *Polnoe sobranie sočinenij* (St. Petersburg, 1912), VI, 297-298.
[2] Kuprin, "Reka žizni," *ibid.,* I, 320.

on a dog's ear: you tear it out, but the head remains and it once again grows into a whole, foul insect.[3]

These horrible lacerations, these images so offensive to human dignity, are those of a man who is about to kill himself because he was "born and raised a slave of insolence, cowardice and stupidity".[4]

Like the Underground Man, the hero of "River of Life" is tormented by this very consciousness of disfigurement, by the realization that he cannot change; he knows that he cannot free himself from all the slavishness he despises. In this he resembles those half-heroes of the "underground", Glazkov and Aleksey Petrovich, men with dreams, but shattered personalities. Everywhere in the student's suicide-letter one senses a malice of impotence, a moral self-disgust that is finally expressed in suicide. Significantly, Kuprin's hero observes:

All my life I have been frightened of something that is in the majority of people and which I cannot explain. That was the way it was with the whole young generation of the preceding period of the transition. In our minds we despised slavery, but ourselves grew up cowardly slaves. Our hatred was profound, passionate, but fruitless, and was like the mad love of the castrate.[5]

These terrible words bring to mind not only Glazkov and Aleksey Petrovich, but also the Underground Man and Arkady Dolgoruki (*Raw Youth*). These "underground" men impotently rebel against the consciousness of slavery.

In the hero of "River of Life" one recognizes that "antithesis of the normal man" about whom the Underground Man speaks, that "retort-made man" who is "sometimes so cowed before his antithesis that he himself, with all his heightened consciousness, honestly considers himself a mouse and not a man".[6] Kuprin's hero is not afraid to die, but he fears people. He was frightened by the shout of the huge police colonel, a "dull, limited man" who trampled upon him (he involuntarily betrayed his comrades at a police interrogation). But "what was more odious than anything" was that while the colonel did not dare shout at the others, "in me he at once recognized a yielding and shrivelled will. This is felt among people without a word, by a glance alone."[7]

Thus the Underground Man, describing how he would dart about like

---

[3] *Ibid.*, I, 317.
[4] *Ibid.*, I, 318.
[5] *Ibid.*, I, 317.
[6] Dostoevskij, *Zapiski iz podpol'ja, op. cit.*, IV, 114.
[7] Kuprin, "Reka žizni," *op. cit.*, I, 314.

a "groundling" on Nevsky Prospect, always retreating before the generals and officers, exclaims that it was "sheer torture, a constant unbearable humiliation" to realize that in the eyes of this society world he was a fly, "a disgusting, obscene fly — more intelligent, more cultivated, more noble than anyone else, needless to say — but still a fly continually yielding to everyone, humiliated by everyone, insulted by everyone."[8]

The fear — and hatred — that Kuprin's hero experiences before the "dull, limited" police colonel is the same that he feels before those "wooden people, rigidly fixed in their world view, stupidly self-confident people who know no hesitations",[9] before all those

definite, self-satisfied, stereotyped, sober people who know everything in advance: professional orators, old, longhaired, ruddy-faced professors coquetting with innocent liberalism, imposing and unctuous archpriests, police colonels, radical women-doctors breathlessly repeating snatches from leaflets, but with a soul that is cold, cruel and smooth like a slab of marble. When I speak with them I feel that on my face, like a loathesome mask, is an alien, servile, officious smile, and I scorn myself for my wheedling, thin voice . . . The souls of these people are dead, their thoughts have become petrified in straight, hard lines, and they themselves are merciless, as only a self-assured and stupid person can be merciless.[10]

In the hero of "River of Life", "underground" hatred of the vulgar, self-confident man of action (here given a certain anti-rationalistic turn) serves to formulate his hatred of a stupid, banal, brutal and faceless society — a society that is for him everything that the army is to Romashev in Kuprin's *The Duel* (*Poedinok*, 1905). Like Glazkov and Aleksey Petrovich, the hero of "River of Life" feels estranged from society, despises himself because of his fear of it, and destroys himself in self-disgust.

The hero of "River of Life" is spiritually crippled by poverty and begging; his mind is filled with humiliating recollections of the abasement and exploitation of his personality as a child in the service of "benefactors" who looked upon him as upon an inanimate object. Even more was he morally corrupted by seven to ten years in a state school — years filled with spying, thievery, onanism, vodka, prostitutes, and venereal disease. In this, in particular, the hero of "River of Life" recalls the Underground Man and Arkady Dolgoruki, two heroes of the "under-

8   Dostoevskij, *Zapiski iz podpol'ja, op. cit.,* IV, 142.
9   Kuprin, "Reka žizni," *op. cit.,* I, 314.
10 *Ibid.,* I, 315-316.

ground" whose pathology of humiliation developed in school years.
"They were monstrously depraved," wrote the Underground Man of his
school comrades. "I hated them horribly, although, I dare say, I was
worse than even they." [11] And when the hero of "River of Life" emerged
from school, his "soul was already permanently devastated, dead and
disgraced". [12]

I was not the only one who perished from this moral poisoning. I,
perhaps, was the weakest of all. But after all, the entire past generation
grew up in a spirit of pious tranquility, forced respect to elders, without
individuality and voiceless. Cursed be that odious time, a time of silence
and squalor, that blissful and peaceful existence under the silent shadow
of pious reaction! Because the quiet degradation of the human soul is
more terrible than all the barricades and executions in the world. [13]

The sensitive individual rebels against this way of life. Arkady Dolgoruki, who also played the role of a lackey, gave the "underground"
formulation to this rebellion: "I could keep up a passive hatred and
underground malice in this way for years." [14]

Kuprin's hero has this passive hatred and "underground" malice. But
the "underground" theme of humiliation in "River of Life" does not
serve as a focus of interest in itself, as it does in large part in *Notes from
the Underground*. Kuprin is not interested in developing a psychology
of the "underground", a philosophy of the irrational. Kuprin, like Albov
and Garshin, is interested in the "underground" only in its social context,
only as an expression of the individual's alienation from society. It is
the fact of protest, rather than the manner of protest, that primarily
interests Kuprin.

What is significant, however, is that Kuprin approaches the psychological aspects of the plight of the lonely intellectual in the context of
the Dostoevskian "tragedy of the underground". Kuprin's hero is a
typical man of "heightened consciousness" who, together with Glazkov
and Aleksey Petrovich, illustrates the contention of the Underground
Man that "every decent person of our time is and must be a coward and
a slave". [15]

The "River of Life" will wash away the vulgar, the stupid, the philistine
and cruel. This is the dream of the hero of "River of Life". In his story
"The Toast", Kuprin sketches the utopian society of the future. The

[11] Dostoevskij, *Zapiski iz podpol'ja, op. cit.,* IV, 153.
[12] Kuprin, "Reka žizni," *op. cit.,* I, 316.
[13] *Ibid.,* I, 317.
[14] Dostoevskij, *Podrostok, op. cit.,* VII, 279.
[15] Dostoevskij, *Zapiski iz podpol'ja, op. cit.,* IV, 137.

Year 2906 finds the earth covered with a gigantic earth-magnetic system which has revolutionized industry and life. On the North Pole there is a huge Council Hall, a "magnificent building of glass, marble and iron"; on the South Pole there is a glass palace, and in both buildings, illuminated by artificial sunlight, men and women at the moment are celebrating the 200th year since the last country — Germany — joined the "universal anarchic union of free peoples".[16]

An orator toasts an eternally young, beautiful life which is free of slavery and triviality. The old world was horrible. But the new was made possible by "heroes with flaming souls", who voluntarily gave up all joys except one — the joy of dying for the free life of future humanity. A "bridge of human corpses" unites the old and new; a "river of blood" has carried humanity to the "shining sea of universal happiness".[17]

Such is Kuprin's utopia in "The Toast". But an irrational spirit enters Kuprin in his story "The Royal Park" ("Korolevsky park"). Once again the scene is a utopia of the future, the 26th century, when the "genius of humanity has tamed the most savage climates, drained swamps, penetrated mountains, united the seas, transformed the earth into a flourishing garden and into a huge workshop. . . ." There is a four-hour workday and obligatory work for all. Vices have disappeared, virtues have flourished. But — it seems as though something is missing. Kuprin is not exultant.

To tell the truth — all this was rather boring. And it was not accidental that in the middle of the 32nd century, after the great South African uprising directed against the boring public regime, all humanity in a kind of joyful and drunken madness plunged into war, blood, conspiracies, debaucheries and savage unprecedented despotism — plunged and — for the nth time in the long history of our planet — destroyed and turned into dust and ashes all the great conquests of world culture.[18]

Thus, Kuprin appears to reaffirm the Underground Man's belief that mankind prefers to construct buildings, but not to live in them; and more, that mankind also loves destruction and chaos because it instinctively fears completing the building. In "The Royal Park" the rationalistic utopian dream is shattered by elemental destruction from within.

[16]   Kuprin, "Tost," *op. cit.,* VI, 294-295.
[17]   *Ibid.,* VI, 298.
[18]   Kuprin, "Korolevskij park," *op. cit.,* VI, 273-274.

CHAPTER XI

V. Y. BRYUSOV'S
"REPUBLIC OF THE SOUTHERN CROSS"

> Now I, for example, would not at all be surprised if
> suddenly and for no reason whatever some gentleman
> with an ignoble or, better, with a reactionary and
> sardonic countenance were to arise amidst universal
> future common sense and, putting his arms akimbo,
> say to us all: what do you say, now, gentlemen, shall
> we kick over all this common sense all at once, letting
> it scatter into dust, with the sole purpose of sending
> all these logarithms to the devil and enabling us once
> again to live according to our own foolish will!
>
> The Underground Man

In his story "Republic of the Southern Cross" ("Respublika yuzhnogo
kresta", 1904-05), Bryusov treats a theme which occupied him in his
poetry: the fate of modern urban civilization. Bryusov was strangely
fascinated by visions of the huge, mechanized, rationalistically-con-
ceived city. Yet at the same time, he was frightened by the possibility
of complete mechanization of life, he was alarmed by the idea of a world
in which the human spirit would be imprisoned by dead forms and
routine. In his poem "The Incarcerated Ones" ("Zamknutye", 1900-
1901) Bryusov writes:

> And a terrible dream tormented me in those days:
> What if my City is the harbinger of the centuries?
> What if Vulgarity is the fateful force,
> And man is created for slavery and chains?
> What if my City is the first, small prototype
> Of that which some day life will display in plenitude,
> What if the world, despondent and weary,
> Stands, like a belated wanderer,
> At the approaches of a quagmire, on the fateful brink?

> And, like a nightmare, there appeared before me
> The future City-Dwelling in a cruel vision,
> Like a huge evenly-proportioned monster,
> With a glass skull covering the earth.
> Refuge of earthly tribes, marked by numbers,
> Bound by life (machine of machines!)

> To wheels, blocks, yokes,
> I saw you, last son of the earth!
> I sensed the life of incarcerated generations . . .[1]

But Bryusov foresees an end to slavery; he foresees a time filled with the "delirium of blood and battles"; this will be followed by ruin and desolation. But, "Out of the darkness of thousands of years / The horrors and joy of being will rise / People will laugh like children. . . ."[2] The theme of urban development, degeneration, of elemental-irrational rebellion followed by a kind of Rousseauesque primitive new life, can be found in Bryusov's urban poetry, for example, "Pale Horse" ("Kon bled", 1903), "Spirits of Fire" ("Dukhi ognya", 1904), "Young Earth" ("Zemlya molodaya", 1913).

Bryusov, like Dostoevsky, is tormented by the vision of a final ordering of human existence, the idea of a completed culture, "all the horror of discovered words".[3] One recognizes in Bryusov's "despondent and weary", "belated wanderer", that weary and weak, once rebellious mankind that gratefully submits to the terrible authority of the Grand Inquisitor. But Bryusov, again like Dostoevsky, found elemental, irrational forces in man which counteracted and negated rationalist claims upon the individual.

The story of "Republic of the Southern Cross" is that of the elemental, irrational, and anarchic rebellion of the citizens of a strictly regulated utopia. Bryusov observed in his introduction to his collection of stories *Earth's Axis* (*Zemnaya os*, 1907) that "in such stories as 'Republic' or 'Now, When I Awake', the influence of Edgar Poe is quite evident".[4] Just as striking is the identity of Bryusov's basic idea of irrational rebellion with the irrational philosophy of the Underground Man and with the dream of Raskolnikov in the epilogue of *Crime and Punishment*.

In "Republic of the Southern Cross", Bryusov depicts a geometrically designed, utopian society, situated in the extreme part of the Southern hemisphere, with the capital located on the pole. Marvellous work, health, educational and cultural conditions prevailed. But life, seemingly free, was regulated to the finest detail. Buildings, clothes, food, etc. were all identical; a Council of Directors, despite universal ballot, was

---

[1] V. Brjusov, "Zamknutye," *Puti i pereput'ja, Sobranie stikhov* (Moscow, 1908), I, 200-201.
[2] *Ibid.*, I, 201.
[3] "Ja provižu gordye teni," *ibid.*, I, 113.
[4] Brjusov, "Predislovie," *Zemnaja os'* (Moscow, 1907), p. viii.

the political-economic heart of an autocratic tyranny; the secret police was omnipresent; the Council did not balk at political murder.

But life was rarely interrupted by disturbances until the fateful epidemic, the *mania contradicens* struck. When affected by this "psychic disorder" people began to say "no" when they wanted to say "yes"; in their words and actions they constantly contradicted their wishes. Recognizing the "irrationality" of his conduct, the sick citizen fell into a state of extreme anxiety, and sometimes frenzy. The inevitable end was death.

The epidemic spread, and horror and madness, anarchy and chaos, "bestial revels and animal malice" replaced the rational life of the capital. Dark, atavistic feelings emerged in the citizens.

Culture, like a thin bark, grown over thousands of years, fell from these people and in them was bared a wild man, a man-animal, such as once roamed the virgin earth. All conception of right disappeared, only force was recognized.[5]

The people of the Republic began to exterminate one another.

In those days Star City was a huge, black box where several thousand people resembling human beings were cast about in the stink of hundreds of thousands of rotting corpses, where among the living there was not a single one who was conscious of his position. This was a city of madmen, a gigantic insane asylum, the most tremendous and repulsive Bedlam that ever appeared on earth. And the madmen were destroying each other, stabbing each other, biting each others' throats, they were dying from madness, dying from horror, dying from hunger and from all the diseases which reigned in the poisoned atmosphere.[6]

The picture of mankind destroying itself, divested of its self-control, helpless before its primitive and irrational instincts, is developed in Raskolnikov's dream of a society reduced to chaos and madness by evil spirits endowed with intellect and will. People who became infected with them at once became as if possessed, went mad. . . . Whole villages, whole cities and people were infected and went mad. . . . Men killed each other in a kind of senseless malice. They gathered against each other whole armies, but the armies, when already on the march, suddenly began to tear at each other, the ranks broke and soldiers threw themselves on each other, bayoneted and stabbed, bit and devoured each other. . . . Here and there [in the cities] people gathered together in groups, came to mutual agreement on something, swore not to part — but immediately something else started quite different from what they themselves had just agreed upon, they began to accuse one another, fought and cut each other up.[7]

[5]   Brjusov, "Respublika južnogo kresta," *ibid.,* p. 19.
[6]   *Ibid.,* p. 22.
[7]   Dostoevskij, *Prestuplenie i nakazanie, op. cit.,* V, 444-445.

This is the same kind of *mania contradicens* that seizes the citizens of Bryusov's Republic.

The future historian, Bryusov suggests, will have to determine how much the rationalistic life of the Republic was responsible for the epidemic which destroyed the Republic. The rebellion of the citizens of Bryusov's Republic was elemental, irrational. As in *Notes from the Underground,* the choice of something harmful (from the standpoint of reason), the choice of suffering and negation over and against prosperity and well-being, symbolizes man's inner insistence on the right of free choice. Man, the Underground Man believes, is phenomenally ungrateful and ever ready to introduce his "ruinous fantastic element" into all rationalist thinking, economic prosperity and well-being. He will invent destruction and chaos and even go mad in order not to have reason and to maintain his free will. This very destruction, chaos and madness prevailed in the Republic. The fact that the citizens' rebellion was involuntary (reason told them that they were ill) only serves to emphasize the existence in man of an independent, irrational core.

In its wild, anarchic, repulsive character, this rebellion of the Republic's citizens is easily recognized as a rebellion of the "underground". It is "underground", too, in the terrible means it chose to defend man's self-respecting, inner "I". For it cannot be said that the man-animal that awakened in the souls of the citizens of Bryusov's "Republic" will restore the rights of the individual any more than Andreev's dying beast or Sologub's sullen rebel Peredonov. This contradiction between ends and means is typical of "underground" rebellion.

Like the Underground Man, the citizen of the Republic understands only two ways of life: a submissive, totally regulated existence or the wild, monstrous anarchism of the "underground". These two extremes reflect the organic disharmony of reason and will in the Republic's citizens. It is in the conception of this citizen as a split and irrational being, and of the inevitable and terrible end of a rational order, that Bryusov's "Republic of the Southern Cross" follows in the anti-rationalist, anti-utopian tradition of *Notes from the Underground.*

CHAPTER XII

A. M. REMIZOV'S "SISTERS IN THE CROSS"

> And yet I am convinced that man will never renounce
> real suffering, that is, destruction and chaos. Suffering
> —why after all, this is the sole cause of consciousness.
> Although at the outset I announced that consciousness,
> in my opinion, is the greatest misfortune for man, yet
> I know that man loves it and will not exchange it for
> any satisfactions. Consciousness, for example, is infi-
> nitely superior to twice two is four.
>
> The Underground Man

The Dostoevskian theme of human suffering is the pivot of A. M.
Remizov's "Sisters in the Cross" ("Krestovye sestry", 1910). The
protagonist of this story, Petr Alekseevich Marakulin, contains in himself
many Dostoevskian features, some of which recall *Notes from the
Underground*.

The Underground Man affirms the primacy of suffering in human
experience. Without suffering there is no real life, only "twice two is
four" which is death to the individual.

Marakulin has led a placid, unreflective, rationally ordered existence
as a clerk. His accuracy and precision gained him the nickname of "the
German"; but he makes an error and is discharged. Marakulin is unable
to find other work immediately. He takes a room in "Burkov's Court",
a miserable rooming establishment in Petersburg. "Blind chance" has
cast him into an "underground".

It is blind chance that descends on Murka, the cat, which dies in
Burkov's Court in horrible agony. It is blind chance that causes the
misery and anguish of the poor, suffering men and women of Burkov's
Court. Indeed, as in the refrain of the half-idiot Akumovna, "One can't
blame anybody".[1] But "the earth in its woe, its misery, need, sorrow,
misfortune — in malice and hatred — rolls about and meows like
Murka . . .".[2]

Struck down in the middle of an ordered existence, gripped by a fate
as incomprehensible as those of Murka or the human inhabitants of
Burkov's Court, Marakulin, like Ivan Karamazov, wants

---

[1] A. M. Remizov, "Krestovye sestry," *Sočinenija* (St. Petersburg, [no date],), V, 85.
[2] *Ibid.*, V, 30.

absolutely, and at all costs, to know for whom all this was necessary and for what purpose, for the satisfaction of what thief, scoundrel and good-for-nothing — crook — and he wanted to know so as definitely to ask himself whether it was still worth drawing the whole thing out — enduring, only so as to be able to carry on a bit?[3]

"Suffering, why after all, this is the sole cause of consciousness,"[4] remarks the Underground Man. Marakulin, no longer living a vegetable existence, experiencing loneliness and shame, suffers and thus, begins to think. He has enacted one of the truths of the "underground".

It is, however, in Marakulin's attitude towards Kholmogorova, a general's wife — the "louse" as she is called in Burkov's Court — that an "underground" pattern especially emerges. She is the object of a truly "underground" hatred and malice — the hatred and malice of the suffering for those who live in complacent ignorance of suffering. Kholmogorova can live on interest until the end of her life; she is strong and alive, goes to the bath to steam herself on Tuesdays, has nothing to repent of. "She has not killed and has not stolen and will not kill and will not rob, because she only nourishes herself — drinks and eats — digests, strengthens herself. . . ."[5] Humanity suffers, but the "immortal louse" goes on living. Marakulin, the tormented Akumovna, the actress Verochka who becomes a prostitute, and many others who pass through Burkov's Court desperately search for a reason to go on living, but Kholmogorova "like some chosen vessel has not merely a right to existence but an *imperial* right".[6]

She is as hateful to Marakulin as the old pawnbroker is to Raskolnikov and as Zverkov is to the Underground Man. She seems to dominate life like Andreev's Novikov ("The Story of Sergey Petrovich"); she belongs among those self-confident and self-satisfied people who repel the hero of Kuprin's "River of Life".

Kholmogorova's monotonous, self-satisfied, vegetable happiness, it seems to Marakulin, is the happiness for which mankind yearns:

And now it is necessary to consider . . . and decide for oneself firmly and once and for all: how would humanity act if, let us say, the great powers . . . were to offer . . . to all humanity the louse-like carefree, sinless and immortal life of the general's wife . . . [Someone might arise] and would announce himself to the world as a *leader* and *judge* — the redeemer of

[3]   *Ibid.,* V, 22.
[4]   Dostoevskij, *Zapiski iz podpol'ja, op. cit.,* IV, 131.
[5]   Remizov, *op. cit.,* V, 33.
[6]   *Ibid.,* V, 64.

original Murka-sin, and he would build without the aid of human hands a New Zion where there would be peace and kindness, and he would do so quickly, simply, cheaply. How would humanity respond, what answer would it give? Well, I think . . . that without any superfluous words and ceremonies . . . it would jump into this *pothouse style* New Zion which had been built without the aid of human hands and where there was peace and kindness, in order to begin a new, louse-like, *carefree, sinless, immortal,* but chiefly *tranquil* life. . . . And one must realize that all *reasonable* and *good* people would act this way — indeed who would act against his own interests! — and would act this way legitimately, correctly, wisely and humanly: after all, now who likes to be tormented, to lie awake and choke, losing both patience and peace of mind![7]

The New Zion of which Marakulin speaks is, of course, but another name for the crystal palace of *Notes from the Underground*. For the Underground Man such a palace is no more than a chicken coop; for Marakulin it is a pothouse. But Marakulin is not certain that man would resist the temptation of the New Zion. Indeed, at times Marakulin himself would pray to God to grant him "just a minute" of Kholmogo-rova's kind of life.

But in the end, Marakulin, like the Underground Man chooses suffering rather than the satisfactions of a Kholmogorovian life. His choice of suffering, however, is rather in the spirit of Aleksey Petrovich, hero of Garshin's story "Night", than in that of the Underground Man in whom suffering has a particularly egotistical, anti-social character. Like Aleksey Petrovich, Marakulin chooses to identify himself with suffering humanity; and like Aleksey Petrovich, he perishes. "If people would look at one another and notice one another, if all were given eyes, then only an *iron* heart could withstand the whole horror and mystery of life."[8] But Marakulin's is not an iron heart and he joins the line of suicides touched by "underground" feeling and moved by the pessimism of the "underground".

---

[7]   *Ibid.*, V, 64-65.
[8]   *Ibid.*, V, 109.

CHAPTER XIII

M. P. ARTSYBASHEV'S *AT THE LAST BOUNDARY*

> Man likes to create and to clear paths; of this there
> can be no doubt. But just why does he also love
> destruction and chaos, and to a passion?
>
> The Underground Man

Artsybashev's novel *At the Last Boundary* (*U posledney cherty*, 1911-12) is a paean to the "underground"; its motifs are fear of death, disillusionment with all social idealism, and nihilistic despair. Artsybashev's heroes, many of them "underground" men, pursue a lonely, tortured existence in an atmosphere "uniformly gloomy, puzzling, alien to man".[1] The scene is a provincial steppe town — stupefying in the banality and senselessness of its existence.

Artsybashev's man-alone, like the Underground Man and Peredonov, is a victim of cosmic humiliation; he feels impotent and insignificant before an inscrutable world order. Against this world order Artsybashev hurls his curse. This "underground" curse, filled with fear and despair, is the heart of *At the Last Boundary*.

Two heroes of *At the Last Boundary,* the engineer Naumov and the student Chizh, are typical representatives of Artsybashev's "underground" gallery. Artsybashev assigns the role of spokesman for the "underground" to Naumov.

The egomaniac Naumov cries out: "I declare war on life. . . . I do not recognize it, I negate it and curse it!"[2] "I will cry out, beat my head against the wall, exhort, push!"[3] The "underground" character of his personality and ideas is striking. He has divorced himself "from the whole world" and in his loneliness has turned on the world with "hatred and malice." His "underground" rebellion, like that of Ippolit Terentiev in Dostoevsky's *The Idiot,* is a protest against the humiliation of death. ". . . Every death," Naumov declares, "is unnatural, even though it be a hundred times according to the law of nature."[4] His "idea" is the destruction of the human race by means of suicide or abstention from procreation.

[1] M. P. Arcybašev, *U poslednej čerty, Sobranie sočinenij* (Moscow, 1913), VI, 5.
[2] *Ibid.,* VI, 195.
[3] *Ibid.,* VII, 44.
[4] *Ibid.,* VI, 191.

Naumov responds to the humiliation of death with typical "underground" malice: by declaring war on life, that is, by trampling in the scorn of humiliation upon the very things of which he complains he is deprived. But in Naumov, as in the Underground Man, malice towards the offender is nourished also by the consciousness of impotence, of his inability to carry out his own "idea".

Two people live in him: one believes in his idea with the stubbornness of a fanatic, wants destruction and death, and the other fears it, is choked with malice, revenges itself on everybody for its own cowardice and despair.[5]

Ippolit Terentiev faced the blank "Meyer's wall" and rebelled. Naumov first faced his "wall" when, in prison, he faced execution as a socialist. The thought that life would remain the same as it was and that his death would be "dissolved in sunlight" killed all social instinct in him. And he vowed to war on "this cursed and insolent life which did not want to consider man".[6] Naumov not only set out to war on this life, but on all future life from which he was excluded. "What is it to me," he declares, "that my *spirit* is glowing there, like a morning star, when I am here in the stink of senselessness and pain, choking like a dog."[7] Naumov's "underground" egotism recalls that of Arkady Dolgoruki who renounced the future in which he was to get "neither love, nor future life, nor recognition for my efforts".[8]

Naumov's war on life is conducted in the name of "putting an end to the vain sufferings of mankind", an altruistic striving which also has its echoes in the "underground". He justifies his nihilistic program by a typically "underground" view of life and history.

Mankind has existed for thousands of years. For thousands of years it has been nourished and maintained by the foolish hope of a happiness which cannot be and must not be by the very nature of human life. Happiness is complete lethargy. Man who does not suffer, who is not in need and does not fear, will not fight, will not in torment strive forward and forward. He will wander about and lie about like a boar. Suffering is the motive force of everything, and this is an old truth known to everybody. Give us happiness now and we will get nowhere; we chase after happiness and this is the essence of life. But in the name of just what will mankind suffer endlessly? Remember: the history of the earth is just one bloody river! Misery, suffering, illness, anguish, malice —

[5]   *Ibid.*, VII, 55.
[6]   *Ibid.*, VII, 48.
[7]   *Ibid.*, VII, 139.
[8]   Dostoevskij, *Podrostok, op. cit.*, VIII, 47.

everything that is blackest in the fantasy of man — this is the life of people.[9]

Life and history are bloody and irrational, suffering is the motive force of everything, happiness is lethargy — these are but variations of salient ideas of *Notes from the Underground*. Naumov, however, concludes that it is necessary to put an end to all this horror by destroying everybody. This is his "humane idea".

Naumov's "underground" outlook quite logically leads him to the conviction that happiness is impossible for mankind — the "colossal suffering herd" — and that thinkers, prophets, poets, scholars, and, especially, socialists are guilty of "cramming into man's stupid head dreams about the future of mankind, about a golden age of justice!"[10]

Once and for all it is necessary to understand that nothing — neither revolution nor any form of social order, capitalism or socialism — can bring happiness to man who is doomed to eternal suffering. What is your social order to us if death stands behind everyone's shoulder. ... But we will not talk about death. ... Let us take life: you can reduce existence to one level, but you will not bring into line the endless diversity of strivings, characters, accidentalities. The elixir of immortality will be smashed by the stone that crushes your head, equality will perish in the torments of unattainable desires. You may equalize people in wealth, rights and pleasures, but you will not equalize the fools and the wise men, the beautiful and the ugly, the sick and the strong. . . . Man will not be satisfied with any single situation, and immortality itself would become unbearably boring.[11]

The socialists do not understand that "socialism and the proletariat are only moments of this limitless future", that the "golden age" would be boring and everyone would be asking: "What next?"[12] But Naumov himself cannot conceive of any other future but one of boredom. Even now he finds human life boring and stupid. He predicts:

A time will come when the field of human activity will be deserted. For distraction people will begin to shoot at one another as targets, will in masses drown themselves, hang themselves, throw themselves from cliffs.[13]

The little student Kirill Dmitrievich Chizh at first argues with Naumov,

[9] Arcybašev, *op. cit.,* VI, 193.
[10] *Ibid.,* VI, 255.
[11] *Ibid.,* VI, 254.
[12] *Ibid.,* VII, 137.
[13] *Ibid.,* VI, 195.

but finally embraces his nihilistic outlook on the world. In the characterization of Chizh, Artsybashev declares his break not only with socialist idealism, but with all idealism. Chizh is a typical dreamer in the process of passing into the "underground".

When the fat, thick-necked merchant Tregulov, this symbol of crude force, throws Chizh out into the street, Chizh is oppressed by the "terrible consciousness of ignominy, of terrible insult and complete helplessness".[14] But the main thing that torments him is the pitiable and comic impression he creates.

Chizh is a lonely student with a permanent feeling of grievance, an irascible, angry "little man" tormented to distraction by the boring, grey, philistine life around him. He lives in a state of "permanent nervous malice" and dreams with delight of an earthquake which introduces chaos and convulsions into the dull monotony of the life around him. His malice is aimless, despairing. Chizh is a little "underground" man and his story is the story of his gradual recognition of this fact, his gradual acceptance of "Naumovism".

The fundamental conflict in Chizh is that between realist and dreamer. Personal humiliation, disgust with his environment, consciousness of suffering (his own and others) coexist in him with a faith in the people, the proletariat, in humanity which has laid the "foundation of a huge colossal building".[15] He is convinced, like the hero of Kuprin's "River of Life", that the filth and vulgarity around him, the "chaotic and hopeless character" of human life, is only temporary and that in the future "some kind of great wave will come and completely wash away all the old and filthy and there will reign an harmonious, mathematically just happiness in which even he, a small exiled student, a tiny mortal, will have some part, some meaning, some duty".[16]

Chizh has faith in a beautiful future, but it is a faith that is collapsing. The suicide of the hero of "River of Life" symbolizes a rejection of self as loathesome and unworthy of the future-dream. On the other hand, Chizh's suicide, following on his complete disillusionment, symbolizes the collapse of the dream itself before triumphant, vulgar reality. In the "underground" sense it is the inevitable collapse of rationalistic utopian formulae before the reality of human suffering. Chizh unsuccessfully counters Naumov's "underground" pessimism. His own convictions, as he increasingly realizes, have no relation to reality.

[14] *Ibid.,* VII, 15.
[15] *Ibid.,* VI, 170.
[16] *Ibid.,* VI, 12.

All that Chizh knew about the coming triumph of socialism, about brotherhood, equality and freedom was not suitable here. For the first time he felt that in his ideas there was a certain theoretical quality and not the living human body.[17]

Artsybashev here echoes Dostoevsky's basic criticism of the socialists: they are not concerned with the living soul.

The triumph of the "underground", of "Naumovism" in Chizh results from an increasing sense of self-interest over altruistic feelings, an increasing sense of alienation from the "herd". Chizh, in essence, divides people into thinkers, dreamers and sufferers, on the one hand, and the vulgar, stupid and self-satisfied men of action on the other. He, Chizh, is thinking and suffering, but fat-skinned animals will reap the benefit of his labors.

Very simple! The best people, the prophets to whom mankind hypocritically prays, the heroes who do not balk at any sacrifice, will perish and go on perishing while the dull, multitudinous herd marches forward over their corpses! They live, then, only in order with their blood to cement the bricks of universal happiness, while in each level of flats erected by them will settle triumphant pigs who will scornfully grunt at them. Is this not so? The whole history of mankind is the history of the destruction of the martyrs of thought and word, and every epoch is the apotheosis of triumphant banality! To them — to the dull animals — everything: wealth, new inventions, beautiful buildings, beautiful women, honor, luxury, while misfortune, agonizing hesitations, want and suffering is the lot of the Chizhs, the little and the big Chizhs! Thus it was and thus it will always be! [18]

Chizh — at the brink of the "underground" abyss — wants none of the self-sacrifice that Kuprin's idealistic heroes ("The Toast", 1905) take on for the sake of the future golden age. He is one with the Underground Man who will not lift a hand to build an ideal apartment house. Man, the Underground Man believes, prefers not to live in the completed building: he would rather leave it *"aux animaux domestiques, such as ants, sheep, etc."*.

Chizh can dream of a "glorious future", but when he ponders the thousands of years that separate the Tregulovs from the "unknown man of the future with the clear face of artist and wise man", his spirit falls; when he concludes that at that time he, the little student, will no longer exist or be remembered, he is filled with "malice":

[17] *Ibid.,* VI, 197.
[18] *Ibid.,* VII, 6.

And is all this much-vaunted happiness, all this golden age, all this future humanity still worth the unnoticed sufferings of one little, hungry, insulted student? . . . And you, happy people of the future, and what will you be like? And won't you be hostile and alien to the little student? Are you worth his sufferings, will you justify his dreams? And how many more such little, unnoticed dreamers, how much blood and pain will be necessary in order that you, people of the future, will enjoy life! Isn't the price too high, aren't the sacrifices too great for you — happy pigs of the future? [19]

Chizh's ruminations are auguries of coming misfortune for the "little man". When the little Chizhs awaken in the post-revolutionary period they will regard the great socialist building as occupied by "*les animaux domestiques*", by men of action who have no interest in the hesitating thinkers and suffering dreamers. There will be no place for the new little men, like Kavalerov (Olesha's *Envy*); they will scorn the new tenants of the great building, but they will also envy them. This envy is first felt in the little student Chizh.

Chizh, like Ivan Karamazov, returns his entrance ticket to future harmony. The price of universal happiness is too high; blood is too precious to be used as "cement". He, too, wants a bit of happiness. As such thoughts occur to Chizh, he exclaims: "You have lost your sentimentality, Kirill Dmitrievich!" [20] Indeed, a process of moral-spiritual disintegration is taking place in Chizh: overcome by the unbearable consciousness of his isolation and insignificance as a "little man", comparing himself to a "dusty and blind fly swept aside by a broom", he ceases to struggle and sinks to the "bottom of senseless stagnation, drunkenness, vulgarity and a filthy liaison with a fat, old and stupid vixen". [21]

All right, I believe, I believe that life is beautiful and great, but not for me! . . . Go ahead, live, be happy, let the unknown horizons of a free, magnificent human existence unfold. But I have fallen! I feel my thoughts growing calm, my soul growing more petty and vulgar! I am not to blame for this: I struggled, believed, dreamed and aroused others to believe! I lack strength? But who is to blame that I was not granted this strength? I am a little man, an unhappy man, an insulted man — insulted by fate and by people! [22]

---

[19]   *Ibid.,* VII, 8.
[20]   *Ibid.,* VII, 8.
[21]   *Ibid.,* VII, 293.
[22]   *Ibid.,* VII, 295.

Thus Chizh laments as he sinks into hopeless despair. All that remains
for him is the path indicated by Naumov: suicide.

The collapse of Chizh's idealism before "Naumovism" is symbolized
by his surrender to the vulgar embraces of his landlady. "Naumovism"
is the admission that the forces of darkness and vileness cannot be held
back. "Naumovism", a doctrine of despair, triumphs in the lives of all
the heroes of *At the Last Boundary*. One by one they commit suicide.
Shortly before he kills himself, Chizh remarks:

Naumovism! . . . Perhaps it is really right for modern society which has
exhausted all values of science and art and has reached the last boundary.
Of course, society, having exhausted all pleasures, naturally must arrive
at the question: what next? and resolve it in the Naumov sense.[23]

The "last boundary", like the "last wall" in *Notes from the Underground,*
justifies "underground" nihilism: the destruction of life and all values,
if necessary. "Naumovism" is the "underground" outlook of a society
in disintegration. And just such a society — Russia in the decade before
1917 — was reflected in Artsybashev's *At the Last Boundary*.

---

[23]   *Ibid.,* VII, 277.

CHAPTER XIV

MAKSIM GORKY AND
NOTES FROM THE UNDERGROUND

> In a novel a hero is necessary, whereas here all the
> features for the anti-hero have been *deliberately* gather-
> ed, and mainly, all this is certain to produce an ex-
> ceedingly unpleasant impression, because we are all
> divorced from life, all crippled, each of us, more or less.
> The Underground Man.

Maksim Gorky's relation to Dostoevsky is interesting not only for itself,
but because it has been a determining factor in the orientation of Soviet
literature and criticism to Dostoevsky. Important writers like Leonov
and Erenburg, who in their early period show the marked influence of
Dostoevsky's "underground", in their later work struggle with the
"underground" after the manner of Gorky.

Gorky developed as an artist in a period marked by the domination
of Dostoevsky in literature, but this influence for the most part is disclosed in him negatively, in the form of a struggle with the moods and
ideas of Dostoevsky's heroes. Gorky does not dispute the artistic genius
of Dostoevsky, but he is the "evil genius of cultured Russia", Gorky
wrote D. Ovsyaniko-Kulikovsky in 1911, "a man who with the greatest
power and lucidity depicted the spiritual illnesses ingrafted upon us
from the Mongol, from the mutilation inflicted on our soul from tormenting Moscow history."[1] Several years later, in an article entitled
"On Karamazovism" ("O karamazovshchine", 1913), Gorky spelled out
these "illnesses" as the

sadistic savagery of the completely disillusioned nihilist and, its opposite,
the masochism of the beaten, frightened creature who is capable of
enjoying his suffering, not without malicious pleasure however, parading
it before everybody and before himself; he has been mercilessly beaten,
and he brags about it.[2]

Dostoevsky's creative work, Gorky believed, was the "genius-inspired
embodiment of the negative qualities and attributes of the Russian
national character".[3] Gorky's polemic with Dostoevsky's work — both

---

[1] S. Ja. Balukhatyj and V. A. Desnickij (eds.), *M. Gor'kij: Materialy i issledovanija*
(Leningrad, 1931), III, 136.
[2] Gor'kij, M., "O karamazovščine," *Stat'i 1905-1916* (St. Petersburg, 1918), p. 151.

in his *belles-lettres* and journalism — becomes, in this sense, a focal point in his struggle for the regeneration of Russia.

Gorky attached central significance to *Notes from the Underground* in Dostoevsky's works. In it, Gorky wrote, "all the basic ideas and motifs of his creative work are united".[4] In his address before the 1934 Congress of Soviet Writers, Gorky singled out Dostoevsky's *Notes from the Underground* as a work which poses the problems of modern anarchic, egocentric individualism for the nineteenth and twentieth centuries.

To Dostoevsky belongs the credit of having painted with the most vivid perfection of word portraiture a type of egocentric, a type of social degenerate in the person of the hero of his *Notes from the Underground*. With the triumph of one who is insatiably taking vengeance for his personal misfortunes and sufferings, for his youthful enthusiasms, Dostoevsky, in the figure of his hero has shown the depths of whining despair that are reached by the individualist from among the young men of the nineteenth and twentieth centuries who are divorced from life. This type of his combines within himself the most characteristic traits of Friedrich Nietzsche and of the Marquis des Esseintes, the hero of Huysman's *Against the Grain*, *Le Disciple* of Paul Bourget, and Boris Savinkov, the author and hero of his own composition, Oscar Wilde and Artsybashev's *Sanin* and many other social degenerates brought forth by the anarchic influence of the inhuman conditions of the capitalist state.[5]

In his polemical orientation to *Notes from the Underground* Gorky rejects all approaches which would idealize or tend to universalize the Underground Man, his strivings and problems, his misery and despair. Gorky removes the problems posed in this work from their ideological and metaphysical context and examines them on a specific social-historical plane. He is concerned with what he regards as the objective content of "underground" rebellion: its anarchic and destructive nature.[6]

---

[3] Gor'kij, "Ešče o karamazovščine," *ibid.*, p. 159.

[4] Gor'kij, "Dve duši," *ibid.*, p. 181.

[5] "Doklad A. M. Gor'kogo o sovetskoj literature," *Pervyj vsesojuznyj s'ezd sovetskikh pisatelej 1934* (Moscow, 1934), p. 11.

[6] An entry in V. Bryusov's notebook for October, 1900 suggests that Gorky was not unresponsive to the attractions of rebellious individualism in *Notes from the Underground*.

"Here's what is dear to me in Dostoevsky [Bryusov cites Gorky]. You remember in *Notes from the Underground*, in Part I, that man who, in the midst of the reign of universal common sense, will suddenly say: 'well, now oughtn't we to send all this common sense to the devil?' And Gorky with a movement of his leg showed how this man would kick that common sense into the abyss. Indeed, he himself is capable of doing this." (Brjusov, *Dnevniki: 1890-1910* [Moscow, 1927] p. 94.)

The Underground Man as used by Gorky emerges primarily as a proto-type for an unidealized anti-hero: a spiritually impoverished, sometimes pitiful but always socially harmful ultra-individualist, without moral pivot and divorced from life.

Gorky carries on a polemic with Dostoevsky in many of his works; his most direct response to *Notes from the Underground* is found in "The Story of a Hero" ("Rasskaz o geroe", 1924), the story of the transformation of a weak and frightened boy into a lackey, informer, gangster, and murderer, and in "Karamora" ("Karamora", 1924), the tale of a provocateur in the Russian revolutionary movement. Both stories are set in the two decades preceding the 1917 revolution.

Fear of life leads to the "underground". The boy Makarov ("The Story of a Hero") feared life. "In my childhood," he observes, "before I became frightened of people, I feared cockroaches, bees, rats; later I began to be tormented by the terror of storms, blizzards, darkness."[7] Fear of the phenomena of life and people were the formulating elements in his character. He was observant ("Yes, cowardly, shy people are very observant")[8] and watched nature, people, life from a detached world of his own, separate and distinct like the "underground".

Makarov read about adventures in the world, but felt no connection with that world. He liked to ponder on the difference between himself and criminals — a pondering that seems detached from any knowledge of good or evil. He was vain and his family fed his vanity. He felt himself cleverer than his school comrades, but he had no friends. He was the butt of jokes. He was cowardly. The Underground Man, hating his school fellows, shut himself away from them in his wounded pride. Makarov soon "felt the pride of loneliness and vaguely understood it as the only realm where independent personality can freely develop".[9]

The schoolboy Makarov recalls the Underground Man at school. A type resembling the Underground Man's classmate, Zverkov, is Rudometov, "a gallant, a powerful lad, and a drunkard", who was feared and envied and who looked upon everybody with the "scorn of an unusual man . . .".[10] Makarov says of Rudometov:

I liked Rudometov's independent relation to the teachers, and I envied his ability to utter certain special words which stuck in my memory.

[7]   Gor'kij, "Rasskaz o geroe," *Sobranie sočinenij* (2d ed.; Moscow, 1932-1934), XXI, 67.
[8]   *Ibid.,* XXI, 85.
[9]   *Ibid.,* XXI, 85.
[10]   *Ibid.,* XXI, 74.

Once at Zhdanov's lesson he said: "I prefer crooked lines, they seem to me more alive, capable of independent movement, whereas straight lines are hopelessly dead." [11]

That Gorky has the cynical and corrupt Rudometov voice a preference for the "crooked" over the "straight" line is characteristic of his method of ridiculing "underground" clichés. Rudometov is as much a part of the "underground" as Makarov.

Fear of nature and distrust of human reason are integrally related in the personality of Makarov. Nature for Makarov was like the huge, filthy, corrupt laundress Karaseva who had frequent periods of drunkenness and savage destructive spells. And "human reason" took the shape of the policeman who used to knock Karaseva down with a blow of his fist and tie her up. This allegorical comparison of nature with the laundress and human reason with the Tatar policeman always remained in Makarov's mind.

Here are gathered a number of themes of the "underground": fear of life, loneliness, vanity, alienation from people, distrust of reason, and the suggestion of a moral vacuum. Yet here there is neither a tragic hero of the "underground", nor a "tragedy of the underground". Gorky takes the "underground" experience and localizes it. In the characterization of Makarov he identifies the themes of the "underground" with narrowness, mediocrity, banality, with the limitations of milieu and education, with a more or less defined petty bourgeois social group.

Gorky consciously emphasizes the philistine character of Makarov's "underground" features. "You might think that I was a sick boy," Makarov says, as though hinting at his weak and sickly counterparts in Russian literature, "but this is not so. ... I was physically healthy and I think that the source of fear before the phenomena of nature lay precisely in my healthiness — this is the natural, biological fear of man before a threatening catastrophe which he cannot comprehend." [12]

In *Notes from the Underground,* the Underground Man serves to disclose not only the irrationality of his own being, but that of human nature in general. In "The Story of a Hero", the irrationality of Makarov is disclosed as exceptional; it is rationally explained. Gorky defines his rational view of the "underground" attitudes with the allegory of the laundress and policeman in which the "underground" attitude towards reason and nature is reduced to daily life. The "underground" theme of distrust of reason and nature is thus rendered impotent as an eternal

[11]   *Ibid.,* XXI, 74.
[12]   *Ibid.,* XXI, 68.

verity. Gorky is not trying to discredit reason; he is trying to rescue it from the "underground".

Gorky's approach to the "underground", therefore, is entirely different from the approach of Andreev who shares the "underground" distrust of reason and who sees in the tragedy of the "underground" a tragedy for all mankind. The "curse" of the beast is the curse of man, rising from the "dead centuries" of the past, a mournful wail of emptiness, hopelessness and horror.

Skotoprigonevsk produced Fedor Karamazov, Skorodozh — the school teacher Peredonov. The school teacher Mily Novak, a baldheaded man with a huge Adam's apple and "small, colorless, inflamed eyes without eyelashes",[13] must be added to these moral deformities. In the image of this cowardly, sadistic person, Gorky seems to establish the kinship between Peredonovism and the Monarchist-Black Hundred movements that developed during the first Russian revolution in 1905.

Mily Novak is a propagator of Carlyle's cult of the hero, he is a disciple of Dostoevsky, Nietzsche, and Konstantin Leontiev. In his savage philosophy of cruelty and power, and in his cowardice (he even trembles when crossing a street), Novak is a true expression of the malice of impotence.

Novak and Makarov complement each other. Novak introduced into his pupil Makarov's life what the Underground Man obtained through his study of history: a fixed idea of history's cruelty and irrationality. His horror-filled picture of history, his justification of the savage cruelty of tyrants against people, his conception of man-the-individual as the "enemy of the reality affirmed by the people", his idea of history as the "enmity of one against the multitude"[14] — all this helped to lay the foundation for Makarov's "underground" development. Novak, in essence, provided a social-philosophical foundation to Makarov's instinctive fear of life and distrust of human reason; he give him what was necessary both to activate and to justify an "underground" relationship with society.

In the deranged thinking of Mily Novak, Gorky parodies ideas of Dostoevsky, Leontiev, Nietzsche, and Carlyle, he parodies Dostoevsky's fear of the irrational in man, his distrust of reason, his rejection of socialism. The socialists, Novak warned, are too confident of "reason", they forget the irrationality of life; they are not arousing the energy of

13   *Ibid.*, XXI, 70.
14   *Ibid.*, XXI, 73.

reason in the masses, but only the instincts of envy, malice and revenge. Only "monarchy, merciless, fearless authority can lead us most quickly of all to anarchism, to the absolute freedom of personality". Makarov notes:

He [Novak] sternly advised me, nay, ordered me to read Dostoevsky, Konstantin Leontiev, Nietzsche. "Yes," he said, "precisely these ones." Anarchists — in the essence of their spirit; monarchists — in the consciousness of the need to be monarchists.[15]

The revolution of 1905-06 was a fateful influence in the life of Makarov. The clerk Makarov's fear of life and people quite naturally broadened into a fear of revolution and of the masses of people. His language even has a certain "underground" flavor. He speaks of the "ant work" of people, the "ant procession" of workers. The people appeared to him like a "herd of sheep" led by leader-heroes. And Makarov, for whom the world of "heroes" had hitherto been alien and unnecessary, set out in search of a hero; he offered his services to Novak, at this time active in the monarchist cause. "What do you want, what are you defending?" Novak asked. "I am defending myself from everything hostile to me,"[16] Makarov significantly replied.

But events soon destroyed Makarov's image of Novak as a hero; he soon learned that Novak's man-the-individual was also a coward, that he, too, feared the people. A blind rage arose in Makarov's fear-ridden soul. The man who had been afraid of people now declares that if he possessed power he would leave behind him in the world "a terrible, blinding memory" of himself. "I would eclipse the fame of all the tyrants of the world", Makarov declares, "I would wash and iron people like handkerchiefs." [17]

This is the terrible despotism of the "underground", the venomous malice of a trembling creature who has discovered a secret source of power. That source is fear.

Fear of people . . . gives to the instinct of life in man the right to be mercilessly savage with people, an indisputable right, because its root is in the instinct of self-preservation. Ivan the Terrible was probably a coward like all so-called tyrants. The politics of cowards is always the politics of savagery, all politicians are merciless.[18]

---

15 *Ibid.*, XXI, 84.
16 *Ibid.*, XXI, 83.
17 *Ibid.*, XXI, 92.
18 *Ibid.*, XXI, 92.

Precisely this violent, uncontrolled rage is characteristic of the Underground Man. His fury with Liza is no more than the rebellion of a man who but a moment before recognized with profound humiliation his own helplessness before others, before the world.

Makarov's disillusionment with his hero Novak was the necessary requisite to his assumption of the role of anti-hero. Makarov discarded his hero, but he appropriated his teacher's philosophy of history and life, his politics of savagery. Makarov passed from clerk to informer, gangster and murderer. "I may be a hangman," he observes at the conclusion of his story, "it's all the same thing." [19]

Novak plays a decisive role in the development of the "underground" personality of Makarov; he functions in the story largely as a carrier of the ideas of Dostoevsky, Nietzsche, Leontiev, and Carlyle. His relation to Makarov, in this respect, is similar to the relation of Novikov to Sergey Petrovich in Andreev's story. It seems fairly certain that Gorky's "The Story of a Hero" is a response to "The Story of Sergey Petrovich" which is concerned with the effect of Nietzsche's teachings on the "little man". In matters of plot and detail there are many similarities between the two stories, but Gorky and Andreev differ completely in their attitude towards the Nietzschean superman.

Both Novikov and Novak are men inspired by ideologies of a master race; both are mentors to weak men. But whereas Andreev tends to idealize Novikov and his Nietzschean philosophy, Gorky discloses Novak as a fraud and exposes the superman as a trembling coward. Gorky, finally, carries through the rebellion of the weak hero — where Andreev cuts it short — and emphasizes the sick content of "underground" rebellion; where Andreev is concerned with the personal tragedy of the "little man," Gorky is concerned with the social tragedy symbolized by the advent of the anti-hero.

An examination of Gorky's story "Karamora" (1924), a study in the causes and psychology of betrayal in the Russian revolutionary movement before 1917, discloses an absorption in moral questions raised by the revolution. Not the "golden dream" of Gorky-the-social-romanticist emerges here, but a grim nightmare of Russian life. "I have written a story," Gorky wrote V. Khodasevich August 17, 1923. "It seems to be frightening. I called it 'Karamora'." [20]

[19] *Ibid.*, XXI, 93.
[20] "The Letters of Maksim Gor'kij to V. F. Xodasevič, 1922-1925," Translated and Edited by Hugh McLean. *Harvard Slavic Studies* (Cambridge, Mass., 1953), I, 297.

The morality of the revolution is not an isolated problem in Gorky's thinking and writing, but is a part of his total sensitivity to the moral and spiritual life of the Russian people and his concern with the pervasive influence on Russian culture of the ideas, attitudes and moods of Dostoevsky's heroes — with all that has been called *dostoevshchina*.

The morality of revolution, the morality of the people and of the men lifted by the revolution to positions of leadership, were in the forefront of Gorky's mind at the outbreak of the March revolution of 1917. In April 1917 in his journal *Chronicle* (*Letopis*) Gorky welcomed the Russian revolution as a liberating force, but warned that "we grew up in an atmosphere of the 'underground' . . . poisoned by the cadaver of dying monarchism".[21] The moral disintegration in the pre-revolutionary period was echoed in the socialist movements by the prevalence of agents of the Tsarist police, adventurists, men without inner law, who found in "police socialism" a source not only of revenue but also of gratification. The publication in 1917 of lists of people who had worked for the secret police came as a shock to Gorky. He had known many of them. "This is one of the most ignominious mockeries of my faith in man,"[22] he wrote in a sketch entitled "Nightmare", published in *New Life* (*Novaya Zhizn*) in March 1917.

In "Nightmare" Gorky describes his revulsion at a woman spy who entreated him to protect her from the revolutionary authorities. The experience is a depressing one and casts a "dark shadow" over Gorky's spirit. "Am I not responsible for all this vileness of life which is seething around me," he asks in a strangely Dostoevskian mood and manner; "am I not responsible for this life, at dawn so foully smeared with the filth of treachery?" At the dawn of the revolution sombre thoughts weigh upon Gorky. Outside in the streets the "liberated element is tumultuous"; he hears the "sharp smell of new words", he rejoices. "But I feel myself nailed to some kind of rotten wall," Gorky concludes his sketch, "crucified on it by bitter thoughts about disfigured man whom I cannot, I cannot help, in any way, ever."[23]

Gorky's "Karamora" is a study in the disintegration of personality. In writing his story, Gorky wrote Romain Rolland, he had in mind various provocateurs he had known: M. Gurevich, E. Azef, and others.[24]

[21] Gor'kij, *Revoljucija i kul'tura. Stat'i za 1917*. (Berlin, [no date]), pp. 5-6.
[22] Gor'kij, "Košmar," in "Zabytye rasskazy M. Gor'kogo," *Znamja*, No. 8-9 (1946), p. 142.
[23] *Ibid.*, p. 143.
[24] Gor'kij, *Sobranie sočinenij v 30 tomakh* (Moscow, 1949-), XVI, 594.

"Karamora", however, is a story with a double objective: an inquiry into the psychology of the *agent provocateur,* it is at the same time an inquiry into the nature of the Dostoevsky "underground" hero (with particular attention to *Notes from the Underground*). In "Karamora" Gorky posits the moral-psychological "underground" of Dostoevsky as the state of mind of betrayal. The full implications of the story, there-fore, can only appear in the light of Gorky's life-long polemic with Dostoevsky. In analyzing "Karamora" it is necessary, also, to consider Gorky's subtle parody and at the same time direct use in this story of themes and problems raised in Dostoevsky's *Notes from the Under-ground.*

Six epigrams open Gorky's story "Karamora". The mood they es-tablish is overwhelmingly that of the Dostoevsky "underground" with its themes of the uncontrollable irrational, the compulsion to do vile things, ambivalence and moral chaos.

"You know: I am capable of an heroic deed. And, I may say, a vile one also. At times one has a terrible longing to do something vile and filthy to someone — to someone very close." The words of the worker Zakhar Mikhailov, provocateur, before the trial committee in 1917.

"Sometimes, for no reason whatsoever, I am conscious of ignominious and vile thoughts." N. I. Pirogov.

"Permit me to do something vile!" One of Ostrovsky's heroes.

"Vileness sometimes demands as much self-renunciation as a feat of heroism." From a letter of L. Andreev.

"You don't learn about a person from his conscious acts; you learn about him from his unconscious acts." Leskov in a letter to Pylyaev.

"The Russian man is a capricious fellow." I. S. Turgenev.[25]

So closely is Dostoevsky's name linked with the expression of these moods and ideas that the absence of it is striking. Yet the omission of Dostoevsky's name and the selection of other sources to give expression to these moods and ideas is not without design. It emphasizes in an oblique way a central idea of "Karamora": the typical nature of Dos-toevsky's moral-psychological "underground". The Dostoevsky "under-ground" is posed not just as a creation of Dostoevsky, but as an expression of a social calamity affecting wide sections of Russian society. An

---

[25] Gor'kij, *"Karamora," Sobranie sočinenij* (2d ed.; Moscow, 1932-34), XXI, 114.

embodiment of this calamity is Petr Karazin, protagonist of Gorky's story "Karamora".

Petr Karazin — nicknamed "daddy longlegs" ("karamora") — is in some ways what Gorky called a philistine individualist. In his article "Destruction of Personality" (1909), Gorky warned the "demos" that this type "would like to enter the ranks of the socialists as law-givers, prophets, commanders", but that this "only conceals the same striving of the philistine to the 'self-assertion of his personality'."[26]

Karazin became interested in socialism at the age of 19 around the turn of the century. He liked to command and was used to adventure, conspiracies and danger. He had no real friends. "I had become instinctively suspicious," he writes, "lacked confidence in people; I lived in an epoch of provocateurs."[27] After the defeat of the 1905 revolution he became conscious of an inner division in himself, of someone living within, "an uninvited and unpleasant guest". Caught by the police he quickly and calmly, to his own surprise, assumed the role of provocateur; in the service of the tsarist secret police he would occasionally — for the sake of "diversity" — play a double game and do little favors for his former comrades: arrange for escapes from prison, organize printing presses, etc. In 1917 he was arrested by the revolutionary authorities and imprisoned. Here he began to write his "notes" and to analyze himself. He wanted to know why no inner force stopped him on the path to betrayal, why when he called himself a criminal he could not "in all conscience" feel that there was any crime. "If my notes have a purpose, it is only this: to resolve the question — why am I so jarringly and completely broken up?"[28]

Like *Notes from the Underground* the story "Karamora" takes the form of "notes". The confession of a personality estranged from himself and from humanity, it consists of self-analysis, philosophizing and recollections. The mood is overwhelmingly that of the "underground". Karazin is sitting alone in prison. It is dark. It is raining.

They gave me three quires of paper: write down, they said, how all this happened. And why should I write and write? It makes no difference: they will kill me.[29]

Yes, I am writing. I am not writing in order to stretch out several superfluous days of life in prison, but — at the desire of a third person.

[26] Gor'kij, "Razrušenie ličnosti," *Stat'i: 1905-1916, op. cit.,* p. 19.
[27] Gor'kij, "Karamora," *op. cit.,* XXI, 128.
[28] *Ibid.,* XXI, 141.
[29] *Ibid.,* XXI, 114.

Two people live in me, I say, and one didn't stick to the other, but there is still a third. He watches the other two, their quarrel and at one moment stirs up, inflames this quarrel, and at the next, honestly wants to know: whence this quarrel, what's the meaning of it?

He's the one who is compelling me to write. Perhaps he is really the genuine I who wants to know everything or at least something. But perhaps this third person is my most malicious enemy? This is really guessing at a fourth. . . . There is I dare say, even a fourth; this one is concealed even deeper than the third and — is silent, and watches like a beast biding his time. Perhaps he will remain silent and dumb all my life, concealed and indifferently watching the tangled confusion.[30]

I am not writing for them, but for myself, because I am bored. And to relate one's life to oneself is very interesting. You look at yourself as at a stranger, and it is entertaining to play hide and seek with one's thoughts, to lie, to conceal something from the fourth, to elude him when he is on your track. Such a game is worth not only a candle, but a whole bonfire. After it only ashes remain? Well, what of it***. It's hardly likely that these notes will be seen or read. . . .[31]

All night long I recalled my life. What more can I do. I looked as into a crack, and through the crack there was a mirror, and in it was reflected the stagnation that I have experienced.[32]

The abrupt, erratic quality of these "notes", the mood, the stylistic devices recall *Notes from the Underground*: the background of rain, the boredom coming from nothing to do, the writing for onself alone, the distorted "underground" perspective through a "crack", the intoxication with the "game" of thoughts, yet the consciousness of the futility of all ratiocination, the disintegration of personality and the awareness of disintegration. The wooden-calm, detached, at times bored tone of narration at once betrays the moral void; in this Karazin recalls the protagonist of Dostoevsky's *A Gentle One,* or the impassive Stavrogin in Dostoevsky's *The Devils,* in whom mind functions but feeling is dead.

Gorky is not passively "influenced" by Dostoevsky. In "Karamora," as in "The Story of a Hero" and in other works, he deliberately introduces the material of Dostoevsky in order to act upon it; everywhere he leaves the stamp of his own interpretation of the "underground", of the "underground" type and of Dostoevsky himself. It is not accidental that Dostoevsky's name appears in Karazin's "notes":

You write, and, so to speak, you are not alone on earth; there is still someone to whom you are dear, before whom you are in no way guilty,

---

[30]   *Ibid.,* XXI, 119.
[31]   *Ibid.,* XXI, 120.
[32]   *Ibid.,* XXI, 115.

who understands you well, who does not pity you in an insulting way. You write — and seem to yourself cleverer, better. This sort of thing is intoxicating. This is when I feel Dostoevsky: here was a writer who was completely intoxicated with himself, with the mad, stormy play of his imagination — with the game of many parts of himself.[33]

The attempt through writing to escape from the feeling of estrangement from himself, from a world in which he feels guilty in everything is characteristic of the Underground Man; in his "notes", as in his life, there is a never-ending game of many parts of himself, a game played out, however, with a tragic compulsion that is not felt so strongly in Petr Karazin.

Petr Karazin and the Underground Man have the same "underground" view of humanity. The Underground Man sees, essentially, only two types of people: the "normal man" — the single-minded, direct "man of action" — and the "antithesis of the normal man, that is, the man of heightened consciousness . . .", the self-divided man from the "underground". The men of action have strong nerves, but they are "stupid" and "limited": they roar like bulls but immediately humble themselves before the impossible, in contrast to "thinking people" who cannot do anything, but nevertheless refuse to accept the impossible.

Gorky parodies this "underground" division of humanity through the figure of Karazin:

Of course, people are divided into working people and those living on the labor of others, into proletariat and bourgeoisie. This is an external division, but then people in all classes are divided into whole people and split personalities. A whole person is always like an ox, he's always boring. I think that wholeness is the result of self-limitation for the sake of self-defense.[34]

Karazin, like the Underground Man, identifies himself with the split personality.

The life of a split personality recalls the spasmodic flight of the sparrow. It goes without saying, the whole man is more useful in a practical sense, but the second type is closer to me. Involved people are more interesting.[35]

In *Notes from the Underground* the phenomenon of ambivalence is an essential part of the Underground Man's despairing, irrational defense of his personality against all that oppresses and outrages it — against

---

[33]   *Ibid.*, XXI, 130.
[34]   *Ibid.*, XXI, 124-125.
[35]   *Ibid.*, XXI, 125.

the whole "men of action", the rationalists, reason, the very "laws of nature" which have been humiliating him more than anything else. One manifestation of the Underground Man's ambivalence is that he is constantly undertaking a course of action which he knows can only end in catastrophe and greater suffering. Will and reason in him are in complete discord.

In "Karamora", however, "underground" ambivalence loses its idealized character. It is identified with the depraved personality of a murderer-provocateur — a professional split personality; ambivalence, far from being a function of self-defense, becomes part of an assault on the individual.

Gorky's parody of the "underground" division of humanity into spilt personalities and whole men of action — his re-evaluation of the values the Undergound Man attaches to these categories is suggested in his characterization of Karazin's relations with the Jewish student-socialist, Leopold. As a youth Karazin became a member of a small socialist circle presided over by the sick student, Leopold: "a little hungry Jew", nearsighted, with a crooked nose and a "yellowish phiz". "He struck me as ridiculous and cowardly," Karazin remarks, "like a mouse." The mouse Leopold was brilliant, indomitable in his exposure of evil in society; he "trembled with malice" as he uncovered the truth of life. But Karazin recalls:

For me, a cheerful youth, it was unpleasant to listen to his malicious talk. I was satisfied with life, not envious, not greedy, I made a good living, I saw my path before me like a bright stream. And suddenly I feel: the little Jew has muddied my water. It was insulting: I — a healthy, Russian fellow and here this insignificant alien little runt turns out to be cleverer than I; he teaches, vexes, as though rubbing salt in my skin.

I was not able to say anything to oppose him, and anyway it was perfectly plain: Leopold spoke the truth. Yet I wanted very much to say something. But — just how do you say: "All this is the truth, only I don't need it. I have my own." Now I understand: had I spoken in that way, all my life would have taken another path. I made a mistake: I didn't speak that way. . . .

After a little thought, I decided to take on the work of a propagandist, but I set myself the aim of disconcerting Leopold, of humiliating him in some way in the eyes of his comrades; this was not only because he was a Jew, but because it was difficult for me to reconcile myself with the fact that truth lived and burned in such a frail, little body. Here, of course, it was not a matter of aesthetic feeling, but, so to say, the organic suspiciousness of the healthy man who fears contagion.[36]

[36] *Ibid.*, XXI, 115-116.

Gorky has quite deliberately shuffled the conventional attributes of
"underground" man and "man of action" in his delineation of both
Leopold and Karazin. The depiction of Leopold recalls the image of
the Underground Man — also a short and thin little man, unattractive
in features, ridiculous and cowardly in behavior, an envious "mouse", a
man of sensibility maliciously aiming his barbs at his enemies. Yet
Leopold is not an "underground" man; he is not a split personality; he
is a whole man who can think and act in concert, and his actions do not
degrade him in the eyes of either author or reader. On the other hand,
Gorky has associated the split personality — the mark of "underground"
superiority — with the passionless, morally destitute "health" of Karazin;
the split personality is identified, therefore, not with the sensitive "insulted and injured" little man, but with philistine egoism. Gorky's
purpose is clear: it is to discredit the "underground" idealization of the
split personality and the association of it with sensitivity and intellect,
and to restore to the "whole" personality sensitivity, intelligence, passion.

The Underground Man, humiliated and abased, cannot live without
humiliating others. In power over others he seeks the restoration of that
sense of self-mastery and self-respect which he has lost. The Underground Man is fundamentally a tragic figure and, despite his excesses,
invites sympathy as one of the "insulted and injured" of humanity.
Gorky deliberately eliminates from Karazin's personality and background
all those extenuating circumstances which serve to rationalize the violence
of "underground" behavior (the facts of orphanhood, poverty, heightened
sensibility, depressing environment, etc.) Karazin, unlike the Underground Man, is not one of the "insulted and injured"; he is a "cheerful
man", a "healthy man" satisfied with life.

What is it, than, that leads Karazin to attempt to humiliate Leopold?
It is Karazin's narrow, philistine egotism, his striving for self-assertion.
Karazin likes the feeling of power, and to this fact he ascribes his success
as a socialist organizer. ". . . Power over people is a great satisfaction,"
he remarks. "To compel a person to think and do what you consider
necessary . . . is valuable in itself as an expression of your personal
strength, your importance." [37]

Socialism is a "game" for Karazin. The "game" as the medium for
egoistic self-assertion and a field for the pure play of reason is an "underground" phenomenon peculiarly characteristic of the Underground Man

---

[37]   *Ibid.*, XXI, 123.

and the "underground" hero of *A Gentle One*. The "game" and the "hunt" form the heart of life, according to Karazin's police superior Simonov. And Karazin, attracted to the "game of human reason" in any form, is indifferent to the role he plays in the game of life. When he shifted from revolutionary to police agent, he experienced absolutely nothing except "curiosity", and then surprise over the fact that he felt nothing but curiosity. "With my reason I could recognize that I was doing a so-called vile thing, but this consciousness was not affirmed by a feeling — corresponding to it — of self-condemnation, revulsion, repentance or even fear." [38] The moral sense is dead in Karazin and reason is isolated.

The loss of moral criteria — a central problem for many of Dostoevsky's heroes — was for Gorky a phenomenon that had its roots in Russian society. Gorky raises this problem in response to a letter he received from a one-time provocateur in May 1917. The provocateur wrote:

Yesterday I read your "Nightmare" [the sketch referred to above] and my soul, the soul of a man who had also served in the Tsarist secret police, weeps from the consciousness of the hopelessness of my position, which this sketch awoke in me. I will not begin to tell you how I fell into that pit: it is uninteresting. I will say only that hunger and the advice of a man close to me at that time, a man who was under arrest and thought that I could lighten his lot, pushed me into taking this terrible step.

I will say that I despised myself all the time I was serving there, I despise myself now, too. But, do you know what is painful? The fact that even a sensitive person like you did not understand, obviously, that it was necessary, probably, for each of us members of the secret police to burn much in our soul; that we suffered not at the time when we served, but — earlier when there was no longer any way out; that society, which now throws mud at us, did not support us, did not extend to us a hand of assistance at that time. After all, not everybody is so strong that he can give up everything without receiving anything in exchange! If there had been no faith in socialism, in the Party — but, do you know, in my vile head I reasoned thus: the harm which I can do to the movement is too small, I believe too much in its idea, not to be able to work in such a way that there would be more benefit than harm. I am not trying to justify myself, but I should wish that the psychology of even such a miserable being as a provocateur could still be clear to you. After all, there were many of us! all the best Party men. This is not a phenomenon of purely individual disfiguration, but, obviously, some kind of a deeper, general cause drove us into this blind alley. I beg of you: overcome your

---

[38]   *Ibid.*, XXI, 138-139.

revulsion; come closer to the soul of the traitor and tell us all: just what motives guided us when, believing with all our soul in the Party, in socialism, in everything holy and pure, we were able "honorably" to serve in the secret police and, despising ourselves, still find it possible to live? [39]

"It is difficult to live in holy Rus! It is difficult," Gorky exclaims ironically, immediately after quoting this letter. "It is foul when they sin in it; it is worse when they repent of their sins." [40] Gorky feels compelled to admit that the letter-writer is "sincere" in his perverted reasoning about doing more good than harm. "The most original feature of the Russian man is that he is sincere at every moment. Precisely this originality is, it seems to me, the source of the moral confusion in which we have been accustomed to live . . ." [41] Gorky discloses the "general cause" which the provocateur seeks:

I think that such a "general cause" does exist and that it is a very complex cause. Probably, one of its component parts is the fact that we regard each other quite indifferently, that is, when we are in a good mood*** We do not know how to love or respect one another, there has not developed within us an attentiveness to man; about us it was long ago and quite correctly said, that "we are shamefully indifferent to good and evil". [Gorky quotes a line from a famous poem by the Russian poet M. Yu. Lermontov (1814-1841) entitled "Meditation" ("Duma")]. The comrade-provocateur wrote this letter quite sincerely, but I think that the cause of his misfortune is precisely this indifference to good and evil.[42]

In "Karamora" Gorky seems to fulfill the request of his correspondent-provocateur that he analyze the "psychology of even such a miserable being as a provocateur". But Gorky does not justify Karazin's betrayal. He emphasizes the moral responsibility of the individual for his acts. "No, I do not want to justify myself," remarks Karazin in connection with that "odious time" after the 1905 revolution, when "even people

[39]   Gor'kij, *Revoljucija i kul'tura, op. cit.,* p. 22.
[40]   *Ibid.,* p. 23.
[41]   *Ibid.,* p. 23. Arkady Dolgoruki in Dostoevsky's *The Raw Youth* voices essentially this same thought. ". . . A thousand times," he observes, "I have been amazed at this faculty of man (and, it seems, chiefly the Russian man) for cherishing in his soul the most lofty ideal side by side with the most extreme vileness, and all this absolutely sincerely. Whether this is a special broadness in the Russian man which will take him far, or simply vileness—that is the question!" (Dostoevskij, *Podrostok, op. cit.,* VIII, 321).
[42]   Gor'kij, *Revoljucija i kul'tura, op. cit.,* pp. 24-25.

who had shown themselves capable of heroic deeds did vile things." [43]
"Whatever I was, still — I am I. The conditions of the time played an important role in my life, but only in that they brought me face to face with myself." [44]

When Karazin came face to face with himself he discovered a moral vacuum. Reason never prompted Karazin, telling him what was good and what was bad, for "reason" in him was "indifferent to good and evil".[45] ". . . Without a pure heart," the Underground Man realizes, "there can be no full correct consciousness."[46] Karazin reaches essentially the same conclusion. "Alone, unfertilized by feeling, thought plays with a man like a prostitute, but is absolutely unable to change anything in man." [47]

With my reason I accepted socialist thought as truth, but the fact from which this thought was born did not arouse my feeling, while the fact of inequality among people was for me natural and legitimate . . . in general, I lacked something necessary for a socialist — was it love for people, or something? I don't know what. Putting it simply: socialism was not to my measurements: here it was a little too narrow, there — a bit too broad. I have seen many socialists like that for whom socialism was something alien. They are like calculating machines. It's all the same to them how the figures add up, the total is always correct, but there's no soul in it, nothing but bare arithmetic.[48]

Gorky, unlike Dostoevsky, is not hostile to reason or revolution as such. "The force which all my life has firmly sustained me and sustains me now," he wrote in his journal *Chronicle* in April 1917, "was and is my faith in man's reason. To this day the Russian revolution in my eyes is a chain of bright and joyful manifestations of rationality." [49] Yet Gorky seems to fear the appearance in the revolutionary movement of the same elements that Dostoevsky treats in *The Devils* — the soulless pseudo-socialist "calculating machines", Shigalevs, adventurers like Petr Verkhovensky ("You see, I'm a scoundrel, not a socialist, ha! ha!"), precisely the degenerate, power-hungry creatures who swarm in *The Devils*. "There is no poison more vile than power over people," Gorky warned in December 1917; "we must remember this, so that power does not

[43] Gor'kij, "Karamora," *op. cit.*, XXI, 125.
[44] *Ibid.*, XXI, 126.
[45] *Ibid.*, XXI, 119.
[46] Dostoevskij, *Zapiski iz podpol'ja, op. cit.*, IV, 123.
[47] Gor'kij, "Karamora," *op. cit.*, XXI, 140.
[48] *Ibid.*, XXI, 116.
[49] Gor'kij, *Revoljucija i kul'tura, op. cit.*, p. 9.

poison us, transforming us into cannibals even more abominable than those against whom we have fought all our life." [50]

"Karamora," like *Notes from the Underground,* is more than a study of the moral-spiritual disintegration of one individual; it purports to be a study of a whole generation. The Underground Man, Dostoevsky wrote in his prefatory note to *Notes from the Underground,* is a "representative of a generation that is still with us". He is conceived as a kind of representative of the Russian intelligentsia, inwardly consumed by rationalism, divorced from life and from the people. In his recollections the Underground Man emerges as a "dreamer", a "bookish" lover of humanity who conceals behind a sentimental desire to "embrace humanity" both a desire to escape reality and an implacable egotism.

Gorky leaves no doubt that Karazin is related to the intelligentsia. Like the Underground Man's, Karazin's relation to socialism was bookish and egotistical. ". . . Formerly," Karazin observes, "I talked to people in words that were alien, bookish and, overwhelmed by them, I did not pay heed to my [real] self." [51] He had the reputation of a man "ideologically unstable, capricious and . . . inclined to romanticism, to 'metaphysics.' " [52] Karazin has been "spoiled by the intelligentsia, by books". [53] Karazin, in fact, finds in the intelligentsia — the "comrade-intellectuals", "poets, lyricists or something, preachers of love for the people" — the same mechanical, fabricated love for the people, the same striving for self-assertion, the same chameleon-like characteristics that define his own personality. At the conclusion of his "notes" the Underground Man rationalizes that he only "carried to an extreme" what others did not dare carry through even half way. Karazin might have reasoned in this way. He is, in Gorky's conception, a sick son of his epoch — an epoch of provocateurs — a representative of a generation that lacked the "habit of living honorably". In the final pages of his "notes" Karazin sets forth some keen generalizations which illuminate the symbolical role Gorky gives him and which sum up Gorky's message in "Karamora":

In 1907-1914, observing how easily people abandoned their beliefs, I became convinced that something was lacking in them, something that had never been there. What was it? The feeling of physical squeamishness towards that which their thought negated? Was it that the habit of living honorably was lacking?

---

[50]   *Ibid.,* p. 79.
[51]   Gor'kij, "Karamora," *op. cit.,* XXI, 126.
[52]   *Ibid.,* XXI, 136.
[53]   *Ibid.,* XXI, 139.

Here, now, I think I've put my finger on the real thing: the habit of living honorably; precisely this is the very thing that people lack. My comrades also lacked this habit. Their way of life contradicted "convictions", "principles", dogma of faith. This contradiction found particularly sharp expression in the methods of fractional struggle, in the enmity among people of the same beliefs, but of differing tactics. Here there took place the most shameless Jesuitism, here there were permitted the crooked tricks and even foul methods of passionate gamblers absorbed with the game to the point of oblivion, playing now only for the sake of the process of the game.

Yes, yes — people do not have the habit of living honorably. Of course, I know that the majority of them did not have and do not have the possibility of cultivating this habit. But those who place before themselves the task of rebuilding life, of re-educating people — they are mistaken in supposing that "in the struggle the ends justify the means." No, guided by such a dogma you will not educate in people the habit of living honorably.[54]

It is the voice of Gorky that emerges in this passage, as it is the voice of Dostoevsky which declared at the end of *Notes from the Underground* that "all this is certain to produce an exceedingly unpleasant impression because we are all divorced from life, we are all cripples, each of us, more or less". For Gorky, in 1917, the Russian man was morally crippled:

The truth must be told: we ourselves are morally shattered no less than the forces hostile to us. (*New Life*, April 27, 1917.)[55]

Morals, as feelings of organic dislike for all that is filthy and bad, as an instinctive attraction to purity of spirit and to fine behavior, such morality we do not have. (*New Life*, May 12, 1917.)[56]

The conditions of [the people's] life have not been able to develop in it either respect for the human being, nor the consciousness of the right of the citizen, nor the feeling of justice. (*New Life*, May 18, 1917.)[57]

In "Karamora" — 1924, as in 1917 — Gorky directs his words at contemporary Russia, at "those who place before themselves the task of rebuilding life, of re-educating people". Anarchy, cruelty, stupidity, violence against the individual, "indifference to good and evil" — these were the internal enemy, the moral and psychological "underground" with which the new Russia had to contend. The problem of overcoming

---

[54] *Ibid.,* XXI, 140.
[55] Gor'kij, *Revoljucija i kul'tura, op. cit.,* p. 15.
[56] *Ibid.,* p. 23.
[57] *Ibid.,* p. 26.

the legacy of old, autocratic Russia and the problem of overcoming *dostoevshchina* seem to merge in Gorky's writing and thinking. "Kara-mora" brings out particularly vividly the unity in Gorky's mind that is formed by the problems of the morality of the revolution, the moral climate of Russia and the pernicious effect of *dostoevshchina*.

CHAPTER XV

AFTER 1917

The period from 1917 to the early thirties began in the turmoil of the revolution and ended in the turmoil of the first Five Year Plan; the eight years from 1921 to 1928, less outwardly stormy, were nevertheless years of difficult problems, crises and adjustments in every realm of Soviet life.

War, revolution, civil war, foreign intervention, famine and a general breakdown of economic and civil life were succeeded in 1921 by the NEP (New Economic Policy), a partial revival of individual enterprise. A new "second revolution", beginning in 1929 with the inauguration of of the First Five Year Plan, brought the period to a close in a fever of urgency with the furious tempo of a new industrialization program, the new shocks of collectivization.

All these events, reflected in the literature of the period, shattered the lives of Russian intellectuals. Many left the country. Some, remaining, bewailed the tragedies of the epoch. Some passionately embraced the new revolutionary movement, romanticizing its elemental, non-rational aspects. Many, confused and uprooted, could only struggle for survival.

It is not surprising, then, that the dilemma of the individual lost in a changing society that rejects or mistrusts him should occupy a central place in the thoughts of many writers. The intellectual Ozhegov in N. Ognev's novel *Diary of Kostya Ryabtsev* (1929), describes the tragedy of intellectuals:

And thus these intellectuals, and along with them a part of the youth, are placed in the Hamlet dilemma . . . are placed there by history . . . are crucified at the historical crossroads, while life noisily and stormily roars past them. . . . And the crucified — what can the crucified do? Because all of us, all of us intellectuals who went with the revolution, were or will in the end be crucified, not by governmental agencies, no, but by the masses. . . . Thus the question: is it worth living or not? Yes, you can live when you are surrounded by people close to you, your own,

who love you and have faith in you, when they carefully respond to your
words and actions and regard them at least as dictated by an honest
attitude towards life and towards progress. But when this confidence,
this love and this faith are lacking — no, then the answer to the question
thrusts itself upon you quite of its own: no, it is not worth living. . . . We
are in a prison, comrades; it is oppressive in this prison cell, we are
without air, and this is regarded as the natural order of things. . . . And
what are we? a splinter, an amputated limb, a piece cut off from the
main, liquidated emptiness, an inner emigration.[1]

It was only in 1921 that writers began to absorb and transmit in prose
the drama of the upheaval around them. That year the renewal of old
economic relations brought with it a spirit of vulgarity, self-seeking,
riotous living. While some saw hope in the new liberties, cynicism and
disillusionment was the reaction of many. In literature, satire flourished;
nostalgia for the old rural life often marked the interpretation of the
clash of old and new in the village; prose, returning to the literary scene,
began to describe and interpret the revolution and the civil war.

The new prose, however, maintained its ties with the past. Testifying
to the strength of one pre-revolutionary tradition in literature, a Soviet
critic wrote in 1924:

And when I seek the watershed, the boundary line dividing the past of
of our literature from its future, it seems to me that the task — the
resolution of which will open the path to the new generation — consists
of the liquidation of dostoevshchina, of voluptuous self-analysis. . . .[2]

The 1917 revolution was a movement away from the doubting, divided,
conflict-ridden heroes of the past.

Everything which prepared the great movement of our days, was the
striving to get out of this concentration on one's individuality, to seek
out a man of deed, to bury the Rudins and Rayskys, Hamlets and
aesthetes, to exalt the Insarovs and Shtolts'.[3]

Indeed, the Insarovs and Shtolts' — the very men of action envied and
despised by the Underground Man — appeared in increasing numbers
in Soviet literature, as in Soviet life. The new man of action was

---

[1] N. Ognev, *Iskhod Nikpetoža. Dnevnik Kosti Rjabceva. Sobranie sočinenij*
(Moscow, 1929), IV, 47-50.
[2] P. S. Kogan, *Literatura ètikh let: 1917-1923* (Ivanovo-Voznesensk, 1924),
pp. 90-91.
[3] *Ibid.,* p. 91.

glorified by some writers and parodied by others. When this rational and functional new hero self-confidently strode onto the literary scene, the appearance of his antithesis, the self-divided and irrational "underground" man, was inevitable.

The "underground" man entered the Soviet era as a center for feelings and ideas hostile to the new rational man and the new rationalism and utilitarianism; because of his inherently rebellious nature, he was used by writers as a medium for protest. In depicting the "underground" man writers saw both his pathos and his destructiveness. While he symbolized to them the disappearance of a world and the extinction of a type, he often appeared in the role of criminal or wrecker. As a representative of individualism, even violent and uncontrolled, he sometimes enjoyed the complicity of the writer. The "underground" themes, however, were employed after 1917 not to uphold the ego with its tyrannical aspirations, or to give expression to a nihilistic despair, but rather to defend the individual himself; to protest against ideological and cultural conformity and the domination of rationalistic and utilitarian imperatives; to insist upon a morality which is absolute, a morality in which the integrity of the individual is protected against arbitrary assaults of a relativistic class, political, collective morality.

CHAPTER XVI

E. ZAMYATIN'S *WE*

> All human actions, it goes without saying, will then
> be computed according to these laws, mathematically,
> in the form of a table of logarithms, up to 108,000
> and put in calendar form; or, even better, there will
> appear certain virtuous works resembling modern en-
> cyclopedic lexicons in which everything will be so
> precisely calculated and designated that there will no
> longer be any more personal actions or adventures
> in the world. Then—all this you are saying—new
> economic relations will take shape, all quite ready
> made, and also calculated with mathematical exactitude,
> so that in a trice all possible questions will disappear
> for the simple reason that there will be anwers for
> all of them. Then the crystal palace will be built.
> Then—well, in a word, the Golden Age will dawn.
>
> The Underground Man

E. Zamyatin's Single State in *We*[1] could be regarded as a realization of
the utopia outlined by the Underground Man.

The time is one thousand years into the future. D-503, mathematician
and builder of the spaceship Integral, is writing his "notes" for unknown
readers. The title of his notebook is "We". This notebook is a "poem"
on the "mathematically perfect life of the Single State";[2] it is the record
of the spiritual crisis of "number" D-503 — rational citizen of the Single
State.

Zamyatin was familiar with the rich literature in English on utopia
and was undoubtedly influenced by it.[3] Yet Zamyatin's *We*, in its basic
philosophy and in the psychological conception of its central hero D-503,

---

[1]   Zamyatin's novel *We* was written in 1920. It was never published in the
Soviet Union, although writers and critics were familiar with its contents at the
time. Gleb Struve gives an account of the history of this novel abroad in his
study "Novye varianty šigalevščiny. O romanakh Zamjatina, Khaksli i Orvella,"
Novyj žurnal, No. 30 (New York: 1952), pp. 152-163.
[2]   E. Zamjatin, *My* (New York, 1952), p. 6.
[3]   Zamyatin was well acquainted with Herbert Wells' work. He wrote a study
on him in 1922 in which he distinguishes Wells' scientific-fantasy novels from the
utopian literature which presents a picture of an ideal society. The novels of
Wells are "not utopias", he writes, but "social pamphlets clothed in the artistic
forms of a fantasy novel". (Zamjatin, *Gerbert Uèlls* [Petersburg, 1922] p. 43.)
The same might be said of Zamyatin's scientific-fantasy novel *We*.

belongs to the Russian anti-utopian and anti-rationalist tradition. The Underground Man's vision of a society based on reason and science, Shigalev's appalling conception of an earthly paradise, and the terrible philosophy of the Grand Inquisitor all find expression in *We*.

The kinship between *Notes from the Underground* and *We* is, of course, on a broad philosophical plane. In its twin objective *We* is related to *Notes from the Underground*: it sets out, first, to satirize and expose rationalist, utilitarian, utopian socialist ideas and ideals, and, secondly, to show that man is essentially an irrational being.

The rationalists, the Underground Man notes, are searching for a formula of all desires and caprices. In Zamyatin's Single State nothing is left to chance. All life is integrated and organized down to the minutest detail. Everything is based upon reason and science, everything is subject to rational utilitarian criteria ("only the rational is useful and beautiful").[4] Desire is regarded as obsolete in this utopia where even love has been organized and expressed mathematically. People live in geometrically formed glass houses and are guided in their acts by the "Hourly Tables" — a form of schedule that recalls the "calendar" in *Notes from the Underground*. D-503 writes:

Every morning with six-wheeled precision at the same hour and the same minute we, millions of us, arise as one man. At the same hour, millions united, we begin work; millions united, we end work. And fusing into a united million-armed body, at the very same second designated by the Tables, we raise our spoons to the mouth, and in the same second we go out for a walk and go to the auditorium to the hall for Taylor exercises, go to sleep. . . .[5]

Man prefers the process of achieving the goal, rather than the goal itself, the Underground Man believed; the goal "it goes without saying can be nothing else than twice two is four, that is, a formula, and after all, twice two is four is no longer life, gentlemen, but the beginning of death".[6] In the Single State, however, the goal has been achieved (its revolution is the "last" revolution) and it is not surprising, therefore,

---

[4] Zamjatin, *My, op. cit.,* p. 45.
[5] *Ibid.,* p. 14. D-503's enthusiasm for regimentation recalls that of Andreev's memoirist who remarked of the regulated life of his prison: "The hours for rising and going to bed, for meals and walks are arranged so rationally, in accordance with the real requirements of nature, that soon they lose the character of a certain compulsion and become natural, even dear habits." (Andreev, "Moi zapiski," *op. cit.,* III, 204.)
[6] Dostoevskij, *Zapiski iz podpol'ja, op. cit.,* IV, 130.

that above everything looms the god-like authority of the "multiplication table" and the formula "twice two is four".

There is only one truth, and there is only one true path. And this truth is twice two and this true path is four. And indeed, would it not be absurd if these happy, ideally multiplied two's were to think about some kind of freedom, that is, obviously, about a mistake? [7]

What is death to the Underground Man is elevated in the Single State to an axiom of life.

Shigalevian social organization — the equality of the herd — prevails in the Single State. In man's "unfreedom" lies his happiness and his salvation from crime and moral choas. This is the philosophy of the Benefactor who, with his Guardians, spies and instruments of torture and execution, rules over millions of "numbers". In the Benefactor one recognizes a variant of the Grand Inquisitor.

A great "Green Wall" separates the "machine-like perfected world" of the Single State from the "irrational, monstrous world of trees, birds, animals".[8] But man has a "soul", an "irrational" component, an unknown quantity "X" that resists tabulation. Man — the Underground Man observes — "always and everywhere, whoever he be, likes to act as he wishes and not at all as reason and advantage dictate".[9] "What is it to you," the voice of the heroine-leader of a rebellion I-330 declares, "if I do not want others to desire for me, but want to experience desire myself — if I want the impossible."[10] I-330 — and the MEFI living in primitive freedom outside the "Green Wall — like the Underground Man do not accept the impossible: their aim is to smash the "Green Wall" and "all walls".

The symbol of the "wall" is an important one in the social psychology of the Single State; it is particularly meaningful to D-503. The "direct" men of action, the Underground Man observes, "immediately humble themselves before the impossible. The impossible means the stone wall! What stone wall? Well, it goes without saying, the laws of nature, the deductions of natural sciences, mathematics."[11] For D-503 the simple "wall" is the "foundation of everything human".[12] It is a symbol of absolute — and therefore infantile — security. It is concomitant with reason, science, mathematics. "Oh, great, divinely limiting wisdom of

[7]   Zamjatin, *My, op. cit.,* p. 60.
[8]   *Ibid.,* p. 81.
[9]   Dostoevskij, *Zapiski iz podpol'ja, op. cit.,* IV, 124.
[10] Zamjatin, *My, op. cit.,* p. 178.
[11] Dostoevskij, *Zapiski iz podpol'ja, op. cit.,* IV, 116.
[12] Zamjatin, *My, op. cit.,* p. 38.

walls, barriers!"[13] he declares. ". . . It is such a joy to stroke the cold wall with one's hand."[14]

The inventor of the "sacred formula of the iron grate" — Andreev's memoirist — would wholeheartedly subscribe to D-503's love of reason. D-503 exclaims:

I am not afraid of this word "limited": the work of the most lofty faculty in man — reason — consists precisely in ceaseless limitation of the infinite, in splitting up the infinite into comfortable, easily digestible portions — differentials. Herein lies precisely the divine beauty of my element — mathematics.[15]

This is the language and psychology of Andreev's memoirist. Andreev's hero observes:

Why is the sky so beautiful through these bars? . . . Is this the effect of the aesthetic law of contrasts according to which *blue* stands out prominently besides *black*? Or is it not, perhaps, a manifestation of some other, higher law, according to which the *infinite* may be conceived by the human mind only when it is brought *within certain boundaries,* for instance, when it is enclosed *within a square*?[16]

Andreev's memoirist and Zamyatin's D-503 have many features in common. Both men are mathematicians debauched by reason and logic who address themselves to an outside world. They live a strictly regimented life which they regard as the highest form of existence and which they would like to impose on others. Both are moral cowards. When Andreev's memoirist declares that he has tried to escape from prison, his fellow prisoner, the artist K., remarks: "You are a coward, granddaddy, you are simply a miserable coward."[17] In *We*, the rebellious State poet R-13 ridicules D-503's faith in knowledge:

"What is this — knowledge! Your knowledge is nothing but cowardice. But what's the use of arguing: it's true. You simply want to encircle the infinite with a wall, and you are even afraid to look beyond that wall. Yes! You will look, and your eyes won't stand the glare. Yes!" "Walls are the foundation of everything human," I began.[18]

Yet in D-503, as in Andreev's memoirist, the security afforded by knowledge, reason, the "wall" has not completely destroyed the demands of instinct and the irrational.

[13] *Ibid.,* p. 81.
[14] *Ibid.,* p. 152.
[15] *Ibid.,* p. 59.
[16] Andreev, "Moi zapiski," *op. cit.,* III, 199.
[17] *Ibid.,* 213.
[18] Zamjatin, *My, op. cit.,* p. 38.

The antinomy of reason and instinct, of the rational and the irrational, forms the basic philosophical tension in Zamyatin's *We*. It is manifested in the struggle between the integrated, regimented force of the Single State with its belief that its revolution is the last one, and the primitive, free forces of the MEFI beyond the Green Wall, with its concept of "endless revolutions". The heroine-rebel I-330 formulates this antinomy in different terms, but the substance is the same:

There are two forces in the world: entropy and energy. One leads to blessed tranquility, to happy equilibrium; the other to the destruction of equilibrium, to painfully endless movement. Our — or more correctly — your ancestors, the Christians, bowed to entropy as to a God. While we, anti-Christians, we***.[19]

This conception of the dynamic forces in the world is set forth, in essence, in the Underground Man's polemic with the rationalist utopian socialists: reason leads to the idea of finality, to "twice two is four", to boredom and inertia, to the "well-being" of the utopian socialists; on the other hand, man's natural, untabulated drives cause him to love the process of building more than the goal, to love destruction as much as building, suffering as much as well-being. Man, in the Underground Man's view, has no place to go but onwards.

The struggle between reason and instinct, between entropy and energy finds dramatic expression in the conflict that develops in D-503. It is his love for I-330 (personal love is forbidden in the Single State) that brings D-503 into tragic conflict with himself and with the Single State.

D-503, like Andreev's memoirist, is not a monolithic personality. He has always hated irrational roots, and his fear of the irrational is a fear of his unknown self which is symbolized in his "shaggy paws", those "vestiges of a wild epoch". It is this irrational self, this "new, alien", uncontrollable self that grips D-503 when he falls in love with I-330.

There were two "I"s. One "I" — the former D-503, number D-503, and the other. Formerly it only barely stuck out its shaggy paws from its shell, but now it crawled out entirely, the shell cracked, and now it is going to pieces, and — and then what?[20]

The tragedy of D-503 is that the conflict of two "I's", of reason and instinct is never resolved in a new synthesis.

[19] *Ibid.*, p. 142.
[20] *Ibid.*, p. 52.

Consciousness to the Underground Man is the painful awareness of singleness; consciousness is an "illness", but in just this "illness", however tragic, that is, in continual pain and suffering, the Underground Man finds the essence of individuality.

The growth of consciousness in D-503 — the bifurcation of "We" into "I" and "They" is painful just because it involves a conflict with reality, a break with the infantile condition of dependency upon the Single State. Not without reason does the Underground Man open his rebuttal against the rationalists with the words: "Oh, the babe! Oh, the pure innocent child!" [21] The growth of consciousness involving a conflict with the Single State is profoundly disturbing to the fledgling-individual D-503. "I am conscious of myself. But really, consciousness is the lot only of an inflamed eye, a sore finger, a sick tooth. . . . Surely it is clear that consciousness of oneself is only a disease." [22]

The words are almost the same as the Underground Man's words. But D-503 — in contrast to the Underground Man — wavers in his attitude towards the illness of consciousness. "I . . . consider my former self the real one," he observes at one point; "the present one is, of course, only illness." [23] "But I want even this pain . . ." he cries out as he is swept away by his feelings, his instinct; but his reason quickly adds: "Great Benefactor! What an absurdity — to wish pain." [24] The new, alien D-503 recognizes that "we must all go crazy". But in the end D-503 finds freedom with its pains, its question marks, its responsibilities, its loneliness insupportable. He cannot really break with the "former" D-503 and events hurl him into isolation; he feels trampled and crushed, cast aside. Individual consciousness has led D-503 to the miserable and despairing state of alienation and self-alienation of an "underground" man.

Man is ever ready to introduce his "ruinous fantastic element" into all rationalist thinking, the Underground Man believed. Just this fantastic element — "imagination" — is removed when D-503 voluntarily surrenders himself to the Great Operation. Like the hero of Andreev's "My Memoirs", the mathematician D-503 survives his spiritual crisis. ". . . I am confident that we will win," he remarks in connection with the efforts to crush the rebellion against the Single State, "because

[21]   Dostoevskij, *Zapiski iz podpol'ja, op. cit.,* IV, 121.
[22]   Zamjatin, *My, op. cit.,* p. 111.
[23]   *Ibid.,* p. 56.
[24]   *Ibid.,* p. 117.

reason must triumph." [25] These are the concluding words in D-503's notebook.

"Let we tell you, sir," remarks Murin in Dostoevsky's "The Landlady", "a weak man cannot stand alone. ... Give a weak man freedom, and he will bind it himself and bring it back to you." [26] D-503 looked beyond the "wall", but his eyes — as R-13 predicted — could not stand the glare.

"I want to think, write and talk about life tomorrow," wrote Zamyatin in 1920. "Because man will not content himself in heaven with superb electrification, sewage and sanitation systems." [27] The spiritual crisis of D-503, the heroism and integrity of I-330, the vitality of existence (albeit a primitive one) beyond the "Green Wall" and the fact of rebellion against the Benefactor and his Guardians — all seem to reaffirm the Underground Man's conviction that man will never allow himself to be transformed into an organ stop. But the spiritual struggle of D-503 ends in catastrophe, the heroine is murdered and the success of the revolution is left in doubt. For one thousand years mankind has accepted the "beneficent yoke of reason" and Zamyatin sees no end to this voluntary slavery. The Great Operation will remove the last obstacle — man's imagination — to transforming man into a completely obedient and reliable citizen of the Single State. Truly, the sombre optimism of the Underground Man in his belief that man would never allow himself to be deprived of his will and desires is overshadowed by the sinister words of the Grand Inquisitor: "I swear that man is weaker and more vile than you ever imagined him to be." [28]

Zamyatin's *We*, as an early Soviet critic observed, is "not a utopia, but an artistic pamphlet on the present and an attempt at a prognosis of the future".[29] This prognosis is interesting in two respects: as an anticipation of certain aspects of totalitarianism and as a criticism of the modern civilization that engendered totalitarianism. Zamyatin looked with a troubled gaze upon his world. He wrote:

The imperialist war and the civil war turned man into material for war, into a number, a cipher. Man is forgotten. ... *Man* is dying. The proud *homo erectus* is on all fours***. The value of human life is

[25]   *Ibid.*, p. 200.
[26]   Dostoevskij, "Khozjajka," *op. cit.*, I, 352.
[27]   Quoted by T. Tamanin in "E. Zamjatin," *Russkija zapiski*, No. 16 (Paris, 1938), p. 102.
[28]   Dostoevskij, *Brat'ja karamazovy, op. cit.*, IX, 253.
[29]   A. Voronskij, "Evg. Zamjatin," *Literaturnye siluèty*, III, *Krasnaja nov'* No. 6 (1922), p. 318.

falling precipitously. It is impossible to be silent any longer. It is time to cry out: man must be a brother to man.[30]

Zamyatin is imbued with the values of Western civilization, in particular a respect for the individual, but he finds no spiritual resources in contemporary Christian civilization to enable it to perpetuate itself and make possible a future more worthy of man's potentialities. The Single State — Zamyatin suggests in *We* — arose on the ruins of Christian civilization.

In *We*, as in *Notes from the Underground*, reason is equated with dogmatic rationalism, science is discredited and man's capacity to live rationally and at the same time creatively is placed in serious doubt. Conflict is regarded as the essence of consciousness. The conception of personality as essentially irrational and of freedom as freedom from all obligations and limitations, follows directly in the tradition of *Notes from the Underground*.

The place of Zamyatin's novel in early Soviet literature is an important one. It was one of the first post-revolutionary novels to use the anti-rationalist, anti-utopian theme as a means of expressing alarm at trends in the new Soviet era. Other writers developed this same theme, though circumspectly, in works devoted to the contemporary scene.

[30] Quoted by T. Tamanin, *op. cit.*, p. 107.

CHAPTER XVII

YU. OLESHA'S *ENVY*

> Well, such a direct person I regard as the real, normal
> man as tender mother nature herself wanted to see
> him when she graciously brought him into being on
> earth. I envy such a man till I am green in the face.
> He is stupid, I won't quarrel over that with you, but
> perhaps the normal man really has to be stupid, how
> do you know? Perhaps it is even very beautiful.
>
> The Underground Man

Elena Goncharova, heroine of Olesha's play *A List of Benefits* (*Spisok blagodeyany,* 1931), rejects the idea that the "theme of socialism" provides universal material for great acting; that which is universal and stirring, she observes, is rather the "theme of the lonely human fate. The theme of Chaplin."[1] The theme of lonely human fate is a central one in Olesha's writings.

In an autobiographical fragment, "I look into the Past", Olesha writes of the man whose "fate it is to remain alone everywhere and in everything". Such a man is regarded as a dreamer and people laugh at him; he is insignificant, ugly; "he goes alone, head drawn into his shoulders: here there is vanity, haughtiness, self-abasement, scorn for people alternating with tenderness. . . . sometimes he turns to the person who is laughing, and the latter then sees flickering on the face which amused him a dog's snarl."[2] Olesha's dreamer has much in common with the little man from the "underground".

Such a dreamer is Nikolay Kavalerov, hero of Olesha's short novel *Envy* (*Zavist*, 1926), a lonely man in whose fate is expressed all the complex and painful poetry of the "underground". The "happy pigs of the future", Artsybashev's Chizh predicted, would have no place for the "little man". It is the misfortune of Nikolay Kavalerov, heaved to the surface by the revolution and stranded among the new, functional men of action, to confirm this prediction by his experience. "Have they insulted you? Have they cast you out?" asks Ivan Babichev, the eccentric dreamer, inventor and buffoon who is Kavalerov's spiritual mentor.

---

[1]   Ju. Oleša, *Spisok blagodejanij* (Moscow, 1931), p. 36.
[2]   Oleša, "Ja smotrju v prošloe," in *Višnevaja kostočka* (Moscow, 1932), p. 97.

"They have insulted me terribly," said Kavalerov passionately, "they have been humiliating me for a long time."[3]

The new, rational-minded utilitarian society has no use for useless Kavalerovs. Nikolay Kavalerov, 27, is a poet in a world of hands. Yet Kavalerov is a victim of his own fantasy. He sees the world as in a distorting mirror, and his irrational perception is followed by typically irrational responses. He had a misunderstanding with the real world. "Things don't like me," Kavalerov observes; "things like him," he says of Andrey Babichev,[4] the Soviet sausage commissar and brother of Ivan Babichev. The poetic vision of Kavalerov is a real tragedy for him; but it brings into sharp focus the basic tensions in his world: the irrational and the rational, the romantic and utilitarian, the creative and the vulgar-philistine.

Kavalerov is more tender, more poetic than the Underground Man, but he is tormented by the same lacerations as the Underground Man, and he is driven to the same tragi-comic extremes. He is sensitive and suspicious, overcome by a feeling of helplessness and insignificance, and consumed by a rancorous envy for the successful men of action of the new order. He is a drunkard, coward and buffoon, but a poet, dreamer and romantic; like the Underground Man he knows the extremes of the lofty dream and ideal, on the one hand, and the vulgar, humiliating reality of the gutter, on the other. The image of himself that he would leave to posterity is that of a man "who had lived in that illustrious period [the first decade of Soviet socialism], who hated and envied everyone, bragged, put on airs, was exhausted with great plans, wanted to do a lot, and did nothing, and ended by committing a disgusting, odious crime".[5]

In Kavalerov, as in the Underground Man, timidity and self-abnegation alternate with wounded pride and vanity. Kavalerov, insulted and humiliated in a bar by a group of fun-seekers, and retreating amidst "a whole volley of jests", recalls the offended mouse in *Notes from the Underground,* who, rattled and offended by the laughter of "judges, dictators" standing about, ignominiously retreats to his hole. Drunk — Kavalerov remarks, "I violently let out with everything in me: self-abasement and arrogance blended into one bitter torrent."[6]

The "man of heightened consciousness", the Underground Man

---

[3]   Oleša, *Zavist'* (2d ed.; Moscow, 1930), p. 97.
[4]   *Ibid.,* pp. 8, 9.
[5]   *Ibid.,* p. 29.
[6]   *Ibid.,* p. 17.

observes, "is sometimes so cowed before his antithesis that he himself, with all his heightened consciousness, honestly considers himself as a mouse and not a man."[7] Nikolay Kavalerov has his antithesis in his benefactor Andrey Babichev, the sausage commissar who lifted him out of the gutter and gave him temporary board but ignores him as a nonentity.

Kavalerov's relation to Andrey Babichev has many of the elements to be found in the Underground Man's ambivalent relation to Zverkov — the vulgar, self-confident, successful man of action. Andrey Babichev — in Kavalerov's words — is a "man of action", a "perfect male individual", but an "ordinary seigneur, egotist, sensualist, dullard who is confident everything will go fine and dandy with him. . . ."[8] Yet while Kavalerov with all his soul scorns and derides Andrey Babichev, while he has utter contempt for his "sausage" mentality, he is conscious at the same time of his insignificance before him, and he envies his glory. Kavalerov, like the Underground Man, envies the fact of success of the man of action, but despises the vulgar character of that success. Kavalerov expresses his feelings towards the maker of sausages, Andrey Babichev:

I am eaten up with malice. He, an administrator, a communist, he is building the new world. But glory in this world flares up when a new type of sausage emerges from the hands of a sausage maker. I do not understand this glory — just what is the meaning of it?[9]

The envious Kavalerov regards the successful Andrey Babichev as a usurper. Ivan Babichev reads Kavalerov's thoughts:

You are certain that it is he [Andrey Babichev] who is preventing you from displaying yourself, that he has usurped your rights, that where in your opinion you ought to dominate — he dominates. And you are fuming. . . [10]

Kavalerov wants to display the force of his personality, he wants glory, yet he lives in a society where "personality means nothing . . .". "In our country," he complains, "there are no paths for individual achievement of success."[11] Kavalerov, therefore, has no hope of becoming anything. The rationalistic man of action is hero of Kavalerov's epoch. Volodya Makarov — that hero — a young Soviet citizen, is a true candidate for citizenship in Zamyatin's Single State. He writes in a letter:

[7] Dostoevskij, *Zapiski iz podpol'ja, op. cit.,* IV, 114.
[8] Oleša, *Zavist', op. cit.,* p. 53.
[9] *Ibid.,* p. 37.
[10] *Ibid.,* pp. 93-94.
[11] *Ibid.,* p. 24.

I am — a man machine. . . . I have been transformed into a machine. If I have not yet been transformed then I want to be transformed into one. . . . I want to be a machine. . . . I want to become proud through my work, proud because I work. Only to be indifferent, do you understand, to everything that is not work! I am seized with envy for the machine — that's what it is! In what way am I inferior to it? [12]

In Volodya Makarov the cult of the machine reaches its highest point. Olesha, like Zamyatin, sees in this cult of the machine an impoverishment of personality. And it is personality — in all its fantastic and subtle moods and variations — for which Olesha's hero, [13] Kavalerov, stands. "I war . . . for tenderness, for pathos, for personality," [14] Kavalerov declares, and indeed these words might stand as an epigraph to Olesha's *Envy*. But it is impossible to argue with a machine, it is impossible logically to refute "twice two is four". Kavalerov's war is conducted with the "underground" weapons of irrational will, negation, ridicule, deliberate nonsense.

The Underground Man observed that he would not be surprised at all if suddenly in a future society based on common sense a "certain gentleman with ignoble or rather with a reactionary and sardonic countenance", were to propose kicking over all that common sense so as to enable man once again to live according to his "own foolish will". [15] Kavalerov has just such dreams as he watches the utilitarian lines of development in the society about him:

And now just imagine that in our times — when everybody is talking so much about purpose, usefulness, when a sober, realistic approach to things and events is required of people — just imagine that in these times somebody suddenly came up and out with something obviously absurd, that he was to commit some genius-inspired piece of mischief, and then say: "Yes, now that's the way you are, and this is what I am like!" Then out to the square he'd go, to do something with himself, and to bow: I lived, I did what I wanted. . . . For example, he takes it upon himself to do something like this: to put an end to himself. Suicide without any cause. Out of mischief. In order to demonstrate that everyone has the right to take charge of himself. Even now. [16]

[12]   *Ibid.*, p. 59.
[13]   "Yes, Kavalerov looked at the world through my eyes," Olesha declared at the 1934 Congress of Soviet Writers. ("Reč' Ju. Oleši," *Pervyj vsesojuznyj s'ezd sovetskikh pisatelej 1934* [Moscow, 1934], p. 235.)
[14]   Oleša, *Zavist'*, *op. cit.*, p. 53.
[15]   Dostoevskij, *Zapiski iz podpol'ja*, *op. cit.*, IV, 124.
[16]   Oleša, *Zavist'*, *op. cit.*, p. 25.

And Kavalerov imagines hanging oneself at the entrance to the Supreme
Council on National Economy. "It would be very impressive there," he
observes ironically.[17]

All the pent-up resentment and frustration of an offended little man
overflows in Kavalerov's description of the irrational rebellion of the
individual. This is Kavalerov's imaginary affront, "out of mischief," to
a utilitarian order which would bind his will, this is his malicious slap
in the face at society. This is "underground" rebellion: frenzied, irrational, mocking and despairing.

Kavalerov experiences all the lacerations of "underground" personality
— humiliation, envy-hatred for the man of action, deliberate malice.
But it is the eccentric Ivan Babichev who formulates for Kavalerov the
psychology and philosophy of "underground" resistance to the new
Soviet epoch. It is Ivan Babichev who reads Kavalerov's thoughts and
attempts to instill in him a sense of his historic mission. Ivan Babichev
would organize a "conspiracy of feelings", a last parade of sentiments
banished from the heart by the new rationalist-utilitarian order. In
Kavalerov he finds a true representative of the old world: a man suffering
from the passion of envy.

"The dying age envies that which is going to replace it";[18] Kavalerov
is the embodiment of envy. Ivan Babichev's program is — malice. "It
is clear: everything is going to ruin, everything is predestined, there is
no way out. . . . Every minute will bring fresh humiliation."[19] Therefore
Kavalerov must slam the door behind him with a bang. "Smash it! [the
epoch] Leave an honorable memory of yourself as the hired assassin of
the century!"[20] Ivan Babichev faces the new world with a mixture of
frenzied hatred and envy, love and despair:

Oh, how beautiful is the rising world. . . . Everything comes from it.
. . . I love it — this world advancing on me — more than life, I bow to
it and with all my strength I hate it! I choke, tears stream down my
face, but I want to dig my fingers into its clothes, tear them to ribbons.
Don't try to eclipse me! Don't try to take anything that can belong
to me.[21]

The peculiarly "underground" character of Ivan Babichev's personality
emerges in a story he tells of his youth — a story which reveals the whole

[17]   *Ibid.,* p. 25.
[18]   *Ibid.,* p. 94.
[19]   *Ibid.,* p. 97.
[20]   *Ibid.,* p. 98.
[21]   *Ibid.,* pp. 96-97.

pathos and despair of his relation to the rising world. He was at a ball. A young, beautiful girl of twelve was queen. She was the first in everything, won the best prizes, did everything she wanted, gained the admiration and applause of everyone. Ivan Babichev relates:

I was thirtéen then, a student in the gymnasium. She eclipsed me. But I, too, I too was accustomed to exalted praise. I too was spoiled by idolization. I also was at the head of my class, won top honors. I couldn't endure it. I caught the slut in the corridor and gave her a thrashing, tore her ribbons, messed up her curls, scratched her charming face. I seized her by the scruff of the neck and knocked her head several times against the column. At that moment I loved this girl more than life, worshipped her — and hated her with all my strength. Rending her magnificent curls, I thought I would shame her, dispel her rosiness, her lustre. I thought I would correct the error made by everyone. But nothing came of it. I was disgraced. I was expelled. ... When I was clawing at her there, in the corridor, clawing at her, a victim snared, tears rolled down my face. I choked — and still I tore at her ravishing dress, trembling from the contact with satin. It almost set my teeth on edge, made my lips tremble. ... All forces rose against me in defense of that nasty slut. ... I don't know whether I came out with any exclamations while I was meting out my justice. In all probability I whispered: this is your place! Don't try to eclipse me! Don't try to take anything that can belong to me.[22]

Ivan Babichev might have remarked, like the Underground Man, that "all this is from Silvio". Like Pushkin's egoistic hero Silvio in "The Shot" ("Vystrel", 1830) and like the Underground Man, Ivan Babichev finds his vanity wounded and his position usurped.[23] In Ivan Babichev's frenzied envy of the queen of the ball there is a special "underground" strain, a certain perverse relish in defiling that recalls the Underground Man's debauchery of Liza when he discovered that he was no longer the "hero". "How I hated her," the Underground Man relates, "and how I was drawn to her at that moment! One feeling intensified the other. It was almost like revenge!"[24]

But "underground" revenge, "underground" malice against the rising world is really possible only in fantasy. The heroes of the "underground" are dreamers and doubters, not men of action. Ivan Babichev invents — all in the imagination — an all-purpose machine, "Ophelia", the "very

[22] *Ibid.*, pp. 95-96.
[23] See Wacław Lednicki's discussion of the thematic links between Pushkin's "The Shot" and Dostoevsky's *Notes from the Underground* in *Russia, Poland and the West* (London, 1954), pp. 181-213.
[24] Dostoevskij, *Zapiski iz podpol'ja, op. cit.,* IV, 191.

genius of mechanics". "One fine day, he observes, "I realized that to me had been given the superhuman power of avenging the whole of my epoch. I defiled it. Deliberately. Out of malice." [25] Ivan Babichev's hatred of the machine is an expression of his contempt for the new rationalist-utilitarian minded society which rejects the emotions of the old world.

In Ivan Babichev's fantastic "Story of the Meeting of the Two Brothers", "Ophelia" is the instrumentality of a terrible revenge against the new society; it destroys the gigantic industrial kitchen built by Andrey Babichev. "It will destroy your building," declares Ivan Babichev. "Screws will unscrew themselves. . . . It will instruct every single beam to disobey you. . . . It will turn all your figures into useless patterns." [26] "Ophelia" is the embodiment of the irrational will of "underground" man. Like the *mania contradicens* that destroyed Bryusov's Republic of the Southern Cross, "Ophelia" introduces an irrational element into the rational inanimate world bringing chaos and destruction.

The imaginary destruction of the giant industrial kitchen is a supreme triumph of "underground" deliberate malice. The identification made here between destruction of the machine and the psychology of the "underground" is not accidental. It is because the machine is the purest embodiment of rationalistic-utilitarian thinking that it is a natural object of "underground" malice.

The struggle that Kavalerov and Ivan Babichev wage against the new order is futile. In the end, Kavalerov's romantic illusions about winning the hand of the beautiful girl Valya are smashed; like Artsybashev's "underground" dreamer Chizh, his defeat is symbolized by his surrender to the embraces of his disgusting landlady, to the vulgarity from which his romantic illusions had hitherto shielded him. Kavalerov and Ivan Babichev drink to "indifference".

All attempts at revenge, as the Underground Man himself discovers, end in only one thing: inertia.

The influence of *Notes from the Underground* on *Envy* appears in specific "underground" themes: the pathological humiliation of the "little man", hatred-envy for the man of action, "underground" malice, malicious rebellion against a rationalistic-utilitarian order which would annihilate man's free will. The influence of *Notes from the Underground* also relates to a basic ambiguity in *Envy*.

Olesha uses the "underground" dialectic of Dostoevsky in which the hero is both exposer and one who is exposed. Both Ivan Babichev and

[25]   Oleša, *Zavisti, op. cit.*, p. 107.
[26]   *Ibid.*, 116.

Kavalerov in their ideas, strivings and way of life are critics of various aspects of the social order. But as individuals, as representatives of the idealism they defend, they arouse feelings that range from pity to disgust. Kavalerov wars for tenderness, pathos and personality, but if he — the little man — allies himself with the Ivan Babichevs in the role of "hired assassin of the century", it seems probable that something very different from respect for personality will emerge from this war. Olesha seems fully aware that "underground" defense of the individual is a contradiction in terms.

One critic has noted that "at the basis of the design of *Envy* lay . . . the Erenburg conflict between mechanization . . . and the living, feeling man". He goes on to observes that Olesha's vacillations towards his heroes, the dualism in their very depiction, is beyond any question. "And this duality, of course, is the greatest inadequacy of Olesha's interesting tale." [27] Indeed, Olesha vacillates in his attitude towards his heroes, but this duality itself is one of the most interesting features of *Envy*; it is expressed by the "underground" dialectic in which both Kavalerov and Ivan Babichev emerge as heroes, and at the same time, as anti-heroes.

The use of this dialectic gave Olesha an especially flexible means of indirectly making fundamental criticisms of the new society. At the same time, this dialectic of *Envy* undoubtedly expressed the author's complex and vacillating attitudes towards the new Soviet society. Soviet society, as viewed in *Envy*, is threatened by a rationalistic-utilitarian spirit, but on the other hand, it has youth, vitality in comparison with the "dying age". There is a strange pathos in Kavalerov's consciousness of being by-passed by the new life, in Ivan Babichev's despairing love-hatred for the "rising world".

But the dominant mood in *Envy* is not that of the new life. Indeed, the novel seems to express the "horror of the discord between everyday life and the striving for poetry, for romanticism" —in the words of the partisan Trofimov in N. Ognev's *Diary of Kostya Ryabtsev*.[28]

Olesha, like many Russian intellectuals in the 1920's, is imbued with a sense of crisis, a feeling of irrevocable break with the past. "We ponder over what has disappeared," Paul Valéry observed after World War I; "we are almost destroyed by what has been destroyed; we do not know what is going to be born, and we can justly fear it." [29]

---

[27] A. Ležnev, "O 'Zavisti' Ju. Oleši," *Literaturnye budni* (Moscow, 1929), p. 215.
[28] N. Ognev, *Iskhod Nikpetoža. Dnevnik Kosti Rjabceva. Sobranie sočinenij* (Moscow, 1929), IV, 210.
[29] Paul Valéry, "La Crise de l'esprit," *Variété [I]* (Paris, 1948), p. 34.

CHAPTER XVIII

A. SOBOL'S "MEMOIRS OF A FRECKLED MAN"

> Everybody ignored me and I sat crushed and annihilated.
>
> The Underground Man

Andrey Sobol's satirical work, "Memoirs of a Freckled Man" ("Memuary vesnushchatogo cheloveka", 1927), like Olesha's *Envy,* focuses attention on the isolated "little man" in Soviet life.

The freckled man is a familiar little man from the "underground" suddenly emerging from his den in a Godforsaken blind alley to offer his "memoirs" to the world. The voice is that of an anguished and lonely man, acutely self-conscious, comic in the misadventures of his life, but always pitiful in his tragic helplessness. Like the Underground Man, he seems intoxicated with language; he is always breathless and his words pour forth in wild disorder.

The freckled man is in distress. As a last resort he is addressing his long-winded "memoirs" to an editor, Aleksey Kiprianovich. It appears that the writer Petr Pismenny has disseminated a terrible calumny to the effect that the freckled man is "an impossible, parasitic individual", with "important connections with the tsarist secret police".[1] It is true that among the fantastic adventures of the freckled man was a ridiculous episode as courier among emigré circles abroad and that, much to his anguish and despair, the counterrevolutionary Svitsky smilingly sent him back to Russia with a passport reading "Aleksandr Pushkin". But now, thanks to Petr Pismenny, he again sees before him the "movement of locking doors" before which he feels impotent to assuage his "inhuman thirst for a life of law and order without fear of the agencies of arrest and exclusion".[2]

The freckled man, like the Underground Man and Kavalerov, does not act; he is acted upon, he is a victim. He is sent flying from a door at the end of a boot, or beaten, or robbed, or ordered about, or persecuted by calumny. Life has conspired to humiliate him. "I have abased myself

[1] Andrej Sobol', "Memuary vesnuščatogo čeloveka," *Sobranie socinenij* (Moscow, 1927), IV, 138.
[2] *Ibid.,* IV, 142.

even to the physical contact of a stranger's hand."[3] The freckled man is, after all, a "little man" a "most unhappy creation", a "harmless creature", and "insignificant personality", a man endowed with an overabundance of "repulsive freckles" which destroy his "human dignity". Like Andreev's Sergey Petrovich this "profoundly pedestrian personality" is humiliated by his looks, to which he ascribes many of his misfortunes; his freckles make him a person easily remembered, "a fact which was intolerable and unendurable in the period of the civil war, to say nothing of the repulsiveness to the stranger's eye, and owing to which I have endured no little suffering and have been marked by blows of fate, and for which reason I grieve and pine, finding no psychological rest. . . . "[4] In his consciousness of humiliation, and in the stamp that this humiliation has placed on his personality, the freckled man is close to the Underground Man.

The freckled man faces especially painful humiliation in the new utilitarian-minded society. Utilitarian society, Sergey Petrovich recognized, transformed the "little man" into a nameless unit; it had no use for individual personality. And Sergey Petrovich bitterly complained of his role in literature as one of the innumerable Sergey Petrovichs. Petr Pismenny, the freckled man's one-time patron, has a similar role in mind for the freckled man. He wants to employ the freckled man as a model for a "collective portrait". He has no use for the little man's autobiography; "I see through you and all your baggage,"[5] he observes simply and sharply. Petr Pismenny had no use for the freckled man's soul:

You — he says — cannot understand the Marxist method in literature. All the souls aren't worth a lead penny. The feeling for everyday life is necessary, local color is necessary. And you barge in with a soul.[6]

The freckled man will not put up with this "castration of soul", and, breaking down with loneliness, he leaves Petr Pismenny. No more successful, however, is his sojourn with the peasant poet Alesha Kavun; this writer, "bored with the smooth phizes of the NEP" and thirsting for variety, saw in the freckled man a "remarkable smudge".[7] Individuality, it appears, is not for the "little man".

[3]   *Ibid.*, IV, 135.
[4]   *Ibid.*, IV, p. 122.
[5]   *Ibid.*, IV, p. 128.
[6]   *Ibid.*, IV, p. 129.
[7]   *Ibid.*, IV, p. 136.

The freckled man, poor, ragged, miserable in spirit, does not participate in the great socialist construction of his day. He is worried about
his illegal entry into his "legal motherland", and every day, after finishing
his vain labors, makes his way in the most extreme fear to his poor
dwelling. He prefers — like a true man of the "underground" — "psychologically to observe the national fermentation of Moscow".[8] His
observations fill him with lofty joy in the reflection that there are no
limits to Soviet achievements.

Because, most respected Aleksey Kiprianovich [the freckled man writes
to the editor], in all consciousness of the fact that I have not even
touched with my little finger the building of the creative power of our
reborn motherland, and, indeed, on the contrary, at one time in every
way interfered with the erection of the stronghold of the fortress and
was something in the nature of a vampire whom spiders compelled,
together with them, to suck the blood of peasants and workers, who are
raised now to the pinnacle of Soviet Power, and in all consciousness of
the fact that at the present time in my country I am a most insignificant
personality, incapable of contributing even five kopecks for the benefit
of *Dobrolet* [Russian Society for a Volunteer Air Fleet], I cannot renounce the pride that wells up in my soul when I view the stores of the
Mosselprom [Moscow State Trust for Processing of Products of Agri-
cultural Industry] or the *Zhirkost* [The Fat and Bone Processing Industry
Trust] with their fragrance of aroma, and I suppose that the outstripping
of such a despicable city as Berlin, and, if possible, Paris, is the pressing
task of our leaders — so in good time I bow low and gratefully to all
portraits, not daring even to myself to call them by their name and
patronymic — something which Mr. Pismenny once permitted himself
without having the slightest right to do this.[9]

The humble posturings of the freckled man — characteristic of his
approach to all things Soviet — only lightly veils the biting satire of his
words. The satire here consists not in the author introducing any
conscious malice into the mind of his hero, but in overdoing his hero's
naiveté and self-effacement. The "underground" malice which is felt in
various parts of these "memoirs" derives not from the hero (who is too
afraid to be malicious), but from the contrasting elements of the local
incident or situation.

The freckled man lacks the peculiar malice of the Underground Man
to conduct a war with the Petr Pismennys and the authority of the new
order. He admits his weariness — a weariness filled with despair.

[8]   *Ibid.*, IV, p. 126.
[9]   *Ibid.*, IV, p. 127.

I am very tired, I can sincerely say that I am immeasurably tired, ca-
tastrophically tired, and there is not a living spot on me, and, if I, after
turning aside so as not to burst into tears, uncover my rags, you will see
endless wounds, a figurative expression, but it is full of significance,
because there are terms, the significance of which*** but there are even
terms for which they will not pat you on the head in the GPU. But
really, now, really I am a completely harmless creature, and in vain,
undeservedly am I punished for my freckles whose indecency is beyond
my control. . . . I conceal myself with rags but I do not conceal myself
from the legal authorities, because it is not the law I fear, but doors, and
if in the GPU a door is closed behind me, then I swear to you with my
word of honor, and it is firm as the revolutionary will of the Russian
socialist people, that I will hang myself on my rags without ado, having
a long time ago rejected religious prejudice.[10]

There is a tragi-comic quality to the fears of the freckled man, fears
which reach a pathetic intensity. Here is that exaggeration of the
morbidly sensitive, always apprehensive personality of an "underground"
man. At the same time, what is real, and what is symbolized by the
"movement of locking doors", is that terrifying sense of isolation experienced by the "little man" in an increasingly impersonal and hostile
world. "Dear, precious Aleksey Kiprianovich," the freckled man writes
at the conclusion of his "memoirs", "I beg of you in the name of Christ;
it is terrible for me, and there is nobody to take my part." [11]

The humiliating consciousness of self as a nonentity, the feeling of
hopeless separation from people and society, and the feeling of hostility
everywhere is the spiritual nexus between the freckled man and the
Underground Man, as well as Kavalerov.

The protest of the "little man" against offending life is the heart of
the rebellion of the Underground Man. The freckled man rebels against
loneliness, against playing the role of a nonentity, against the "movement
of locking doors". But it is a rebellion of pure despair rather than of
malice. The freckled man's rebellion is expressed most of all by his
quixotic personality; like his contemporary Kavalerov, he has nothing
rational or responsible in his nature. His adventures are a senseless
collection of misadventures, wild, stupid, fantastic and irrational.

If it were necessary to invent a life to demonstrate that man "whoever
he be, likes to act as he wishes and not at all as reason and advantage
dictate" [12] the external life of the freckled man would serve as a model.

---

[10] *Ibid.*, IV, pp. 146-147.
[11] *Ibid.*, IV, p. 147.
[12] Dostoevskij, *Zapiski iz podpol'ja, op. cit.*, IV. 124.

Yet the paradox here, as in the case of the Underground Man, is that precisely in his chaotic movement from one misadventure to the next the freckled man is profoundly unfree — is helpless, forever acted upon, forever following the direction of the ineluctable pointed boot.[13]

[13] The hero of Zoshchenko's short story "Madonna"—the clerk Vinivitkin—is another little "underground" man very close to Kavalerov and the freckled man. The story is told in the form of Vinivitkin's diary. He has received a raise, and as soon as he gets the money he will "step into the arena of life. It is time. For five years I've lived like a pig. For five years—or perhaps ten? Or all my life? Ha-ha, all my life!" (M. Zoščenko, "Madonna," in *Uvažaemye graždane* [Moscow, 1927] p. 91). The hero relates his meeting with a prostitute (whom he does not recognize as such) and his final disillusionment with his "madonna." There is no way out of his "underground". "But if I had noticed [that she was a prostitute]?" he asks himself, and answers: "And even if I had noticed it, it would be all the same. Some, of course, soar like eagles, while in my case***. Yes, life is pretty foul. I was never much drawn to it. There is some kind of foulness in it." (*Ibid.*, p. 99.)

CHAPTER XIX

B. PILNYAK'S

THE VOLGA FALLS TO THE CASPIAN SEA

> As far as I am concerned, I, after all, only carried to
> an extreme in my life what you do not dare to carry
> through even half-way . . .
>
> The Underground Man

The half-mad Ivan Ozhogov in Pilnyak's *The Volga Falls to the Caspian Sea* (*Volga vpadaet v kaspyskoe more*, 1930)* "asserted that communism was the renunciation of things; the first concern of genuine communism must be trust in, great attention to, and respect for man and humanity".[1] This is certainly the belief of Pilnyak in his novel — a study in the impact of collective morality on human relations.

Ivan Ozhogov is close in spirit to the Pilnyak who saw in the Russian revolution the triumph of primitive, elemental Russia over Petrine Russia with its cities and factories, its rational ideas and imported Western culture. It was the elemental, spontaneous, egalitarian idealism of the early years of the revolution which stirred Pilnyak. In *The Volga Falls to the Caspian Sea,* Ozhogov laments the passing of this stage of the revolution.

The great dam — the monolith at Kolomna (the "Russian Bruges") — is going to sweep away a whole historical era. Ancient Kolomna is dying; it is part of old village Russia. Pilnyak recognizes that this world is dying, but seems drawn to it by a strange nostalgia; for it is the

---

*   B. Pilnyak's novel was published in the Soviet Union in 1930. The Russian edition, however, in contrast to the translation by Charles Malamuth which is used here, does not contain important passages which appeared in Pilnyak's original manuscript. Charles Malamuth writes that he "translated the Pilnyak book from a manuscript before it was approved for publication in Russian". (Letter from Charles Malamuth, May 24, 1956.) All quotations which appear only in the English translation are placed in square brackets.

[1]   Boris Pilnyak, *The Volga Falls to the Caspian Sea,* trans., Charles Malamuth (New York, 1931), p. 303. Pilnyak published a novel entitled *Mohogany* (*Krasnoe derevo*) in Berlin in 1929. This novel was denounced by Soviet critics and banned in the Soviet Union. Paris of it, however, were incorporated into Pilnyak's *The Volga Falls to the Caspian Sea,* an edition of which was published in the Soviet Union in 1930—Boris Pil'njak, *Volga vpadaet v kaspijskoe more* (Moscow: Nedra, 1930).

"Russian Bruges", while the construction camp at Kolomna has nothing to replace it.[2]

Pilnyak's *Volga,* despite the assent it gives to socialist construction, to the triumph of the industrial new over the primitive old, is essentially a criticism of communist rationalism. The old world, the world of antiquarians, of the brothers Bezdyetov (dealers in antiques), of "mahogany", in this respect, plays a double role; it is not only a contrast to the constructive activity of the revolution. As B. Aykhenvald observed:

... The world of "mahogany", of Pauls, of Catherines, of baroque, rococo, the world of the Bezdyetovs' frock coats passing into antiquity has, it seems to me, another meaning for Pilnyak. Seen in the light of Pilnyak's symbolism, this is the world of the inert, unmastered, primitive instincts of man, this is the biological antiquity which has not melted in the revolution of glacial ice.[3]

In Pilnyak's *Volga,* biological, instinctual, irrational strivings on the one hand, and rational, utilitarian strivings, on the other, form the basic tension. All the heroes of *Volga,* in one measure or another, are affected by the conflict of instinct and reason which rages in Pilnyak's world.

Of the heroes of *Volga,* one of the most significant from an ideological standpoint, and at the same time one of the most psychologically complex, is the engineer Evgeny Evgenyevich Poltorak. This man is a hero of the "underground"; like the Underground Man he is a philosopher-immoralist.

Poltorak is man-alone, man at the moment of catastrophe, at the moment of a final reckoning with an offending world order. Poltorak's reality, his "civilization" is collapsing. He is — in the symbolism of Pilnyak — like a wolf surrounded by hunters; he is man cast out of the course of life; his place has been "usurped" by the working class, his enemies.[4] All his life Poltorak has lived by "blood", that is, by instinct, and now he is being "killed — and without blood",[5] by a rational

[2] Joseph Freeman cites Pilnyak as once saying: "Everything that was wonderful in the old Russian culture was rooted in the village ... And now that old village is dying. It should die. Something better, greater, more inspiring will take its place. But before that new something comes, there is a vacuum. And I am living in that vacuum, in that no-man's land between that which is dying and that which is just being born. You have no idea how painful that is for a writer who creates out of nostalgic memory, out of love for his earliest experiences ..." (Joseph Freeman, *An American Testament* [New York, 1936], pp. 578-579).
[3] B. Ajkhenval'd, "O romane B. Pil'njaka 'Volga vpadaet v kaspijskoe more'," *Krasnaja nov',* No. 4 (1931), p. 182.
[4] Pilnyak, *op. cit.,* p. 131.
[5] *Ibid.,* p. 306.

revolution, by the working class; he is being ignored, bypassed, rejected, and he is alone with the fear and hatred of a lone wolf.

Poltorak's relation to the new society resembles Ivan Babichev's in Olesha's *Envy;* both men regard the rising world as a usurper, and both are led to wage "underground" war with the new world.

Poltorak was a Russian nationalist. Since when had he become an enemy of everything Russian, one to whom Sherwood had given English pounds sterling to blow up this dam, built by Russian workers?[6]

The genesis of Poltorak the saboteur is that of the "underground" Poltorak.

Man is neither trusted nor respected in socialist society, according to Poltorak. Hence he lives up to his reputation: roguery, flunkeyism, treason, moral dissolution are everywhere. But the government has only "controlling organizations" to counteract this dissolution. The whole country, relates Poltorak, is transformed into a moral placard — an indication that there is nothing left of morality in mens' souls. In all this Poltorak sees the "bandaged hand" with the seal that doctors affixed to the slings of workers so that they might not injure themselves on purpose, that is, commit sabotage.

The controlling bandage loomed before his eyes. [Man was regarded as without individuality, but with rascally proclivities; man could not be trusted, man did not obligate himself to be honest; he was guilty by virtue of being alive. This stood out like death. Poltorak became a wolf.][7]

[I believe — Poltorak remarks on the night of his death — that it is just such controlling bandages, placed not on our fingers but on our souls, that neither of us recognizes. It is just such controlling bandages that have brought me here into these meadows at this hour of night. Formerly we lived by family morality; now we live by collective morality.][8]

Man — in the view of the controlling organizations — is without individuality, but essentially irrational; therefore he must be controlled for his own good. In these conditions man cannot possibly be good: he is "guilty by virtue of being alive". All that remains for man so labeled and stamped is to resort to deliberate non-conformity. Poltorak becomes a wolf.

[6]   *Ibid.,* p. 300.
[7]   *Ibid.,* p. 301.
[8]   *Ibid.,* p. 307.

This is the psychology of the "underground", the psychology of the Underground Man before the "binding force of nature". The Underground Man feels guilty in everything, and, "what is even more insulting, guilty without guilt and, so to speak, through the laws of nature".[9] The Underground Man, as it were, feels guilty by the mere fact of being alive. It is against these "laws of nature" (the "controlling organizations") which have been offending him all his life, that the Underground Man rebels in all his malice. In rebellion he defends his individuality. The Underground Man becomes a wolf.

"Underground" malice — a form of self-destruction — among the workers takes the form of self-injury; with Poltorak it takes the form of sabotage. Poltorak is involved in a conspiracy to blow up the monolith at Kolomna.

Poltorak is an "underground" man, a symbol of irrational, instinctual man. His rebellion, like that of many "underground" heroes, is total; he rebels not only against the "controlling bandage", but against all controls, against morality in general. Poltorak is an immoralist; his relations with people, in particular with women, are those of a ruthless egotist.

Poltorak is ill. "He was ill because of women, having unchained his instincts."[10] Egotistical, lecherous, incapable of any real love, Polotrak moves from one woman to another, multiplying his liaisons, inflamed by sensualism and revelling in "deliriums replete with abnormalities".[11] Constant duplicity marks his relations with his wife; his respectable life with her is paralleled by a life of cynical debauchery. His complete cynicism is brought out in the scene in which he seduces his sister-in-law on her death bed. Poltorak intones:

What is love, Vera Grigorievna? and what is life? What is death? Who knows? And what is truth? I know many truths which are untruths, and I know many untruths which eventually became great, very great truths. I am not talking about the various virtues — about faithfulness, duties — these are mere trifles before the face of death! You are very ill. Vera Grigorievna, you are very ill! . . . All the truths, all the justices, all sorts of morals are nothing before death, because death is a blank, a zero — and the multiplier zero turns all numbers into zeros. What is love, Vera Grigorievna? What is love? There are many loves clothed in all sorts of truths. . . . All these loves are merely an introduction to

---

[9] Dostoevskij, *Zapiski iz podpol'ja, op. cit.*, IV, 113.
[10] Pilnyak, *op. cit.*, pp. 101-102.
[11] *Ibid.*, p. 121.

that which alone is given by nature and which has been besmirched by
a morality that has survived from medieval Christianity — an introduction to the simply carnal, physical — I am not afraid of words — to
love as physical enjoyment. Before the zero of death — everything is
nonsense. . . . I fear neither words nor the conventionalities of morality.
I want to kiss you, at once — for your sake. Even if all this be outside
the pale of truths and morals![12]

What is suggested by this monologue was concisely expressed by
Dostoevsky's Prince Valkhovsky in *The Insulted and Injured:* "What
isn't nonsense is personality — myself. Everything is for me, the whole
world is created for me."[13] Poltorak is not so frank; in the manner of
the Underground Man alone with Liza, Poltorak spoke to Vera Grigorievna "like a skilled orator; he would lower his eyes and cover them
with the palm of his hands . . .".[14]

This is the atmosphere of the "underground". Here is the familiar
"game" — favorite sport in the "underground" — consisting in half-
sincere, half-simulated preachment. The psychologically complex
"game" is first disclosed in *Notes from the Underground.* If Poltorak
is such a master at this "game", however, it is perhaps, because he has
inherited the rich experience of others who — true epigones of the
Underground Man — codified the rules of the "game". Andreev's Dr.
Kerzhentsev plays it with murder, and Gorky's Petr Karazin applies the
rules to police socialism.

The engineer Poltorak, like his predecessors, is without moral pivot;
he stands above "medieval" Christian morality; he recognizes no truths.
Poltorak's relativism leads to cynical scepticism which destroys all
morality. Scepticism leads him to the extreme limits of egotism: the
identification of life only with self, and the death of the self as the death
of everything. If there is no immortality, if God does not exist, Ivan
Karamazov believed, then all is permissible. Just this nihilism of despair,
nourishing the asocial instincts of a number of Dostoevsky's heroes, is
the unsimulated, "sincere" element in Poltorak's "game" with Vera
Grigorievna.

Poltorak's immoralism has social roots. The zero of death that
Poltorak uses to rationalize his immoral game with Vera Grigorievna
belongs to that everyday life of the revolution and civil war "when each

---

[12] *Ibid.,* pp. 106-107.
[13] Dostoevskij, *Unižennye i oskorblennye, op. cit.,* III, 215.
[14] Pilnyak, *op. cit.,* p. 107.

one had at his back a zero at stake in the desperate game",[15] when life
consisted of inexplicable meetings and departures. And so it was in the
era of socialist construction.

There were two lives: the first life and the second life, the latter like a
wolf's forest path, imperceptible dens, various signs and guide posts.
The first life consisted of the socialist cause, the *camera obscura* of
books, the customs of the home, the laws of friendship. It was possible
and necessary to switch oneself from the first to the second life.[16]

This split in the life of the individual is paralleled by a split in consciousness:

. . . Men have always two lives: the life governed by the brain, by the
feeling of duty, of honor, by the open blinds of consciousness; and a
second life given by the subconscious element in man, by instinct, by
blood, by the sun.[17]

Not only Poltorak, therefore, is a man of two lives; the other inhabitants
of the socialist world, in Pilnyak's view, also have two lives, though
their duplicity is less conscious, perhaps, than that of Poltorak. Immorality, Pilnyak suggests, is the very essence of relationships in a
society in which collective and political morality has replaced individual
and family morality. The engineer Laszlo observes:

I heard the following kind of argument: I was told that every historical
epoch has its morality, bred by the epoch. They say that the sticks of
arguments may break, but that they must not be bent too far, to the
point of snapping, along with the arguments. They say that public
morality of our years is political morality. [You may be an absolutely
illiterate man, who asks what sort of science is chemistry and who
cannot spell the simplest word, an ignoramus and a drunkard. You may
be untrue to your word. You may be unscrupulous about money. You
may be dishonest with a woman, with your wife, with your family,
having lost all idea of family decency. In any case, men with such ideas
confuse the notions of family and prostitution as they were thought of
in the old morality.] They say that it is necessary to be moral only in a
political sense; it isn't necessary to be very moral or very literate, but
just orthodox. But to be politically illiterate is immoral.[18]

---

[15]   *Ibid.*, p. 218.
[16]   *Ibid.*, p. 219.
[17]   *Ibid.*, p. 185.
[18]   *Ibid.*, p. 213.

The heroes of Pilnyak, despite the diversity of their backgrounds, personalities, views, are all caught in the web of collective, political morality. There is Professor Poletika whose wife, Olga, left him for the engineer Laszlo; the latter in his turn abandons Olga after seducing Maria, first wife of the Bolshevik Sadykov; the latter soberly releases Maria who becomes the wife of the engineer Laszlo; Maria, unloved by Laszlo, finally commits suicide. The spiritual lives of these people are cemented together by "blood", by instinct.

The Bolshevik Sadykov, "one of the millers at the millstones of the revolution",[19] is guided by a political morality. He is "what is called a coarse, unrefined man; he had his life's work mapped out for him by the revolution".[20] He has never found time to tell his wife Maria whether he loves her. And when the engineer Laszlo begins to be intimate with her, Sadykov — with a rectilinear forthrightness that recalls the behavior of some of Chernyshevsky's heroes in *What is to be Done?* — voluntarily steps aside and calls upon his rival in love to marry Maria. Sadykov the Bolshevik has his heart in the "silent music of the revolution".[21]

Fedor Sadykov, a Bolshevik man of action, is not portrayed unsympathetically by Pilnyak; the author does not judge him; he is a victim of collective morality — a morality which places rational decisions before the decisions of the heart. The violation of the individual is the inevitable result. Poltorak and Sadykov are really not so very far apart in terms of the objective consequences of their behavior; they are, respectively, negative and positive responses to the same phenomenon — collective morality — a morality which frees man of moral responsibility.

"Let these be sick people," the critic Pereverzev observed of many of Dostoevsky's heroes, "but the illness is not exceptional, not accidental, but represents a widespread phenomenon, a real social illness, a real social calamity."[22] Poltorak emerges in Pilnyak's novel as a man whose illness represents a real social illness — and this illness is the principal concern of Pilnyak. The Underground Man confesses at the end of his notes that he has wasted his life in moral corruption. ". . . We are all divorced from life, all crippled, each of us, more or less." "As far as I am concerned," the Underground Man continues, "I, after all, only carried to an extreme in my life what you do not dare to carry through

[19] *Ibid.,* p. 194.
[20] *Ibid.,* p. 193.
[21] *Ibid.,* p. 195.
[22] V. F. Pereverzev, *Tvorčestvo Dostoevskogo* (Moscow, 1922), pp. 235-236.

even half-way. . . ."[23] These words define the position Pilnyak gave his hero in respect to his contemporaries.

Poltorak-the-philosopher explains Poltorak-the-immoralist in the following way:

It seems that, like boots and grain, the morals of each of us are also property [and not a knowledge that we gradually learn to respect, but precise morality, moral qualities. And it turns out that morality may be squandered just like boots and grain; the revolution has squandered it. Morality will have to be restored like boots and sown areas, because morality is a simple and an actual economic unit, no less necessary than coats or potatoes. When the moral resources are exhausted to the point of zero, then the results are we — or, at any rate, I. This happens when the last calorie of moral qualities has been exhausted. But morality, like cloth, may be of good quality — like English cloth — or of an inferior grade, like our cloth.]. We say that our country is ignorant, ignorance itself; our people are ignorant — having been spoiled, or corrupted, thanks to Russian darkness. This argument is not right, because one can turn sour like molded bread not only through ignorance but through ignorance but through corrupt morality — or perhaps because of absence of any morality, as in my case, for I am a very competent man even in questions of morality and philosophy. The controlling bandage is a matter of morality, not of knowledge or ignorance. . . .[24]

Pilnyak uses his "underground" hero in a role similar to that of the Underground Man and of Gorky's Petr Karazin; the philosopher-immoralist Poltorak is both an exposer and one who is exposed; as philosopher he exposes and indicts the moral vacuum that engenders Poltoraks, and as immoralist he illustrates the deceit and moral chaos he so skillfully exposes.

The theme of *The Volga Falls to the Caspian Sea* — on the surface — is one of revolutionary change; the triumph of the new over the old, the machine over the primitive and elemental, man over nature. But for Pilnyak this war between the old and new conceals another, dangerous struggle: this is the war between the rational and the irrational, the brain and instinct, reason and biology. But reason cannot triumph in this struggle. "Man has reconstructed geography and geology, created a new sociology and changed even psychology," writes B. Aykhenvald summing up a basic idea of Pilnyak's novel, "but he himself in his natural blind substance has remained as before." This critic further suggests

[23]   Dostoevskij, *Zapiski iz podpol'ja, op. cit.,* IV, 194, 195.
[24]   Pilnyak, *op. cit.,* p. 308.

that the title of the novel, *The Volga Falls to the Caspian Sea,* may mean that

the biological Volga cannot be interrupted or recreated by any geological and sociological monoliths — it will continue to fall into the same sea that it has fallen into for a thousand years. The antithesis of affirmation and negation in the title emphasizes and confirms the antithesis of content.[25]

Poltorak is a symbol of the biological-irrational element rampant in man, very much as the Underground Man might be said to symbolize this element in his wild, irrational self-will.

Pilnyak, like Dostoevsky in *Notes from the Underground,* postulates the irrational as the core of man's being and as an elemental force in the life of man which cannot be ignored or denied by reason.

In his attitude towards the Bolshevik revolution, Pilnyak is mainly concerned with social morality. Gorky — through Petr Karazin in "Karamora" — insists that man inculcate in himself the "habit of living honorably". Pilnyak, through the philosophizing of Poltorak and the half-mad ravings of Ozhogov, makes the same demand upon his contemporaries. "What we want," Ozhogov declares, "is a revolution of honor, of conscience, that all may become honest; otherwise we shall perish. We must be honest! We must have a conscience!"[26]

[25] Ajkhenval'd, *op. cit.,* p. 182.
[26] Pilnyak, *op. cit.,* p. 336.

CHAPTER XX

A. I. VOINOVA'S *SEMI-PRECIOUS STONES*

Both the author of the notes and the "Notes" themselves are, of course, fictitious. Nevertheless, such persons as the author of these notes not only can, but even must exist in our society, considering those circumstances which have in general led to the formation of our society. I wanted to bring before the public, more conspicuously than is usually the case, one of the characters of the recent past. This is one of the representatives of a generation that is still with us. In this fragment, entitled "The Underground," this person presents himself, his views and, as it were, tries to explain those circumstances owing to which he made his appearance and had to make his appearance in our milieu.

Dostoevsky's prefatory note to
Notes from the Underground

A. I. Voinova's *Semi-Precious Stones* (*Samotsvety*, 1930) — the story of the Machiavellian immoralist Victor Pavlovich Okromeshkov — concludes with the speech of a Soviet prosecuting attorney; it is a sharp indictment of the morals and mentality of the "secret destroyer" Okromeshkov. ". . . We are forced to struggle with special energy against the abnormal twists of the old, self-centered type of mind," the prosecuting attorney observes at one point. "Personal emotions, separation from the collective, self-analysis, reflexion — all this is the same to us as an illness of the organism. . . ."[1]

The prosecuting attorney's remarks recalls the observation of the Underground Man that "to be too acutely conscious is a disease".[2] Consciousness in Okromeshkov is indeed a disease. The words of the prosecuting attorney, however, provoke a negative reaction in the reader, for it is a commonplace that without "personal emotions . . . self-analysis and reflexion" there can be no true consciousness. The ambiguous content of the prosecutor's words is intentional on the part of Voinova; it relates to the ambiguous design of *Semi-Precious Stones*

---

[1] A. I. Voinova, *Semi-Precious Stones*, trans., Valentine Snow (New York, 1931), p. 602. Voinova's novel first appeared in Russia in 1930. A. I. Voinova, *Samocvety* (Moscow, 1930).
[2] Dostoevskij, *Zapiski iz podpol'ja, op cit.*, IV, 111.

whereby the exposing of the hero, ostensibly the primary objective, is a device for exposing the society that engendered him.

Okromeshkov, consulting technologist at the Semi-Precious Stones Trust, relates the story of the events leading to his personal catastrophe. Soviet reality is seen through his eyes. As in *Notes from the Underground* and Gorky's "Karamora", the presentation of the world through the eyes of the "underground" hero makes it difficult at times to distinguish between the views of author and hero. Just this potential for confusion is an asset in *Semi-Precious Stones* — a work which aims at criticizing Soviet reality, but is forced to criticize by indirection.

Okromeshkov is a specialist from the cultured intelligentsia, a profoundly sceptical man who trembled inwardly because of the insecurity of his position as a member of the intelligentsia. He recognizes the necessity of straddling his epoch, of consciously adapting to new conditions, of using these conditions for self-advancement.

Our task was cleverly to combine chimeras with the most matter-of-fact and practical considerations. Because of this necessity I formed the habit of inventing all sorts of combinations and intrigues, never allowing myself to be sincere and destroying in myself all vestiges of humanity.[3]

Cold calculating egotism, ruthless opportunism, deliberate malice and frank immoralism — these are the principal elements in Okromeshkov's personality. He is an "underground" man who stands for himself, and stands alone, alienated from both nature and the "collective".

Every word, every facial expression, every action is studied, calculated, rationally thought out. Okromeshkov moves from one person to another, plotting, weaving intrigues, dropping malicious hints, launching ugly rumors, bolstering his reputation, blackening the reputations of others, denouncing people, sowing discord in the family, and writing a diary which is to serve him as an alibi when, as he expects, he is arrested by the police. Constant duplicity, inherent in the role of the spy, is characteristic of him.

I had learned so well to follow all the turns and twists of human psychology, had become so accustomed to watching intensely not only myself, but all those with whom I came into contact, that these spy's habits had become an integral part of my personality.[4]

---

[3]   Voinova, *op. cit.,* p. 4.
[4]   *Ibid.,* p. 80.

Okromeshkov is an intriguer and opportunist playing the role of a loyal Soviet specialist; yet his pose as a man devoted to the cause of socialism is not entirely simulation; here there is a certain singular truth. "I was irresistibly drawn to men of broad dimensions," he observes, "and in our time such men were all Communists. I liked at times to indulge in reflections of state importance, since I felt that we alone could bring forth new ideas."[5] An ambivalent attitude towards socialism is characteristic of Okromeshkov as it is of Gorky's Petr Karazin.

This combination of loftiness of purpose with cynicism, immoralism and treachery, this blend of the real and the simulated, is one of the most striking "underground" features of Okromeshkov, and marks his personal relations with his wife as well. He poses before her as decent and righteous, but subjects her to a cruel process of spiritual disintegration. As with the hero of Dostoevsky's "A Meek One", human relations take on the character of an organized game to Okromeshkov. "How, after all, uncomplicated human psychology is!" he observes in connection with his wife. "Given the desire, one can play upon it as on a player organ. You put in the music sheet, press the pedal, and the sounds come forth!"[6] A girl, the object of one of Okromeshkov's intrigues, observes with a shudder:

"What a torturer you are!" she said, with a shudder. "If one falls into your hands — Horrible! You wreck one's nerves!"
"Why, what are you saying? I am a very meek person," I said, but I was displeased, for she had noticed the most touchy side of my character, which heretofore Doussia alone had known.[7]

Truly "Doussia alone" — his wife — understands the real nature of the "meek" Okromeshkov, this "underground" hero who prides himself on his knowledge of human psychology.

Okromeshkov squeezes his wife's emotions like a rag, drives her into the arms of another man, then torments her for the momentary infidelity he had diabolically engineered. On the occasion of the final rupture in their relations, he torments her, then feels "forced to play the symphony of friendship",[8] for fear she would go away. He speaks to her softly, hypocritically, of his feelings of jealousy (half real, half simulated):

"And how you tormented me!" I continued, purposely raising my tone higher and higher. "Who had ever been so insulted, as I have been as

---

[5]   *Ibid.,* p. 122.
[6]   *Ibid.,* p. 534.
[7]   *Ibid.,* p. 169.
[8]   *Ibid.,* p. 534.

a husband and as a human being? . . . I felt incensed by my own words. I had restrained my vengefulness too long, hiding under a mask of friendship and nobility, and when at last I found an opportunity to express myself, I was possessed by a sort of rage. I did not speak, but vomited forth words, paying no heed to her, but solely enjoying my revenge.

"Remember, if you please, how you chucked me out! . . . I was literally shaken now by the feeling of injury for the past. I wanted to force her to suffer, as I had suffered, to offend her mortally, so that she would twist and writhe before me here, and I would feel at last that I had avenged all the humiliations I had borne.[9]

"I have never lied," she said with dignity. "I repeat, if I have been mistaken, it was only because I loved you!"

"Loved? Oh yes, you loved me!" I was moving nervously around her. "If you please, prove it! There's been enough talk!"

"How can I prove it?" she said softly, and did not grow angry or irritable. Only deep in her eyes there lay a cruel pain, as if she were forcing herself with difficulty to bear all my senseless onslaughts and injuries. . . .

"Well, if you love me — lie with me — right now!" I said through clenched teeth.

She looked at me in fright and staggered away. My face was terrible. I sensed it myself. At the same time, I did not want to calm myself. Truth to tell, I had so twisted and broken myself that I had lost all idea of my own personality. Now I was delighting in the process of showing my real self, and showed it unrestrainedly, elementally. . . . I grasped her, and here something incredible happened. I clutched her with such force, that all her bones creaked. She cried:

"What are you doing, let go!"

I threw her on the bed and took possession of her . . . When all was over, I rose. My fury had abated. I had outraged her, and I became aware of a pleasant feeling of satisfaction. I moved away to the table and watched mockingly, while she sat on the bed, as if stunned, then slowly made herself look decent, arose, and looked at me with repulsion.

"Here is your hat, if you please," I said with exquisite courtesy, restraining a smile with difficulty. . . . I bent down, picked up the hat and presented it to Doussia, thus hinting that I had absolutely no desire to see her remain here. She did not brush off the dust, but put it on right away, took her bag, got out the money and threw it on the table in a contemptuous gesture, as if to say: "Go to the devil with your money!"

And went silently out of the room.[10]

This scene in spirit and in much detail resembles the final scene in *Notes from the Underground* in which the Underground Man torments and debauches Liza.[11]

9   *Ibid.,* pp. 535-536.
10 *Ibid.,* pp. 537-539.
11 Glazkov's "rhapsody of malice" directed against Katya (Albov's "Day of

In the inhuman psychological experiments he performs on his wife, Okromeshkov is a true epigone of the Underground Man and the "underground" hero of Dostoevsky's "A Meek One". Okromeshkov loves the game. "Life is a tourney," a "contest in psychological organization. He who has the most agility and inventiveness wins." [12] Socialism for the "underground" Okromeshkov is also an area for the self-assertion, for self-advancement and the exercise of power.

Okromeshkov is the successor in the field of socialism to Gorky's Petr Karazin. Both men have an intoxication with self, a love of the "game" and of dangerous adventure, pathological ambivalence, and an amoral nature which reason can neither control nor comprehend. Okromeshkov is one of the socialist calculating machines about which Gorky writes in "Karamora". Not accidentally Okromeshkov's wife calls him a "soulless egotist". "You, like a book-keeper, are always counting — so much love, so much tenderness, more of this, less of that, this is profit, this is loss. . . ." [13] "You small, insignificant little man!" she exclaims. ". . . you are simply an animal, trembling for your existence — Self-seeker!" [14] Behind the mask of the "underground" self-seeker and sadist, characteristically, is a trembling, insignificant little man.

Reckoning"), Ivan Babichev's despoiling of the queen of the ball (Olesha's *Envy*), the artist Mikhaylov's seduction of Liza (M. P. Artsybashev's *At the Last Boundary*) are variations of this episode. The artist Mikhaylov, a kind of "underground" Don Juan, is a devotee of the "game" of seducing a woman, "the intangibly delicate game in which you attack and she despairingly defends herself . . ." (Arcybašev, *U poslednej čerty, op. cit.*, VI, 65.) The following is a scene from one of Mikhaylov's intangibly delicate games. Liza, a girl, stands at the door. "Mikhaylov looked stubbornly at her and was silent. This was a savage game and he was sorry for her and ashamed, and interested as never before in his life . . . He quickly rushed towards her . . . He pressed her with insane rage, tore her dress . . . With terrible force, almost in a frenzy, he took possession of her . . . Liza went away. Mikhaylov remained alone . . . He was worn out, happy, and satiated with life." (*Ibid.*, VI, 242-243). Another reflection of this episode may be found in Tolstoy's *Kreutzer Sonata*. Pozdnyshev observes that "true debauchery consists precisely in freeing onself from moral relations towards the woman with whom you are entering physical relations. And I worshipped just this liberation. I remember how I was tormented once when I did not succeed in paying a woman who, probably, falling in love with me, gave herself over to me, and I became tranquil only after I had sent her money, in this way showing that I did not consider myself bound to her in any way in a moral sense." (Lev Tolstoj, "Krejcerova sonata," *Polnoe sobranie sočinenij*, e.d., V. G. Čertkov [Moscow, 1936], XXVII, 17.)

[12]   Voinova, *op. cit.*, p. 234.
[13]   *Ibid.*, p. 269.
[14]   *Ibid.*, pp. 347-348.

Okromeshkov, in the words of the Soviet prosecuting attorney, is a man who has "mastered perfectly all our conceptions and the forms of our language . . .".[15] But in the presentation of Voinova, Okromeshkov is not only a simulator, but a real embodiment of the Soviet spirit. Okromeshkov does not feel out of place in the Soviet epoch:

I liked all these dangers which lurked about me, liked the mad instability of our epoch, when life was on the whole sold for less than thirty pieces of silver, while morals and ethics were quoted on the stock exchange as the now worthless securities of the old regime.[16]

Okromeshkov is very grateful that Soviet life has "burned all idealistic conceptions" out of his consciousness and turned him into a "staunch realist".[17] Okromeshkov utters these words quite sincerely, without any irony; there is only the irony of Voinova.

The basic feature of Okromeshkov's world view is a deep-seated scepticism; it is the philosophical counterpart to the moral chaos of his personality. This scepticism, Voinova clearly indicates, is the fruit of the October revolution and of the Soviet era. The "October revolution had upset all values".[18] "This is good about the revolution," another unsavory "underground" character, Mons, says, "that it knows neither pity nor cruelty, neither morals nor immorality, and we are its children."[19]

Okromeshkov, like his spiritual brother Poltorak, is presented as one of these children of the revolution; he denies the existence of any firm, immutable values or truths. "Every epoch has its own truth. . . ."[20] Okromeshkov's thinking on morality has a class orientation. He remarks:

In our time, to be indignant at betrayal [infidelity in family], to occupy oneself with research as to what is good and what is evil, this is madness! We have only one kind of ethics: the ethics of today — and yesterday is a tomb . . . .[21]

Of course, from the point of view of old ethics — I thought — one might say: the betrayal is complete! But . . . to Soviet morals, what is betrayal? That which harms the interests of the proletariat.[22]

---

[15] *Ibid.,* p. 603.
[16] *Ibid.,* p. 80.
[17] *Ibid.,* pp. 121-122.
[18] *Ibid.,* p. 433.
[19] *Ibid.,* p. 45.
[20] *Ibid.,* p. 28.
[21] *Ibid.,* pp. 186-187.
[22] *Ibid.,* p. 444.

Communist morality, Voinova suggests, is relativistic morality, a
morality that leads inevitably to the violation of the individual. The
Bolshevik Khriapin, characteristically described as a "stone wall of a
man", remarks: "Who cares about personalities when the interests of
the country are above everything else?"[23] Not only Okromeshkov
emerges in Voinova's novel as a destroyer of the moral fabric of life,
but Khriapin and, by implication, others like him also emerge as
destroyers, although not "underground" ones. The direct result of
Khriapin's morality is the dissolution of his own family life.

Voinova, like Pilnyak, is primarily interested in exposing the destructive impact of class, political, collective morality upon family life
and human relations in general. Okromeshkov, like the Underground
Man, Poltorak and Petr Karazin, presents himself to the reader, in the
final analysis, as only an extreme manifestation of a moral crisis affecting
all society, a crisis involving the breakdown of all moral standards.
Okromeshkov is conscious that he is not alone in his asocial behavior.

I always saw myself as a representative case. I saw that my characteristics
were those of almost any Soviet employee. The only difference was
that the others changed and adapted themselves unconsciously to the
new reality, whereas I was conducting a profound social experiment,
deliberately revising my psychology in the direction of the governing
modern ideas.[24]

Like the Underground Man, Okromeshkov could truly say that he only
carried to an extreme what others did not dare carry through even half-
way. Okromeshkov is exposed by Voinova, but he is presented as a hero
of his time. The juxtaposition of Okromeshkov the poseur — the man
of self-effacing strivings, the man of lofty Soviet idealism — with the
real Okromeshkov, the completely cynical, egotistical, immoral "underground" man, takes shape as a devastating commentary on the Soviet
bureaucrat.

In the Soviet world, according to Voinova, the individual struggles
to survive against the encroachments of the collective with its political-
utilitarian imperatives. In her novel *East and West* (*Vostok i zapad*,
1932), Voinova characterizes the clash between the individual and the
collective by a colloquy between the young communist Gleb and another
communist, Gravinsky.

---

[23]   *Ibid.*, p. 63.
[24]   *Ibid.*, p. 101.

"One must take into account the individual experiences of each member of the brigade," Gleb said heatedly, "one cannot deprive people of individualism as you want! In your opinion 'man' sounds odious, it is necessary to destroy everything human. I know, you want to drag out your theory of the standard man — everybody like one another — to emasculate him of all experience."

"And you would restore individualism!" Gravinsky coldly parried. "If you develop your thought through, do you know where it will lead? To the affirmation of man, to the affirmation of the human personality, while the collective — all that's just poppycock. No, comrade! We will not back down, we will fight for the collective, we will not give up a single inch to individualism. What is useful for the collective, for the party — that shall be developed, and what is not useful — that shall be cut out."

"And personal life?!" cried Valka. "According to you all that should go to the devil?"

"To the devil!" said Gravinsky irritably.[25]

Gravinsky, with his theory of the "standard man" — a theory reminiscent of Shigalev's in Dostoevsky's *The Devils* — is a type who would easily obtain citizenship in Zamyatin's Single State.

Gravinsky symbolizes everything Voinova rejects in Soviet life. But it is Okromeshkov who discloses the extent of the moral chaos she sees there. He only reveals the multiple layers of his being — and of Voinova's intentions — when he is seen as a true "underground" man.

---

[25]   Voinova, *Vostok i zapad* (Moscow, 1933), I, 52-53.

CHAPTER XXI

ILYA ERENBURG AND
NOTES FROM THE UNDERGROUND

> How do you know, perhaps man loves the building
> only from a distance and not at all at close quarters;
> perhaps he only likes to create it, but not to live in it,
> offering it on completion *aux animaux domestiques*—
> such as ants, sheep, etc. etc. Now ants are of quite a
> different taste. They have a magnificent building of
> the kind that is eternally indestructible—the ant hill.
>
> The Underground Man

"Art is the alembic of anarchy," Khulio Khurenito observes in *The Extraordinary Adventures of Khulio Khurenito and his Disciples* (1922); "artists are heretics, dissenters and dangerous rebels."[1] Such an artist-rebel is the author of *Khulio Khurenito*; he caricatures himself in the figure of the narrator "Ilya Erenburg", a disciple of Khurenito.

This is the story of a great Teacher, and not about a weak, insignificant, contemptible pupil. Ilya Erenburg — the author of mediocre verses, a hack journalist, a coward, an apostate, a petty hypocrite, a despicable creature with intelligent, thoughtful eyes — this Ilya Erenburg howled on his seat in the train.[2]

This "Ilya Erenburg" has the familiar personality of a little man from the "underground"; he reacts to the new, socialist life in a familar way:

"Teacher: these new people about whom you speak are deformed and therefore impossible. Their lives are shorn of the accidental, and therefore of that which is the most beautiful; they live without the unexpected, without contradictions, without romanticism; they have nothing. These are millions of Shmidts, lacking even the most insignificant Napoleon. What boredom!"

"What of it, you will get bored because you are a man of the old species [retorts the Teacher]. Others will grow up according to pattern, they will work and they will not be bored."[3]

The satirical image of "Ilya Erenburg" suggests the affinity that exists between the early Erenburg and the author of *Notes from the Under-*

---

[1] Il'ja Erenburg, *Neobyčajnye pokhoždenija Khulio Khurenito i ego učenikov* (Moscow-Berlin, 1922), p. 301.
[2] *Ibid.,* p. 328.
[3] *Ibid.,* p. 297.

ground. Erenburg himself emerges as an epigone of the Underground Man. This Erenburg feared the "million Shmidts", epigones of the man of action. Irrational, romantic, individualistic man finds his antithesis in the fanatical rationalist Shmidt, the German officer (a disciple of the Teacher) who joined the Bolsheviks because among them he found the best opportunity to apply his organizational instincts, to subject Europe to a "single plan". His plans for combatting chaos seem like a blueprint for Zamyatin's Single State.

Shmidt pointed out to us a most mysterious chart: it resembled the roots of a giant plant. The life of man! I recalled the naive little woodcuts: a boy playing, a youth, in love, with flowers, the father of a family caressing an infant, a mature man for some reason holding a goosequill in his hand and a feeble old man hobbling towards an open coffin. But here there was nothing like that: white squares dissolved into green pyramids which passed on currents to red circles, the circles became transformed into rhomboids and so on for a long time, very complex, and nowhere to be seen was the coffin for repose — but only black triangles of settlements for labor invalids.

And Shmidt, showing to us all these paths and passes, throwing out hundreds of figures and names of organizing centers, declared with pathos: "There you have life! It is no longer a secret, a fairy tale, a delirium, but a labor process which in this pitiful room has been broken down into parts and reunited by the power of reason!"[4]

The opposition between the living, feeling man, the irrational dreamer and rebel and the rational man of action, is an important theme in a number of Erenburg's early works. Erenburg fears the triumph of the machine in modern civilization. The Teacher, Khulio Khurenito, observes:

... The machine demands neither court painters nor poet-courtesans, but the transformation of living flesh into wheels, nuts, screws. Freedom and individuality, the face and the image must perish in the name of the total mechanization of life.[5]

Erenburg sees the spectre of mechanization in both the old bourgeois society and the new socialist society. He approaches the promised land of socialism with a scepticism and pessimism that closely resemble Dostoevsky's. The irrationalism of *Notes from the Unterground* and the pessimism of "The Legend of the Grand Inquisitor" made a deep impression on the early Erenburg.[6]

---

[4] *Ibid.*, p. 295.
[5] *Ibid.*, p. 99.
[6] The very streets of Russia, Erenburg writes in *Khulio Khurenito*, cry out in fear

The antagonism between the irrational anti-hero and the rational
man of action is developed in Erenburg's novel *The Racketeer* (*Rvach*,
1925). The contrasting personalities and activities of the brothers
Mikhail and Artem Lykov form a basic tension in the novel on both an
emotional and philosophical plane.[7]

Mikhail Lykov does not fit the revolution. The very concept of
discipline offends him. He is unpredictable, rebellious, egotistical, lustful,
complex, and filled with a multiplicity of strivings. He is spiritually
akin to the Underground Man. Artem Lykov, on the other hand, fits
the revolution like a cog. He is one of the "millions of Artems" who
made the revolution. He is a "self-conscious sheep" imbued with a
"pure rationalism", a creature for whom life is clear and direct, death

---

and despair: take our freedom away, it is more burdensome than any yoke, it is
too much for us! In the chapter entitled "The Grand Inquisitor outside the Legend,"
a communist, conversing with Khulio Khurenito, remarks: "We are leading mankind to a better future. Some, to whom this is not advantageous, hinder us in
every way ... We must eliminate them, killing one in order to save thousands.
Others resist, unaware that it is really their happiness which lies ahead ... We
lash them onwards, lash them towards paradise with iron whips ... Do you think
it is easy? Easy for you to look on? Easy for them to incur guilt. Here is a burden,
here is pain! Of course, the historical process, inevitability etc. But somebody
had to comprehend it, take the lead, stand at the helm ... We came! Who? I,
dozens, thousands, organization, the Party, authority. We took the responsibility ...
I am not going to roll about before ikons, atone by prayer for sins, I am not going
to start washing my hands. I simply say—it is a heavy burden. But it was necessary
this way, you hear, any other way was impossible!" Thrusting myself forward, I
saw [comments "Ilja Erenburg"] how the Teacher rushed up to him and kissed his
high, severe forehead. I, wild with amazement and horror, took off in flight.
I came to only at the Kremlin gate where the watchman stopped me and Khurenito
and demanded a pass. "Teacher, why did you kiss him, out of respect or out of
pity?" "No. I always respect traditions of a country. Indeed the communists
also, as I have noted, are extremely traditional in their customs. After I had heard
him out, I recalled identical precedents in the works of your Dostoevsky and,
observing etiquette, I bestowed this ... ceremonial kiss." (*Ibid.*, pp. 278-280.)
[7]   The method of employing two contrasting personalities to express conflicts in
Soviet life is a familiar one in early Soviet literature. K. Fedin's *Cities and Years*
(*Goroda i gody*, 1924), for example, resembles Erenburg's *The Racketeer* in that
elements of the rational and irrational, conformist and non-conformist find em-
bodiment in two contrasting personalities, two heroes. "All my life," Andrey
Startsev says, "I have striven to get into the main stream of things ... But I was
always washed away, carried aside." "He has good hands, shoulders and mouth,"
Andrey says of his antithesis Kurt Van. "In his presence the room takes on meaning.
The table, the bed, the windows immediately become pleasant and necessary.
Kurt is a well-organized man." (K. Fedin, *Goroda i gody* [Leningrad, 1924] p. 9).
And Kurt, justifying before a Party Committee the murder of Andrey, declares.
"... I taught myself to think objectively and to act according to the dictates of
reason." (*Ibid.*, p. 10.)

easy, a strong man, but without any special features to distinguish him. Artem acts like everybody else.

It is not difficult to recognize in Artem Lykov an epigone of that man of action for whom the Underground Man felt both hatred and envy, scorn and attraction. Quite understandably Mikhail Lykov hates his brother; at the same time his hatred is easily transformed into a tormenting, passionate liking. He despises Artem, but invariably as a youth seeks protection under his brother's "broad shoulders".[8]

The revolution increases the estrangement of the brothers. To Mikhail — who cannot play the role of a party man — Artem is a sheep, a symbol of everything that is alien. "In Artem he hated the health and the norm, the virtuous one, the party, the state, all humanity."[9] "He hated the leaden man for whom everything is simple and clear. . . ."[10] But most of all he hates the revolution. The revolution takes and caresses the Artems while it rejects him, Mikhail. "Why, because he is not like the others, a goat, a stubborn goat among a herd of filthy sheep, whipped, blindly disciplined, branded with ticket numbers."[11]

The individualist Mikhail faces the revolution with the resentment and malice of an "underground" man who is conscious that he is being displaced, by-passed, ignored. Pilnyak's Poltorak became a wolf when he was cast out of the course of his life. Mikhail Lykov, following his inborn inclinations (he always had hands that liked to "grab"), finding himself alienated from the sheep, degenerates into a grasping Nepman, a speculator involved in shady enterprises. Mikhail Lykov's rebellion, like that of the Underground Man, knows no limits. He becomes a wolf.

Erenburg is unsparing in his scorn for the new man of action. But here there is more than scorn; the writer feels quite nonplussed and helpless as an artist before this new hero.

If in merely mentioning Artem we involuntarily abandon the language of the chronicle of events for that of an editorial, then this is exclusively because the wealth of this person (as all those people like him in the new generation) consisted in a frank and shocking poverty of so-called "personal life". In speaking about him one has to speak about conferences, about the struggle with banditry, about the restoration of Soviet industry, about anything you want, but not about those picturesque occurrences which enliven the chapters of any novel. If one even points out that Artem was at first a political commissar of the X regiment,

8   Erenburg, *Rvač* (Paris, 1925), pp. 80-81.
9   *Ibid.,* p. 366.
10   *Ibid.,* p. 42.
11   *Ibid.,* p. 42.

which went through the whole campaign against Poland, that then he worked in the GUVUZ [Chief Administration for Military Schools] and, finally, entered the Military-Chemical Academy, this hardly will satisfy the curiosity of readers, for it will recall rather a page from the history of the revolution than the biography of a man. But what can be done? In order to become the hero of the novel, Artem would have to cease to be simply a hero and, following the example of his young brother, enliven his days with ravishings, robbery, sentimental tears or the debaucheries of an unrestrained man. Varying a well-known saying, we make bold to say that good communists have no biography. And Artem was without question a communist of the first water. His feelings and acts were dictated not by Party directives, but by the collective of wills — silent, perhaps, but felt — the wills of those building the ant hills, the triangles of cranes on the move, the Cyclopean structures and a new human society. It is enough for us to know the fact itself and the relation to it of ten communists in order unerringly to divine how it was received by the eleventh, that is, in this case, by Artem Lykov.[12]

This passage is remarkable for its satirical "underground" spirit. Erenburg not only rejects the hero-builder of the "ant hill" state as the hero of a novel, but suggests that any true hero must enliven his days after the manner of an unrestrained man, that is, after the manner of an anti-hero.

Erenburg poses perhaps the most important creative problem facing the early Soviet writer who wished to portray sympathetically the face of the new revolutionary hero: how shall one create an individuated hero out of the man of action, out of the "millions of Artems". Erenburg poses this problem in *The Racketeer,* but he does not resolve it.

In his novel *Out of Chaos* (1933), devoted to the period of the first Five-Year Plan, Erenburg suggests that the real hero of the Soviet epoch will neither be the unrestrained man of feeling nor the rationalistic man of action, but a hero in whom the elements of instinct and reason, thought and action achieve a synthesis. Erenburg seeks a way out of the impasse created by the rigid "underground" opposition of instinct and reason, thinking man and man of action, individual and mass man. Erenburg speaks through many voices in *Out of Chaos,* and these voices conflict. Erenburg's sharp, derisive "underground" voice is heard in Volodia Safonov; but this voice is now challenged by others. In *Out of Chaos* Erenburg attempts to isolate, define, and control those "underground" elements which are rampant in many of his earlier works and dominate his world view.

"I am raging because I am filled with envy. I am not at all the hero,

12 *Ibid.,* p. 178.

Irina," the young student Volodia Safonov remarks in words recalling the Underground Man. "Rather a nonentity. Even worse." [13] "Of such as he they wrote in the novels of the old days," Irina significantly observes. "If there is a single living emotion in him, it is hatred. He hates me, he hates Kolka — he hates everybody. He does not love even himself." [14] Volodia decides to straighten everything out, quietly and without fuss. He chooses suicide as the only way out.

Volodia is disclosed in the novel as a spiritual cripple, a man divorced from the life of his times, unfit for constructive work, and perishing in idleness in a "stuffy underground". He is a lonely, tormented, disillusioned idealist, an intellectual, a book worm, a profound "sceptic" and a "coward". He feels very close to Dostoevsky and to his fictional world.

Whenever he read Dostoevsky he felt ill. Those were not books, but letters from a man intimately related to him. He waxed indignant, laughed, conversed with himself. Sometimes, utterly worn out, he threw the book aside. He swore he would not read it any more. An hour later, with guilty stratagems, he opened the book to the exact page which had aroused his resentment. He sighed with relief — the hour's breathing spell was doubly hard. He plunged into the thicket of absurd scenes, hysterical screams, and hot, sticky pain. Sometimes he felt that in one more moment he himself would be writhing in an epileptic fit.[15]

Volodia's whole being is in constant conflict with reality. In the end, he regards his whole being as a "mistake". His conflict with reality, like the Underground Man's, is essentially an internal drama. The Underground Man, safely hidden in his "underground", argues with the rationalists, jeers at them and at his enemies in the privacy of his "notes". Volodia puts his grievances, his arguments with the men of his epoch down in his diary; he too is "condemned to the cautious disguise of an innocent, to swallowed threats, to jeers under lock and key, to a double existence".[16] He withdraws from his epoch in proud scorn. But like Glazkov in Albov's "Day of Reckoning" and Aleksey Petrovich in Garshin's "Night", he cannot come to terms with himself or reality, and he commits suicide.

Volodia is marked by that hypersensitivity and fear of life that is

---

[13] Ilya Ehrenburg, *Out of Chaos,* trans. Alexander Bakshy (New York, 1934). p. 264. This work appears in Russian under the title *Second Day.* Il'ja Erenburg, *Vtoroj den'* (2d ed.; Moscow, 1934).

[14] *Ibid.,* p. 264.

[15] *Ibid.,* p. 229.

[16] *Ibid.,* p. 215.

characteristic of many "underground" heroes. From his earliest years he was afraid to meet life face to face. Spring alarmed him because it drove him out of his hole. Volodia's spiritual development in his early school years recalls in broad outline that of the Underground Man who, repelled by the life of his comrades, shut himself away from people in wounded pride. Volodia, "haughty and dogmatic", cannot compromise with truth, cannot ignore the "absurd and ludicrous", cannot march in time with the collective, and cannot tolerate stupidity, vulgarity, and dishonesty. His idealism soon turns into cynicism and he begins to evade life and nourish his secret injuries in silence. He likes history and poetry, but he falls in love with mathematics because it is aloof and gives the illusion of an absolute truth.

Volodia's uncompromising nature, his egotism, his contempt for his comrades, his absorption in the culture of the old world, isolates him, forces into an "underground life".

"I am one, while they are *everybody* . . ." [17] the Underground Man remarks. Volodia also discovers the frightening singleness of his existence. His reads his diary and becomes aware of his double existence.

Never before had he thought of other people as different, and forming a single body. Now he wrote "They", "They accept", "They have the truth". Then he was just he, and against him were the people. Volodia was frightened. As in his childhood, he pulled the covers over his head and drew up his feet: he was afraid of life.[18]

Volodia cannot communicate with his contemporaries. They are not "animals", he allows, but they are creatures who belong to another spiritual age. They are "infants" and, Volodia notes, he began his diary "in order to fight obligatory infantilism. . . ." [19]

It was impossible to converse with the wheels of a crane. They were capable of sweating, as men sweat. But they had no sentiments — they moved according to plan.[20]

Volodia Safonov, like Mikhail Lykov, has only contempt for the men of his epoch who are guided by the rational considerations of building socialism. Socialism is cultural leveling and cultural leveling is the death of the Safonovs — such is the essence of Volodia Safonov's thinking.

Volodia feels contempt for his contemporaries, but also envy; he envies them as the Underground Man envied the "normal" man; they,

17   Dostoevskij, *Zapiski iz podpol'ja, op. cit.,* IV, 138.
18   Ehrenburg, *Out of Chaos, op. cit.,* p. 96.
19   *Ibid.,* p. 152.
20   *Ibid.,* p. 71.

at least, are living, whereas he is condemned to inaction, and his other life is known only to his diary. "Everything he had done . . . had been only the recoil of an alien life." [21] "I envy him," Volodia confesses about his successful rival in love, the worker Kolka Rzhanov. "For everything. Because he has such shoulders. . . . Because he is really seriously interested in the percentage of silicon dioxide in pig iron. And I am raging because I am filled with envy." [22]

Volodia is conscious that he is "marching to ruin without attempting to destroy even a fragment of the world that was his enemy".[23] And this moves him to sum up his charges against his epoch, to sum them up in an address prepared for a public meeting. In a spirit of egoistic pride and contempt that recalls Glazkov's indictment of society in his impromptu speech at Rozanov's party (Albov's "Day of Reckoning"), Volodia writes:

You are sure to be much surprised at my words. You are accustomed to silence. Some are silent because you have frightened them; others because you have bought them. Simple truths demand self-sacrifice now. As in the days of Galileo they can be spoken only at the stake. You want to discuss the question of culture. It is unlikely, however, that anyone among you understands what culture is. For some, culture is blowing one's nose in a handkerchief; for others it is buying the "Academia" publications, which they do not understand, cannot, indeed, understand. You have eliminated from life the heretics, the dreamers, the philosophers, the poets. You have established universal literacy and equally universal ignorance. After this you gather together and prattle out of your cribbing about culture. Of course, the fact that you do not blow your nose with the help of two fingers merits all praise. But it is not exactly the foundation of culture. You may build a thousand blast-furnaces and you will still be ignorant. The ant-heap is a model of reason and logic. But it existed a thousand years ago, too. Nothing has changed in it. There are ant-workers, ant-specialists, and ant-chiefs. But there never was an ant-genius. Shakespeare wrote of other things than ants. The Acropolis was not built by ants. The law of gravitation was not discovered by an ant. Ants have no Senecas, no Raphaels, no Pushkins. They have a heap, and they work. They build, they carry twigs, they lay eggs, they devour one another, and they are happy. They are far more honest than you are — they do not prattle of culture.[24]

Volodia's eloquent indictment of utilitarian culture is in the main stream of the anti-rationalist, anti-utopian tradition of *Notes from the Under-*

21   *Ibid.*, p. 216.
22   *Ibid.*, p. 264.
23   *Ibid.*, p. 219.
24   *Ibid.*, pp. 218-219.

ground. The symbol of the ant hill is used by the Underground Man to characterize the social utopias of the rationalists.[25]

Volodia mentally rehearses his proposed address, envisages the scene in which he will deliver it, rejoices in the anticipation of an inevitable reckoning. His speech is something of a sortie from the "underground", a collision with reality. His anticipatory feeling and thoughts are in the spirit of those of the Underground Man as he sets out in pursuit of Zverkov in order to revenge himself for the humiliation he suffered at the *Hôtel de Paris*. Volodia's decision to "tell them all", fills him with a joyous feeling. Just as the Underground Man imagines how a beating, arrest, imprisonment and exile may follow his vengeance upon Zverkov, so, anticipating the reaction of his audience, Volodia "drew inspiration from their hostile cries", and is "happy that at last he would stand alone against them all". He ruminates:

They would see what he was. They would roar with rage. Probably they would rush at him to pull him off the platform. Prolonging this pleasure, he glanced even farther into the future: he might be expelled from the university — he might even be imprisoned. The idea of a reckoning elated him. His very face changed — became alert, more youthful. His sickly listlessness vanished. . . . For the first time he thought of Irina [his girl friend] without a sense of humility.[26]

But Volodia Safonov, true man from the "underground", at the last moment fails to act. He is too much of a coward to act (the "Volodia Safonovs are reasoners and cowards"[27]). "I was never a coward in my soul," write the Underground Man, "although I am continually a

---

[25]   There are echoes of Shigalev's "future paradise" (*The Devils*) in Volodia's description of the leveling of culture. Petr Verkhovensky, discussing Shigalev's doctrine with Stavrogin, remarks: "The first task [in the implementation of Shigalev's ideas] will be to lower the level of education, the sciences, and the professions. A high level of sciences and of accomplishment is accessible only to men of the highest abilities—but people of the highest abilities are not needed!" (Dostoevskij, *Besy, op. cit.*, VII, 341.)

[26]   Ilya Ehrenburg, *Out of Chaos, op. cit.*, p. 218.

[27]   *Ibid.*, p. 300. Volodia, as Erenburg makes clear, acts in another way. Like Ivan Karamazov, Volodia implants an idea in a man capable of real action—the hooligan Tolia; he "spoke of Dostoevsky," told him that "man was more important than machines." (*Ibid.*, p. 318.) Tolia subsequently went out and damaged a piece of machinery. Erenburg, like Olesha and Pilnyak, suggests a link between the "underground" anti-rationalist outlook and "wrecking." Volodia's hatred of the machine finds implementation in Tolia's sabotage. "You have reared machine worshippers," Volodia muses; "therefore you have also reared machine fighters." (*Ibid.*, p. 318).

coward when it comes to action. . . ."[28] Volodia does not deliver his
scathing address; instead, another speech, unexpectedly conciliatory
and self-critical, comes forth from him. Later he berates himself for
this conciliatory speech. "He had not said a word about ants," he
bitterly thinks. "He had crawled into the ant-heap himself."[29]

Erenburg suggests, however, that cowardice is not the only reason for
Volodia's abandonment of his original address. Volodia's ideological
flexibility derives from a real ambivalence. "I am simply a double-
dealer," he observes; "like everybody else, I have two lives. I think one
thing and say another."[30] "I spoke at the meeting as I did . . . because
I am a cripple." As in the Underground Man, hypocrisy and sincerity
exist side by side in Volodia.

The most interesting part of it is that I spoke sincerely. In any case, not
out of fear. But I did not speak what I thought. Or rather, I said what
I thought, and yet did not think. It was as if other people were speaking
for me. I have observed this phenomenon before. For example, in
literature. Here people, lies the answer to that unanimity of thought
which has become established. We are all double-dealers, hypocrites
and Tartuffes. But we practice double-dealing with rapture, engage in
hypocrisy with a sincerity which does not stop at tears, and if we are
Tartuffes, we are Tartuffes of a singular kind — with real stigmata.[31]

Here "underground" confusion becomes the basis for penetrating social
criticism. Erenburg, like Pilnyak and Voinova, seems to relate the
appearance of the "underground" type (with double-dealing as an
essential characteristic) to the general social climate. At the same time,
Erenburg's presentation of other men and women in his novel is such
as to suggest that Volodia is projecting his own ambivalence upon society.

Volodia, like the Underground Man, can neither effectively struggle
against reality nor make peace with it. He is immobilized by contradictory impulses. His reason undermines his will to action by telling
him that he is a sick man, a cripple. The Underground Man, seeking a
foundation for action, had malice; but he lacked the consciousness of
the right to be malicious; even in moments of the most intense ex-
asperation with people he would realize that he was not malicious, and
not even a malicious man. Volodia is immobilized by a similar doubt
over his right to place himself above the new society.

---

[28]   Dostoevskij, *Zapiski iz podpol'ja, op. cit.,* IV, 141.
[29]   Ehrenburg, *Out of Chaos, op. cit.,* p. 226.
[30]   *Ibid.,* p. 227.
[31]   *Ibid.,* p. 228.

It is impossible, of course, to despise the bees or the rain. Moreover, I have no right to despise anybody. . . . Whether because of class instinct, or because of my blood, or, finally, because of my frame of mind, I have become attached to a dying culture. It follows that I am not fit for constructive work. . . . Vladimir Safonov is condemned by history as an untimely phenomenon. . . . ahead of me is only darkness.[32]

Like many "underground" heroes, Volodia fails in the one realm which could bring him some happiness: love. He cannot join his life with that of the school teacher, Irina. Albov's Glazkov left the seamstress Katya because he realized that his love was destructive. Volodia has the same awareness with regard to his relations with Irina. He fears that he will pass on his "disease" to her — a disease of consciousness. Irina herself knows that Volodia does not want her to live like other people, but wants to drag her into a "stuffy underground world". Volodia's relations with Irina have a certain "underground" character. Egotism, boredom, spleen, self-dissatisfaction lead, on one occasion, to a scene in which he besmirches his character, tells Irina that he hates her, torments her, and then, finally, confesses: "You are perfectly right. All my talk about hatred is pure affectation, mere venting of boredom." [33]

Erenburg not only indicates that the path of the "underground" man leads to disaster, but he tries to rehabilitate the man of action. Kolka Rzhanov, Volodia's working class antithesis and a central figure in Erenburg's novel, is not a vulgarization of the successful man of action. He is a person capable of genuine feeling, he is possessed of a simple dignity. But he is two-dimensional and is lacking in the rich and varied tones, the genuine passion, of Volodia's personality. At a meeting devoted to the discussion of *Out of Chaos* (the Russian title is *Second Day*), Erenburg recognized that alongside of Volodia Safonov "there is no one else. But, comrades, we have not yet reached the sixth day, and the man who ought to be placed alongside of him has not yet appeared." [34]

It is the school teacher Irina who provides the key to Erenburg's ambivalent feelings towards Volodia. Irina, who at first was in love with Volodia and later marries Kolka Rzhanov, symbolically unites two extremes, two types of personalities. "And that girl who is for me, personally, the main figure in the novel — I will be frank, not Kolka and not Safonov are for me the main characters, because I was at all times

[32]   *Ibid.*, pp. 150-151.
[33]   *Ibid.*, p. 156.
[34]   "Obsuždenie romana Erenburga 'Den' vtoroj'," *Literaturnyj kritik*, No. 7-8 (1934), p. 289.

with Irina — she moves away from Volodia and unites with Kolka." [35]

It is Volodia who teaches Irina to hate the base and the vulgar; it is Kolka who introduces the active element into Irina's life, the determination to do something about the baseness in life. It is not the socialist idea that is base, Irina believes; it is simply that people are full of the old baseness. "I want to join in the common struggle as well as the common mistakes," Irina observes, in what is probably the most unambiguous expression of Erenburg's point of view, "for do something I must, and not merely sit with my hands folded." [36] "After all," remarks the Underground Man, "the direct, legitimate, immediate fruit of consciousness is inertia, that is, the conscious sitting with hands folded." [37] Irina rejects Volodia's "underground" inertia.

Through his characterization of Irina, Erenburg rejects "underground" thinking primarily for its sterility, negativeness and self-destructive nature. His acceptance of Soviet reality seems based not so much on optimistic view of the immediate situation as on the belief that only through participation in Soviet reality can the baseness in life be destroyed. Irina, significantly, approaches her participation in Soviet reconstruction with the realization that it will not be "a heaven of rest, but a veritable hell". [38]

Erenburg's *Out of Chaos* cannot be fully comprehended apart from the author's clear desire to disengage himself from "underground" thinking, from regarding the "underground" as a key to an evaluation of Soviet reality. Yet in rejecting Volodia's "underground" orientation to Soviet reality, Erenburg does not reject Volodia as an individual; he has invested his hero with real pathos. Erenburg, like Dostoevsky in *Notes from the Underground,* is close to his hero and experiences deeply his problems and contradictions.

The long monologues of Volodia are filled not only with the familiar Erenburg irony and sarcasm, but with pain and despair; these monologues disclose the complexity of the position of many Soviet intellectuals — people who were emotionally and intellectually alienated from Soviet life, who saw instead of a new culture only cranes and infants. The tragedy of Volodia Safonov is a record of some of the contradictions and convulsions that have accompanied the revolutionary transformation in the Soviet Union.

[35]   *Ibid.,* p. 289.
[36]   Ehrenburg, *Out of Chaos, op. cit.,* p. 163.
[37]   Dostoevskij, *Zapiski iz podpol'ja, op. cit.,* IV, 118.
[38]   Ehrenburg, *Out of Chaos, op. cit.,* p. 163.

"It would be interesting to see how the heroes of Dostoevsky adapted themselves to the period of dialectical materialism,"[39] Volodia ruminates. Volodia Safonov himself, of course, is an answer to this question. Like the Underground Man he can see nothing but a "wall", and like the Underground Man he cannot reconcile himself to it. "For me they are not human," he remarks of his contemporaries. "All alike — it's called a 'collective' — in simple words — a wall. Inevitably I crushed my head. I cannot be cross with them. They are made of different clay."[40]

Out of Chaos is Erenburg's attempt at reconciliation with the "wall" of Soviet reality. In his panorama of Russia in reconstruction — in the "second day" of creation of a new society — Erenburg depicts the Dostoevsky "underground" as an increasingly isolated part of Soviet life. Erenburg did not crush his head against the "wall" of Soviet life. But the difficulty and complexity of his decision to reconcile himself with Soviet reality is contained in his subtle portrait of one of the last and unrepentant "underground" heroes in Russian literature — Volodia Safonov.

³⁹   *Ibid.*, p. 314.
⁴⁰   *Ibid.*, p. 354.

CHAPTER XXII

LEONID LEONOV AND
NOTES FROM THE UNDERGROUND

> Now I ask you: what can one expect from man, a
> creature endowed with such strange qualities? Go
> ahead and shower him with all kinds of earthly bless-
> ings, drown him in happiness right up to his neck ...
> satisfy his economic needs so that nothing would be
> left for him to do except sleep, eat cakes and worry
> about keeping world history going—and even then he
> will, man will, out of sheer ungratefulness, out of
> spite, play a dirty trick on you.
>
> The Underground Man

Lack of faith in man and in his ability to achieve his dream of happiness, and fear of that dream in its rationalist form, constitute the philosophical axis of *Notes from the Underground*. Man is irrational; man is selfish; man is impotent in his knowledge of good and evil. It is this despairing portrait of man that Dostoevsky holds up before the utopian socialists, rationalists and utilitarians, so that they may compare this image of man with their idealized version.

Leonid Leonov in his early writings shares much of Dostoevsky's lack of faith in man and his fear of a rationalistic distortion of socialism. The revolution to Leonov is a powerful, elemental and liberating force, but man still remains a zoological creature. "The new chairman," writes the chronicler of Gogulev, A. P. Kovyakin, "is continually threatening to put electricity into every home so as to check up on what is going on and who is doing it. ... So we go on living, but civilization as we know it is no more. On the other hand, I have even a greater pain in the small of my back."[1] Leonov is not sure that the revolution can free man from the power of his "underground" instincts.

Among the works in which themes and motifs of the "underground" echo are "The End of a Petty Man" ("Konets melkogo cheloveka", 1924), *The Thief* (*Vor*, 1927), "Untilovsk" ("Untilovsk", 1927), "Provincial Story" ("Provintsialnaya istoriya", 1927) and *Skutarevsky* (*Skutarevsky*, 1932).

---

[1] Leonid Leonov, "Zapisi nekotorykh èpizodov, sdelannye v gorode Goguleve Andreem Petrovičem Kovjakinym," *Rasskazy* (Moscow, [n.d.]), p. 10.

In "The End of a Petty Man" Leonov depicts the perishing ot
members of the old world intelligentsia; all that remains to this intelligentsia is egotism. The Underground Man was sceptical of the highminded — those "wise lovers of humanity" who try to conduct themselves "in as moral and sensible a way as possible . . .". Such moral
people, the Underground Man believed, sooner or later are false to
themselves, "playing some queer trick, often a most unseemly one".[2]
There are no moral or highminded intellectuals in Dr. Elkov's "menagerie" — a stinking "underground" filled with spiteful, frustrated and
disgusting beings. Nobody — shouts the hysterical Captain Titus — has
the right to expect or demand anything of man, any "highminded acts".
What is more, "all highmindedness is meaningless, the highminded will
not survive".[3] Titus resolves the problem of his participation in the
revolution in the egocentric manner characteristic of some of Dostoevsky's heroes: "After all, when he, Titus, dies, then nothing will remain
at all for him, for Titus! So he'll spit on the whole business!"[4]

Professor Likharev descends into Dr. Elkov's "menagerie"; he is a
paleontologist, divorced from life, sunk in the "deaf ice fields and perfect
quiet of antedeluvian times".[5] Complete indifference to the world and
to human beings is his central feature.

Is it really possible to go anywhere with the men of the revolution,
the sceptic Elkov asks Likharev, and goes on to observe:

Indeed, is it really possible, my little dove, to erect delicate buildings
with dirty hands! Moreover, they will, if you please, steal this whole
delicate house brick by brick. What are you laughing at? Just watch,
in about five little years you will see, Maybe, if you give them all a
flogging, then, perhaps, but — no; even then nothing will come of it![6]

The master of the "menagerie", filled with spiteful, cunning creatures
who lie and steal, does not believe in "delicate buildings" (the "crystal
palace" of *Notes from the Underground*); he can visualize society only
as a gigantic "menagerie" dominated by the ethics of the animal kingdom, just as the Underground Man makes of his "underground" a
symbol for the moral-spiritual condition of all mankind.

Here there is "underground" egotism, also. "Now Elkov assures us,"

[2]   Dostoevskij, *Zapiski iz podpol'ja, op. cit.*, IV, 127.
[3]   Leonov, "Konec melkogo čeloveka," *Rasskazy, op. cit.*, pp. 124-125.
[4]   *Ibid.*, p. 127.
[5]   *Ibid.*, p. 97.
[6]   *Ibid.*, pp. 130-131.

Likharev's double — his mocking *alter ego* — observes in conversation with Likharev, "that they will steal brick by brick. ... He wants destruction because in it rests all his justification!"[7] But "joking aside" — Likharev's double goes on to support Elkov's ideas:

Do you think that in reality they will not steal? After all, are these really people? Bubbles on an eternal slime, bubbles and a stench within, that's all. Ah, Fedor Andreich, oh, my dear one — one cannot be such a child in these days. Why fear the truth? Dirt — it is just dirt — why ask from it various highminded acts! ... [What kind of acts — asks Likharev.] Acts of humanity, humanity most excellent sir, that's what! For highmindedness, for truth it is necessary to pay in blood, and blood is worth more than any truths.[8]

Likharev's double returns his ticket to future harmony.

Egotism, selfishness, inertia, the "eternal slime" stands in the way of a bright future. Delicate buildings will never be built on eternal slime. The zoological, proprietary instinct — not highmindedness — will prevail in the end. "Vanka" — the Russian everyman — will go tomorrow to "lay bricks, to construct a delicate building to the amazement of the whole world, and to the terror of the millions of Elkovs".[9] But this same "Vanka" will drag away the bricks.

The "petty man" Likharev found the deprivations and sacrifices of the revolution too great and came to the conclusion, shared by the other members of Elkov's "menagerie", that "blood is worth more than any truths".

Leonov's "The End of a Petty Man" and Dostoevsky's *Notes from the Underground* are linked by an all-pervading scepticism. For both Dostoevsky and Leonov there is an unbridgeable distance separating the miserable reality of man from the realization of earthly happiness. Both Dostoevsky and Leonov measure this distance in terms of man's unfitness for the good life; man is a prisoner of the "underground".

When Likharev burns his manuscripts, his *alter ego* remarks: "Now Russia will shoot upwards. The sky will be filled with concrete, tramroads will line the sky. ... Bread will be made of air ... people will wear velvet trousers. ..."[10] Leonov, like Erenburg, feared in communism the triumph of the machine over man.

---

[7] *Ibid.*, p. 138.
[8] *Ibid.*, p. 139.
[9] *Ibid.*, p. 139.
[10] *Ibid.*, p. 182.

Leonov expresses his fear of rationalistic socialism in the story of the fierce Kalafat in *The Badgers* (*Barsuki*, 1925). The mythical Kalafat, pained by the lack of "system" in his father's kingdom, came to the conclusion that it was necessary to live according to the science of geometry. So he set to work:

He branded the fish, issued passports to the birds and noted down every blade of grass in a book. And everything around him grew sad. . . . And it was no joke: everything in nature was thrown into confusion. The bear pined away; he didn't know whether he was a man or an animal now that he had been handed a passport. And then Kalafat took it into his head to build a tower to the heavens. "I'll have a look," he said, "and see what kind of view there is from there. And in passing I'll brand the stars!" [11]

The tower, five years in building, sank into the ground with each step of Kalafat, and in the end the woods and animals were left as before. "The fields were fragrant with the smell of flowers, and the birds were in the fields. Nature had thrown off Kalafat's passport." [12] Leonov is convinced that nature, elemental life must in the end triumph over any attempt at an ordering of the universe along rationalistic lines, over any attempt to "label the stars".

". . . Every epoch is the apotheosis of triumphant banality," the little man Chizh declares in Artsybashev's *At the Last Boundary*. The New Economic Policy (NEP) appears just such an apotheosis to Leonov in his novel *The Thief* (1927). The "eternal slime" which Leonov writes about in "The End of a Petty Man" is spreading out over revolutionary Russia. The passionate heroism, romanticism and militant idealism of the revolution and civil war has given way to the narrow petty bourgeois habits and aims of the NEP. "You will say again," old Manyukin writes in his notebook, "that the train is still moving through the darkness of the tunnel and has not yet reached the light at the other side of the mountain. But isn't the tunnel rather long, Nikolasha? Has it an exit at all? Look out, or you will be crushed!" [13]

Mitya Vekshin, hero of the civil war and hero of *The Thief*, is lost in the darkness of the NEP tunnel; the revolution for him was "national . . . the wild unrest of Russian blood before a fabulous blossoming". [14]

[11]   Leonov, *Barsuki, Sobranie sočinenij v pjati tomakh* (Moscow, 1953-1954), I, 264-265.
[12]   *Ibid.*, I, 265.
[13]   Leonov, *Vor* (Moscow, 1936), p. 150.
[14]   *Ibid.*, p. 45.

Mitya rebels against the bureaucratic NEP in the name of an almost inarticulate faithfulness to the revolution; Mitya the thief represents a romantic but angry protest against the enveloping darkness, against the new supremacy of the bureaucrat. Mitya cannot comprehend his old friend Atashez, now sitting before four telephones. "Where have you thrown your 'boorka' the nice warm shaggy coat we slept under the night before Lukoyanov?"[15] Mitya asks Atashez. But there is no longer a point of contact between these two men — the one, wild, explosive, irrational, the other subjecting himself to the new rational-administrative orientation of the revolution.

Bolshevism with its practical concerns, its faith in plans, its passion for organization and integration, enters into a strange union with petty bourgeois philistinism and vulgarity in Leonov's *The Thief*. The result is a strange hybrid phenomenon: "Chikilevism" — named after Petr Gorbidonich Chikilev, Chairman of a House Committee in charge of a section of flats. Chikilev is an old acquaintance in a new role: the Underground Man as a Soviet bureaucrat. Chikilev is petty, opportunistic, spiteful, and cowardly. He is the "malicious kind who spits at the world",[16] a shabbily formed creature with a red beard, who has "no face, but only a mask which altered its expression according to what insane devil possessed its master".[17]

The chief characteristic of this guardian of morals is his unrelenting bureaucratic insistence on fulfillment of house regulations. He is always checking up on people, watching them, spying on them. If the state were to think up a thousand degrees, Chikilev declares, "I myself would think out the thousand and first and carry it out with zeal".[18]

"You'll get a tram car to leave its rails," say Chikilev, "before you get me to leave my habits."[19] This petty fiend, with his love of order and regulations, this little despot resembles the Underground Man in many ways. The fact that the Underground Man argued against the "ant hill" state, whereas Chikilev argues in favor of it, does not alter a basic kinship between these two "underground" men. The Underground Man, despite his rebellious nature, as a government clerk "slavishly worshipped routine in everything external", "loved to fall into the common rut",[20] and in his relations with petitioners, in fact with all

[15]   *Ibid.*, p. 125.
[16]   *Ibid.*, p. 34.
[17]   *Ibid.*, p. 160.
[18]   *Ibid.*, p. 400.
[19]   *Ibid.*, p. 197.
[20]   Dostoevskij, *Zapiski iz podpol'ja, op. cit.*, IV, 139.

people, friend or foe, exhibited a despotism and craving for power that
knew no bounds. The failure of the Underground Man in the service
was no more than a failure to alter his status in the "ant hill" from that
of a humiliated and abused ant into one that does the humiliating and
abusing.

It is Dostoevsky's Liputin (*The Devils*) — a "despicable little figure
of a provincial official, a jealous husband and coarse family despot, a
miser and a money-lender . . . and at the same time a fiercely fanatical
believer in God knows what kind of a future 'social harmony', who at
nights went into ecstasies over fantastic pictures of the future phalanstery . . ." [21] — it is this "Fourierist with a strong leaning towards police
work"[22] who is the bridge connecting the Underground Man with
Chikilev. "You're simply the golden mean which will get on everywhere
in your own way,"[23] Stepan Verkhovensky observes to Liputin. With
these words Dostoevsky stamps "underground" man's passport to the
future. It is just this "underground" lack of principle, this opportunism
and readiness to adapt to, and profit from, any situation, that characterizes Chikilev; he has, as Leonov notes, simply "adapted to circumstances".[24]

Chikilev, like Liputin (and the Underground Man in his idealistic
youth) is a passionate believer in social harmony of a well-organized,
well-integrated sort. But Chikilev is most clearly connected, in his ideas,
with Dostoevsky's Shigalev (*The Devils*). The name Chikilev itself
seems an obvious play on Shigalev.[25] Chikilev's plan for the future
state — in which people will be of the same size and weight — recalls
Shigalev's plans for future harmony. Chikilev declares:

In the future state which will come in a thousand years, no secrets will
be permitted. Anyone, please note, will be able to come to anyone else
and observe his life at any time of the day or night, as though through a
magnifying glass! For, perhaps you are entertaining the idea of destroying humanity? With the modern achievements of science — the
death ray, sneezing gas! — in one moment you could blow the whole
world to smithereens. Man must be watched, man must not be left
unwatched. No little secrets, come out, come out onto the square please,
citizen, and make a clean breast of it. Then willy-nilly everybody will

[21]   Dostoevskij, *Besy, op. cit.,* VII, 45.
[22]   *Ibid.,* p. 184.
[23]   *Ibid.,* p. 28.
[24]   Leonov, *Vor, op. cit.,* p. 158.
[25]   Gleb Struve notes the parallel between Chikilev and Shigalev in his book,
25 Years of Soviet Russian Literature (London, 1946), p. 48.

be honest; whether you like it or not, you'll have to put up with it. If I, say, was the ruler of the earth, I would put on every man's head a sort of machine, with a kind of telegraph tape. In the morning a specially appointed official would read off the ribbon and affix his resolution — and everybody would be able to look in the same way into the head of his controller. Thought — there is the source of suffering. The one who destroys thought will be eulogized by a grateful mankind.[26]

Chikilev's blueprint of the future state yields nothing in boldness of conception to Zamyatin's Single State.

Characteristically, Chikilev imagines himself the ruler of such a society.

If I were a ruler I should order all authors to look at life from its cheerful side: let everyone laugh. I would even impose laughter on the whole globe under penalty of being torn to pieces by wild beasts if you disobeyed!![27]

Leonov, like Dostoevsky, discloses the Shigalevian dream-ideal of the man from the "underground". "Without power and tyrannizing over someone I cannot really live,"[28] the Underground Man confessed.

Chikilevism for Leonov is the rot of the NEP. Chikilev emerges as the symbol of the rationalism threatening the revolution, of the degeneration of revolutionary idealism. The rationalistic ideal also permeates the thinking of the worker Matvey:

When one day men discover everything, and measure and weigh and calculate everything, when they get to know the numbers, temperatures and the color of things, when they are in a position to change everything, then there will be happiness. Happiness, my dear, can be made as easily as galoshes or that electric bulb there. . . . One must learn! Then happiness without suffering will come.[29]

But Zinka, Matvey's sister, inquires laughingly: "Happiness without suffering, you say? . . . Then happiness is to be manufactured in factories, is it?"[30] Happines without suffering — happiness that was as simple and certain as "twice two is four" — this was the rationalistic ideal which Dostoevsky attacks and ridicules in *Notes from the Underground*.

[26] Leonov, *Vor, op. cit.,* pp. 217-218.
[27] *Ibid.,* p. 255.
[28] Dostoevskij, *Zapiski iz podpol'ja, op. cit.,* IV, 191.
[29] Leonov, *Vor, op. cit.,* p. 168.
[30] *Ibid.,* p. 168.

Leonov in *The Thief* finds in suffering a permanent condition of human existence, and a force capable of transforming the individual. In *The Thief*, the living, suffering complex human being contrasts with the debased man that would be the product of Chikilevism.

In his play "Untilovsk" (1927) Leonov again expresses his fear of the influence of the "underground" on the revolution. But now the "eternal slime" threatening the revolution is confined to Untilovsk, a place of exile in the far north. The ex-priest Buslov speaks of the "Untilovsk stink" and remarks of the world beyond Untilovsk: "They are frightening the world with new words, and what words! The more threatening their madness, the sweeter the Untilovsk home brew. With them it's an eagle — with us, a grating. . . ."[31]

Untilovsk is the "underground" and, as in Andreev's cage filled with filthy birds ("The Curse of the Beast"), the atmosphere is foul and disgusting. ". . . I am a disgusting creature," the Underground Man says of himself, "I am the nastiest, most ridiculous, most petty, most stupid of all worms on earth. . . ."[32] Such a worm is the rat exterminator Pavel Chervakov[33] — the living symbol of Untilovsk.

"I am Untilovsk!" profoundly declares Chervakov. "Our snows are empty and our hearts are humble, shrivelled up. Our sun is small, not very powerful."[34] "You are darkness, Pashka, gloom," Buslov says to Chervakov.[35] "I am more complex than you," says Chervakov. "The insides of a spider are always more complex than the stellar system," Buslov retorts.[36] Leonov has no doubt as to the real character of "underground" complexity.

Pavel Chervakov is a grimacing, disgusting vulgarian, but like his predecessor the Underground Man he is "a man of the head, a thinker". Chervakov is a philosopher who views the future with the same scepticism as the Underground Man. He observes of the tranquility of life around Untilovsk:

And in three hundred years, how this tranquility will screech, set off, transfixed by some electric beam there. He! He! Along the lacquered avenues, under an electric moon walk smart, red-cheeked humble

[31] Leonov, "Untilovsk," *Novyj mir*, No. 3 (1928), p. 46.
[32] Dostoevskij, *Zapiski iz podpol'ja, op. cit.,* IV, 190.
[33] The name Chervakov is an obvious play on the Russian word "červjak" which means "worm."
[34] Leonov, "Untilovsk," *op. cit.,* p. 68.
[35] *Ibid.,* p. 42.
[36] *Ibid.,* p. 43.

descendants! Humble people who have developed beyond their very selves. Oh, and it will be boring in that wished-for time, Raisochka, bo-o-oring.[37]

With frank cynicism Chervakov opposes the pure egoism of Untilovsk to the utopian future, just as the Underground Man opposes man's egoistic self-will to the utopian plans of the rationalists. "Untilovism," Chervakov declares, will give battle to man's humble descendants.

... We will still battle with our intrusive descendants. (He cries out, raging:) Comrades! Observe strict order in centuries! Put to death before its time, Untilovsk will rise like the Phoenix. We are for peace, but if we have to fight — we have enough spittle for three hundred years! We have one horse, but a faithful one.[38]

Such is the "underground" Chervakov's challenge to the thousands of "frantic" Buslovs who are "piling up a tower there so that it will collapse more terribly and kill with its bricks. But we will live in hovels! We are bored with Babylonian structures!"[39] Chervakov's ideal is the stagnant tranquility of frozen Untilovsk, the "underground" security of the hovel.

The future belongs to Untilovsk, according to Chervakov. A scholarly fool, Chervakov relates, built himself a time machine, a lounge car without wheels, in which to travel about. When the Bolsheviks took away his piano, shot his son, he conceived the idea of taking off — "not out of the city, my little charmer, but out of his great and troublesome epoch." But instead of shooting "twenty years to the other side of our heaven", he shot a million years ahead (the little lever in the machine broke), into the 10,000th century. And when he looked out of his little window he found neither land, nor sun, just naked emptiness — "a great hole", "one continuous Untilovsk".[40]

Leonov exposes the "underground" in his play "Untilovsk". "Untilovism" is "underground" egoism, cynicism and stagnation. Leonov, like Erenburg in *Out of Chaos*, links "underground" psychology with political counterrevolution.

But while Leonov in "Untilovsk" exposes the "underground", he still remains fearful of the power of the "underground", the power of "Untilovism". An element of Leonov's own scepticism is felt in Chervakov's sarcastic tirades against the future utopia.

[37] *Ibid.*, p. 67.
[38] *Ibid.*, p. 67.
[39] *Ibid.*, p. 67.
[40] *Ibid.*, p. 68.

Leonov's scepticism is felt again in his story, "Provincial Story" ("Provintsialnaya istoriya", 1928), in which the brothers Andrey and Yakov Pustynnov stand in relation to one another as "underground" man to man of action. Yakov — to whom everything comes easily and painlessly, Yakov — with a forehead "stubborn as a battering ram which beats at the gates of a besieged city", this Yakov will be an engineer. The father of Yakov and Andrey observes to Akhamazikov:

Yakov is clever, but he is a queer one. He thinks they [the Bolsheviks] will give him palaces and towers to erect. They will make him build sheds and dog houses! . . . They will construct machines which will milk the world like a cow. . . . But the soul will remain the same as in the beginning of time. And nevertheless I am proud of Yashka, Akhamazikov. I bless you, Yashka! And over your shed strong people will pass, not vile people, not us — they will pass and say: "Doff your hat, here a man labored!" But Andrey, my elder son, — who, who will say in a thousand years: "Doff your hat, — here a man suffered!" Hey? you don't think they'll say it? Descendants, I despise you! [41]

"Suffering is an infirmity; it must be cured. And we will cure it," declares the self-confident new man, Yakov. But Leonov, like Dostoevsky, rejects the rationalist simplification of human existence, rejects a state of society in which suffering is ignored or denied. Besides, the optimism of Yakov must contend with dark, inert forces. "Yashka thinks that life can be stirred up by a paragraph," the old Pustynnov remarks. "No — life exists on an earth that is dark and — not innocent." [42]

In his novel *Skutarevsky* (1932) Leonov, like Erenburg in *Out of Chaos,* tries to disengage himself from "underground" thinking; he evaluates it in class terms and interprets it as an aspect of counter-revolution. This class approach is implicit in "Untilovsk", but it is only in *Skutarevsky* that Leonov's tragic view of man is counterbalanced by a confidence in the Bolshevik path.

". . . Dostoevsky," Gorky observed in his address before the First Soviet Writer's Congress (1934), "in the figure of his hero [the Underground Man] has shown the depths of whining despair that are reached by the individualist from among the young men of the nineteenth and twentieth centuries who are divorced from life." [43] Arseny Skutarevsky, son of the scientist Sergey Skutarevsky, is such an "individualist".

---

[41] Leonov, "Provincial'naja istorija," *Izbrannye proizvedenija* (Moscow, 1934). pp. 238-239.
[42] *Ibid.,* p. 206.
[43] "Doklad A. M. Gor'kogo o sovetskoj literature," *Pervyj vsesojuznyj s'ezd sovetskikh pisatelej 1934* (Moscow, 1934), p. 11.

Egocentric, weak-willed and self-pitying, Arseny Skutarevsky is torn between the old world, to which he is drawn by temperament, and the new world in which he works. Behind Arseny looms the ponderous figure of the anti-Soviet Petrygin, and before him is the figure of the Bolshevik worker-engineer Cherimov, his civil war comrade. Arseny is drawn into Petrygin's underground world of inner emigrés, but his romantic soul reaches out towards Cherimov.

In *The Thief*, Leonov sides with the romantic revolutionary Mitya in his conflict with the Bolshevik bureaucrat Atashez; in Skutarevsky, Leonov sides with the Bolshevik Cherimov as opposed to the romantic revolutionary, Arseny Skutarevsky. Leonov rejects the romantic revolutionism of Arseny as something which only created "a justification for himself and his existence . . .".[44] Arseny's romanticism is disclosed as an unwillingness to meet the demands of reality. "Go away for a while to some new construction work," Cherimov tells Arseny, "where any one stroke is worth a whole page of the sort of thing we did at the front."[45] But Arseny cannot face the task of building socialism with the exuberance, strength and confidence of Cherimov; he says:

And if we are weary? We are striding through history barefoot and you think it doesn't hurt. And must one be ashamed to speak of this? Once there was youth and romance; now we have the state, law. And then — this Socialism, isn't it for human beings? I am even prepared to recognize anyone's right to sit around and paint pictures of cottages, if he gets sick of battling, struggling, not sleeping at night, if he gets sick of pleasing you and every minute trying to earn your approval. And perhaps some man — I, for example — wants to go to the Malay Archipelago to cut down baobab trees with his own hands?[46]

"I agree that twice two is four is a magnificent thing," the Underground Man observes, "but when everything is said and done, twice two is five is sometimes an exceedingly pleasant thing."[47]

Arseny Skutarevsky, like the Underground Man and Kavalerov (*Envy*), supports the individual's absolute right of self-determination. There is a familiar "underground" malice — a deliberate desire to mock — in Arseny's insistence on man's right even to the most absurd behavior. Arseny Skutarevsky is repelled by a land in which they always look for "guilty people" when there is an accident. Arseny accuses the Bolsheviks

[44] Leonov, *Skutarevskij, Sobranie sočinenij v pjati tomakh, op. cit.*, III, 76.
[45] *Ibid.*, III, 109.
[46] *Ibid.*, III, 77-78.
[47] Dostoevskij, *Zapiski iz podpol'ja, op. cit.*, IV, 130.

of what the Underground Man accuses the rationalists: a lack of respect for human beings. Arseny sees in his father — a scientist supporting the Bolsheviks — a symbol of deadly rationalism. He tells his father:

. . . No, I know your views about the state having a right to dispose in a rational way of its stock, so to speak, of human material. And if the experiment fails, one must wash out the retort and pour it all down the drain. Or then again, perhaps, simply break it. These are your own words: there's no use pining over the loss of every single species. I heard that when I was a boy. Even then, you know, you forgave this earth everything: wars, brothels, crusades, dreams à la Jenghis Khan and Torquemada. And this not out of any weak goodheartedness, not from any inadequacy of intellect, but simply because all this appears to you as electro-chemical processes. . . . You don't even see political economy whose cruel mandates we feel upon us. All you can see is the movement of atoms along Laplace co-ordinates, a complex chemical reaction, an accumulation of billions of laws, a draught of electrons — that's what the world means to you! [48]

You see, I'm only a retort in your eyes, but then so is everybody else, eh? And mankind as a whole? Does it fit your dogma? . . . Tell me, now, you bulwark of Soviet power, where is the man in whose name all this is being done? [49]

Arseny Skutarevsky's impassioned protest is in the spirit of all "underground" protest against those who place themselves above history and above suffering, who regard men not for their intrinsic worth but only as a means to an end.

But Arseny Skutarevsky's voice is isolated in Leonov's *Skutarevsky*. Soviet society, as Leonov presents it in *Skutarevsky,* is not Chervakov's regimented, boring utopia transfixed by some electric beam. Arseny is presented as a weak, whining, self-indulgent egotist, spiritually disintegrating because of a fundamental divorce from real life.

Arseny perishes because of his ambivalent orientation towards Soviet society. He does not accept Soviet reality, but neither does he accept, in the last analysis, the conspiratorial, moribund world of his uncle, Petrygin. He is unable to get out of the "Dantesque depths" into which he has been drawn. He could see clearly that the rising class was easily overcoming the resistance of the few that opposed it.

And suddenly there arose in his diseased imagination the roar and cannon smoke of a new intervention; he saw children burned by gas, people mown down by bacteria, red hot metal dancing among devastated

[48]   Leonov, *Skutarevskij, op. cit.,* III, 56.
[49]   *Ibid.,* III, 56-57.

cities. He wavered, and this split in him threatened catastrophe. .... He fled from phantoms created by his own imagination, and all the time there was a something which was chasing him from which he could no more escape than he could escape from his own shadow.[50]

Like the Underground Man, Arseny is essentially a romantic and a dreamer; he is ready to meet Cherimov on a lofty plane of reconciliation. Even at the moment of complete psychological breakdown, Arseny imagines himself telling all to Cherimov. "And were it only in response to his greatness of heart — he clung to that phrase! — Cherimov would offer him the hand of friendship and even, possibly, consent to go with him on an expiatory trip to Garass' grave, to the taiga."[51] But Arseny's sentimental dreaming is only a manifestation of his complete separation from reality. Unable to resolve the contradictions of a divided consciousness, Arseny commits suicide. Like Erenburg's Volodia Safonov, Arseny Skutarevsky could neither adapt to Soviet reality nor live outside it.

The "underground" in Leonov's *Road to the Ocean* (*Doroga na okean*, 1935) is disclosed as an anachronism in Soviet life, a disgusting but impotent survival of the old world. Two aged human beings, Dudnikov and Pokhvisnev, rivals for a woman's love fifty years ago, sit opposite each other in a dark, musty basement; they sit in silence and are filled with hatred. This is a grave, a "miserable and doomed underground".[52] Dudnikov — like the poet Khromulin in "The End of a Petty Man" — regards Russia as dead; but he envies the new.

Here one thing was clear: he was mixing up the visitor's profession solely out of obduracy and the frenzy of boredom. The new era appeared to him only as a dishonest and senseless bustle of ignoramuses — but he heard the songs of youth flowing above his cave, and he envied them with the greediness of a huge body growing progressively colder.[53]

Leonov illuminates the "underground" just at the moment when its inhabitants are literally perishing. Dudnikov dies in his "underground" — together with his boredom, his envy and his impotent malice.

Leonov's scepticism over the future socialist society is displaced in *Road to the Ocean* by the sober optimism of his hero, Kurilov. The future that Kurilov envisages is not the rationalistic utopia of Chikilev. Kurilov, on his imaginary tour of the world of the future, called Ocean, remarks:

[50]   *Ibid.*, III, 238.
[51]   *Ibid.*, III, 238.
[52]   Leonov, *Doroga na okean, Sobranie sočinenij v pjati tomakh, op. cit.*, IV, 70.
[53]   *Ibid.*, IV, 73.

Not astonished at the technical cunning of our descendants, we looked attentively at the people themselves. It seemed to us that human nature itself had improved. These people stood more erect, seemed more self-assured — whether because each one felt the presence of his neighbor and was not afraid of anything, or because the pure air of the new period did not contain the bacillus of falsehood. I was always expecting that they would boast of the perfection of their social order, and I would not have condemned their just pride, but they simply did not notice it. Here the natural state of man had been attained — he was free, he delighted in the work of his hands and thought, he was not exploited by anyone. But although they had everything — bread, work and fate itself, we often came across people with careworn faces. We understood that even among them there was sadness, that even they knew tragedy, but of a kind more worthy of man's dignity.[54]

There can be no happiness without suffering, Leonov asserts in *The Thief*. Leonov regards suffering and tragedy as an integral part of human existence in Ocean. Man has reached his "natural state", but he has not ceased to be a man; man has achieved "perfection" in social order, but he has not been transformed into a mathematical unit. Leonov's Ocean is free of the tyranny of dogmatic rationalism; it is not a crystal palace. What distinguishes Leonov's Ocean is that reason and feeling are reunited in the individual, science is dominated by man (and not man by science) and, above all, suffering remains an integral part of human existence.

[54]   *Ibid.*, IV, 397.

CONCLUSION

The long and short of it, gentlemen: better to do
nothing! Better—conscious inertia! And so—hurrah
for the underground! Although I have said that I
envy the normal man to the last drop of my bile, yet
in the condition in which I see him, I wouldn't care to
take his place (although I still won't stop envying him.
No, no, the underground is in any case more advantageous!) There, at least, one can ... Ah! But
even here I am lying! I am lying because I myself
know, as twice two is four, that it is not at all the
underground which is better, but something else, quite
different, for which I thirst, but which I can in no
way find! The hell with the underground!

The Underground Man

The themes and motifs of *Notes from the Underground* became a part
of Russian literature; the Underground Man — a literary archetype.
The Underground Man takes many forms — from the pitiful, humiliated
"little man" through the hypersensitive students and intellectuals to
the noxious professional anti-hero; but all are people whose feelings,
strivings, ambitions and ideals have been driven "underground"; their
tortured natures, their fractured personalities bear witness to their
permanent estrangement.

In the pre-revolutionary period these "underground" men gave expression to the despairing, often nihilistic protest of the individual
against an enveloping isolation, stagnation and darkness. This "underground" protest is directed, after 1917, against conformity, utilitarian
morality and the supremacy of the new Soviet man of action — the
functional and rational new man. The man from the "underground"
remained the same as he had been before 1917: an intransigent "outsider", unable and unwilling to participate wholly in the life about him,
condemned by his nature and by his social situation to insecurity, suffering and the disintegration accompanying estrangement, a fatality of the
centrifugal force of the revolution which hurls to destruction all those
who do not cling firmly to the "wheel of history".

What distinguishes the "underground" man in both periods is his
wholly conscious — and therefore often cynical — recognition and
acceptance of his condition, a readiness to follow to the end the logic

of his alienated position. His alienation is not a temporary refuge or defense, but a permanent position, the basis for his entire personal and ideological assault on the world; forced into unnatural isolation, he becomes asocial; compelled to lead an irrational, conflict-ridden existence, he seizes upon irrationalism as a way of interpreting the meaning of life and combatting all the forces bearing down upon him. For his epigones the Underground Man provides a weapon of defense of the totally negated individual — a philosophy of "malice"; that this weapon cuts both ways, that it destroys both offender and offended is immaterial; it is protest, it is resistance, it is self-expression, however deformed. In this lies the paradox: these wild distortions of personality and behavior are expressions of a craving for self-respect, indeed, for a self to respect. This contradiction between the humane origins of "underground" rebellion and the nihilistic character of that rebellion is characteristic of the literature of the "underground". Gorky alone rejects this Dostoevskian paradox; he points to Dostoevsky as the source of much idealizing of psychic disorder, of petty bourgeois anarchism and of moral abandon.

Notes from the Underground is a monument to human suffering and despair and to the catastrophe of irrational rebellion. At the same time, it testifies to the truth that — as Dostoevsky wrote in *Notes from the House of the Dead* — "despite all measures, it is impossible to turn a living man into a corpse; he will remain with feelings, with the thirst for revenge and for life, with passions and with the need to satisfy them."[1]

Notes from the Underground and the literature of the "underground" are corrosive and depressing. It focuses attention directly upon the individual in his extreme distress; it dwells upon the dissonances, the discontinuities, the irrationalities in human life and upon the divorce of the individual from the world about him. That many writers have found in the "underground" the only refuge for the individual is a measure of his despair, but even more a measure of the forces oppressing him.

The literature of the "underground" from Dostoevsky to Leonov is part of a literary current — a sombre chapter in Russian literature which reflects the anxieties, contradictions and upheavals of the period. The West, too, has found in the "underground" type vital expression of some of its own most elusive and most difficult questions. Today the "underground" has not disappeared, and the "underground" man continues to live his tormented, angry and alienated existence.

---

[1] Dostoevskij, *Zapiski iz mertvogo doma, op. cit.*, III, 348.

BIBLIOGRAPHY

SOURCES

Al'bov, M. N., *Sobranie sočinenij*. 8 vols. St. Petersburg: A. F. Marks, 1908.

Andreev, L., *Polnoe sobranie sočinenij*. 8 vols. St. Petersburg: A. F. Marks, 1913.

Barbellion, W. N. P., *The Journal of a Disappointed Man*. With an Introduction by H. G. Wells. London: Chatto & Windus, 1919.

Brjusov, V., *Puti i pereput'ja*. Vol. I of *Sobranie stikhov*. Moscow: Skorpion, 1908.

——, "Respublika južnogo kresta," *Zemnaja os'*. Moscow: Skorpion, 1907, pp. 1-25.

Camus, A., *La chute*. Paris: Gallimard, 1956.

Černyševskij, N. G., *Čto delat'? Iz rasskazov o novykh ljudjakh*, Vol. IX of *Polnoe sobranie sočinenij*. St. Petersburg: Jablonskij, 1906.

Dostoevskij, F. M., *Polnoe sobranie khudožestvennykh proizvedenij*. 13 vols. Moscow and Leningrad: Gosizdat, 1926-1930. Vols. XI-XII contain *Diary of a Writer* and Vol. XIII contains articles of 1845-1878.

——, *Pis'ma*. Edited by A. S. Dolinin. Moscow and Leningrad: Vol. I, Gosizdat, 1928. Vol. II, Gosizdat, 1930. Vol. III, Academia, 1934.

——, *Ispoved' Stavrogina*. Vol. I of *Dokumenty po istorii literatury i obščestvennosti*. Moscow: Centrarkhiva RSFSR, 1922.

Duhamel, G., *Confession de minuit*. Paris: A. Fayard, 1927.

——, *Journal de Salavin*. Paris: A. Fayard, 1927.

Ehrenbourg, Ilya, *Out of Chaos*. Translated by Alexander Bakshy. New York: Henry Holt & Co., 1934.

Erenburg, Il'ja, *Den' vtoroj*. Moscow: Gozisdat, 1934.

——, *Neobyčajnye pokhoždenija Khulio Khurenito i ego učenikov*. Moscow-Berlin: Gelikon, 1922.

——, *Rvač*. Paris: Tipografy de Navarre, 1925.

Fedin, K., *Goroda i gody*. Leningrad: Gosizdat, 1924.

Garšin, V. M., *Polnoe sobranie sočinenij V. M. Garšina*. S portretom, avtobiografičeskim očerkom, vospominanijami o Vsev. Garšine v raznye epokhi ego žizni i kritičeskimi stat'jami. St. Petersburg: A. F. Marks, 1910.

——, *Pis'ma*. Edited by Ju. G. Oksman. Vol. III of *Polnoe Sobranie sočinenij*. Moscow: Akademija, 1934.

Gide, A., *L'immoraliste*. Paris: Mercure de France, 1946.

Gor'kij, M., *Sobranie sočinenij*. 2d ed. 25 vols. Moscow: Gosizdat, 1932-34.

——, *Sobranie sočinenij v 30 tomakh*. Moscow: Gosizdat, 1949-.

Hesse, H., *Der Steppenwolf*. Berlin: S. Fischer, 1927.

Kafka, F., *The Great Wall of China and other pieces*. Translated by Willa and Edwin Muir. London: Martin Secker, 1933.

Kuprin, A. I., *Polnoe sobranie sočinenij*. 8 vols. St. Petersburg: A. F. Marks, 1912.

Leonov, L., *Izbrannye proizvedenija*. Moscow: Sovetskaja literatura, 1934.

——, *Rasskazy*. Moscow: Krug. n.d.

——, *Sobranie sočinenij v pjati tomakh.* Moscow: Gosizdat, 1953-1954.
——, "Untilovsk," *Novyj mir,* No. 3 (1928), pp. 41-94.
——, *Vor.* 5th ed. Moscow: Gozisdat, 1936.
Ognev, N., *Iskhod Nikpetoža. Dnevnik Kosti Rjabceva.* Vol. IV of *Sobranie sočinenij.* Moscow: Federacija, 1929.
Oleša, Ju., *Spisok blagodejanij.* Moscow: Federacija, 1931.
——, *Zavist'.* 2d ed. Moscow: Gosizdat, 1931.
Pilnyak, B., *The Volga Falls to the Caspian Sea.* Translated by Charles Malamuth. New York: Cosmopolitan Book Corporation, 1931.
——, *Volga vpadaet v kaspijskoe more.* Moscow: Nedra, 1930.
Remizov, A., "Krestovye sestry." Vol. V of *Sočinenija.* St. Petersburg: Šipovnik, n.d., pp. 13-157.
Sartre, J.-P., *Le mur.* Paris: Gallimard, 1947.
Sobol', A., "Memuary vesnuščatogo čeloveka," Vol. IV of *Sobranie sočinenij.* Moscow: Zemlja i fabrika, 1927, pp. 114-147.
Sologub, F., *Melkij bes.* Vol. VI of *Sobranie sočinenij.* 7th ed. St. Petersburg: Sirin, 1913.
——, *The Little Demon.* Translated by John Cournos and Richard Aldington. London: Martin Secker, 1916. With an Introduction to the English edition by F. Sologub.
Voinova, A. I., *Samocvety.* Moscow: Zemlja i fabrika, 1930.
——, *Semi-Precious Stones.* Translated by Valentine Snow. New York: Jonathan Cape & Harrison Smith, 1931.
——, *Vostok i zapad.* Vol. I. Moscow Moskovskoe tovariščestvo pisatelej, 1933.
Zamjatin, E., *My.* New York: Izdatel'stvo imeni Čekhova, 1952.
Zoščenko, M., *Uvažaemye graždane.* Moscow: Zemlja a fabrika, 1926.

CRITICAL LITERATURE

Ajkhenval'd, B., "O romane B. Pil'njaka 'Volga vpadaet v kaspijskoe more'," *Krasnaja nov',* No. 4 (1931), pp. 178-186.
Amfiteatrov, A. V., "M. N. Al'bov," *Slavnye mertvecy.* Vol. XIV of *Sobranie sočinenij.* St. Petersburg: Samoobrazovanie, 1912, pp. 331-369.
Anciferov, N. P., *Peterburg Dostoevskogo.* Peterburg: Brockgaus, 1923.
Bakhtin, M. M., *Problemy tvorčestva Dostoevskogo.* Leningrad: Priboj, 1929.
Balukhatyj, S. Ja., and Desnickij, V. A. (eds.), *M. Gor'kij: materialy i issledovanija.* Vol. III. Moscow: Akademija nauk SSSR, 1941.
Beardsley, Monroe C., "Dostoevsky's Metaphor of the Underground," *Journal of the History of Ideas,* III, (1942), 265-290.
Bel'čikov, N. F., "Černyševskij i Dostoevskij: iz istorii parodii," *Pečat' i revoljucija,* No. 5 (1928), pp. 35-53.
Beljaev, N., *Garšin.* Moscow: Molodaja gvardija, 1938.
Berdjaev, N. A., *Mirosozercanie Dostoevskogo.* Prague: YMCA Press, 1923.
Berliner, G., *N. G. Černyševskij i ego literaturnye vragi.* Moscow: Gosizdat, 1930.
Bjalik, B. A., "Bor'ba Gor'kogo-khudožnika protiv reakcionnykh idej Dostoevskogo," *Gor'kovskie čtenija: 1949-1950.* Edited by A. M. Egolin, B. V. Mikhajlovskij, S. M. Petrov. Moscow: Akademija nauk SSSR, 1951, pp. 418-465.
Bjalyj, G. A., *V. M. Garšin i literaturnaja bor'ba vos'midesjatykh godov.* Moscow: Akademija nauk SSSR, 1937.

Blackham, H. J., *Six Existentialist Thinkers*. London: Routledge & Kegan Paul Ltd. 1956.

Bljakher, B., "Kniga o vreditelstve," *Na literaturnom postu*, No. 23-24 (1930), pp. 45-49.

Brjusov, V., *Dnevniki: 1891-1910*. Moscow: Sabašnikovy, 1927.

Camus, A., *L'homme révolte*. Paris: Gallimard, 1951.

——, *Le mythe de Sisyphe*. Paris: Gallimard, 1945.

Čebotarevskaja, A. (ed.), *O Fedore Sologube: kritika. stat'i i zametki*. St. Petersburg: Šipovnik, 1911.

Čiževskij, D. I., *Gegel' v Rossii*. Paris: Dom knigi i sovremennye zapiski, 1939.

Čukovskij, K., "Plejada Belinskogo i Dostoevskij," in *Nekrasov: Stat'i i materialy*. Leningrad: Kubuč, 1926, pp. 326-349.

Čulkov, G., *Kak rabotal Dostoevskij*. Moscow: Sovetskij pisatel', 1939.

Dolinin, A. S., "Otrešennyj (k psikhologii tvorčestva F. Sologuba)," *Zavety* No. 7 (1913), pp. 55-85.

——, *V tvorčeskoj laboratorii Dostoevskogo*. Moscow: Sovetskij pisatel', 1947.

Dolinin, A. S. (ed.), *Dostoevskij: Stat'i materialy*, Vols. I-II. Leningrad: Mysl', 1922-5.

El'sberg, Z., *Krizis poputčikov i nastroenija intelligencii*. Leningrad: Priboj, 1930.

Ermilov, V., "Gor'kij i Dostoevskij, *Krasnaja nov'*, No. 4 (1939), pp. 157-177; No. 5-6 (1939), pp. 240-272.

Fagin, N. B., "Dostoevsky's Underground Man," *The Antioch Review*, III, No. 1 (1953), pp. 23-32.

Fondane, Benj., *La Conscience Malheureuse*. Paris: Les Editions Denoël et Steele, 1936.

Gercen, A. I., *Byloe i dumy*. Vol. XIII of *Polnoe sobranie sočinenij i pisem*. Petersburg: Gosizdat, 1919.

Gide, André, *Dostoevsky*. With an introduction by Arnold Bennett. Norfolk, Connecticut: New Directions Books, 1949.

G.I.L., "Dve smerty (Pamjati I. L. Ščeglova-Leont'eva i M. N. Al'bova)," *Istoričeskij vestnik*, CXXV (1911), pp. 227-250.

Gorbov, D., "Opravdanie zavisti," *Novyj mir*, No. 11 (1928), pp. 218-230.

Gor'kij, M., *Istorija russkoj literatury*. Moscow: Gosizdat, 1939.

——, *O literature. Literaturno-kritičeskie stat'i*. Moscow: Sovetskij pisatel', 1953.

——, *Revoljucija i kul'tura: stat'i za 1917*. Berlin: J. Ladyschnikow, n.d.

——, *Stat'i: 1905-1916*. Petrograd: Parus, 1918.

Gornfel'd, A., "'Moi Zapiski' Leonida Andreeva," *Russkoe bogatstvo*, No. 1 (1909), pp. 96-120.

Grossman, L. P., *Dostoevskij na žiznennom puti*. Moscow: Nikitinskie subbotniki, 1928.

——, *Bor'ba za stil'*. Moscow: Nikitinskie subbotniki, 1927.

Gurvič, A., *V poiskakh geroja: literaturno-kritičeskie stat'i*. Moscow: Gosizdat, 1938.

Hegel, G. W. F., *The Phenomenology of Mind*. Trans. J. B. Baillie 2d ed. revised. New York: The Macmillan Co., 1931.

Horkheimer, Max, *Eclipse of Reason*. New York: Oxford University Press, 1947.

Ivanov, V., *Dostojewskij: Tragödie-Mythos-Mystik*. Übersetzung von Alexander Kresling. Tübingen: J. C. B. Mohr, 1932.

Ivanov-Razumnik, *Tvorčestvo i kritika*. Vol. II. St. Petersburg: Prometej, 1911.

——, *O smysle žizni: Fedor Sologub, Leonid Andreev, Lev Šestov*. St. Petersburg: Stasjulevič, 1908.

——, *Russkaja literatura ot semidesjatykh godov do našikh dnej*. 6th ed. revised. Berlin: Skify, 1923.

Kaufmann, W., *Existentialism from Dostoevsky to Sartre*. Edited, with an introduction, preface, and new translation by Walter Kaufmann. New York: Meridian Books, 1956.

Kaun, Alexander, *Leonid Andreev: A Critical Study*. New York: B. W. Huebsch, Inc., 1924.

Kaus, Otto, *Dostojewski und sein Schicksal*. Berlin: E. Laub'sche, 1923.

Khodasevič, V. F., *Nekropol', Vospominanija*. Brussels: Petropolis, 1939.

King, Henry Hall, *Dostoevsky and Andreyev*. Ithaca, N.Y.: The Cornell Alumni News Corp., 1936.

Kierkegaard, S., *Fear and Trembling. The Sickness unto Death*. Translated with Introductions and Notes by Walter Lowrie. New York: Doubleday & Co., 1955.

Kirpotin, V., *Romany Leonida Leonova*. Moscow: Gosizdat, 1932.

Kogan, P. S., *Literatura ètikh let: 1917-1923*. Ivanovo-Voznesensk: Osnova, 1924.

Komarovič, V., "Dostoevskij i šestidesjatniki," *Sovremennyj mir*, No. 1 (1917), pp. 129-139.

——, "Mirovaja garmonija Dostoevskogo," *Atenej*, No. 1-2 (1924), pp. 112-142.

Kranikhfel'd, Vl. P., *V mir idej i obrazov: ètjudy i portrety*. Vol. III. Petrograd: Pečatnyj trud, 1917.

Lednicki, Wacław, *Russia, Poland and the West*. Essays in Literary and Cultural History. London: Roy Publishers, 1954.

Ležnev, A., "O 'Zavisti' Ju. Oleši," *Literaturnye budni*. Moscow: Federacija, 1929, pp. 213-216.

Lukacs, Georg, *Der Russische Realismus in der Weltliteratur*. Berlin: Aufbau-Verlag, 1949.

Lunačarskij, A. V., *Russkaja literatura*. Izbrannye stat'i. Moscow: Gosizdat, 1947.

Manning, C. A., "Dostoevsky and Modern Russian Literature," *Sewanee Review*, XXX (1922), pp. 286-297.

——, "T'ma Andreeva i Zapiski iz podpol'ja Dostoevskogo," *Slavia*, V (1927), pp. 850-852.

Maslenikov, Oleg A., *The Frenzied Poets: Andrey Biely and the Russian Symbolists*. Berkeley: University of California Press, 1952.

Mikhajlovskij, N. K., "Ešče o Garšine i o drugikh," Vol. VI of *Sočinenija*. St. Petersburg: Russkoe bogatstvo, 1897, pp. 328-346.

——, "O Vsevolode Garšine," Vol. VI of *Sočinenija*. St. Petersburg: Russkoe bogatstvo, 1897, pp. 305-328.

Mirsky, D. S., *Contemporary Russian Literature: 1881-1925*. London: Routledge, 1926.

Močul'skij, K., *Dostoevskij: žizn' i tvorčestvo*. Paris, YMCA 1947.

Nietzsche, F., *Der Wille zur Macht*. Vol. XVIII of *Gesammelte Werke*. München: Musarion Verlag, 1926.

Nikolaevskij, B., *Istorija odnogo predatelja*. Berlin: Petropolis, 1932.

Nusinov, I., *Leonid Leonov*. Moscow: Gosizdat, 1935.

——, "Ot 'Untilovska' k 'Soti,'" *Krasnaja nov'*, No. 4 (1932), pp. 156-167.

"Obsuždenie romana Erenburga 'Den' vtoroj'," *Literaturnyj kritik*, No. 7-8 (1934), pp. 283-291.

Oleša, Ju., "Beseda s čitateljami," *Literaturnyj kritik*, No. 12 (1935), pp. 152-165.

——, "Ja smotrju v prošloe," in *Višnevaja kostočka*. Moscow: Sovetskaja literatura, 1933, pp. 70-82.

Otveržennyj, N., *Stirner i Dostoevskij*. Moscow: Golos truda, 1925.

Ovsjaniko-Kulikovskij, D. N. (ed.), *Istorija russkoj literatury XIX veka*. 5 vols. Moscow: Mir, 1910-1911.

Parker, Fan, *Vsevolod Garshin: A Study of a Russian Conscience*. New York: Kings Crown Press, 1946.

Pereverzev, V. F., *Tvorčestvo Dostoevskogo*. 2d ed. revised, Moscow: Gosizdat, 1922.
Phillips, W., "Dostoevsky's Underground Man," Introduction to *The Short Stories of Dostoevsky*. Edited by William Phillips. New York: The Dial Press, 1946.
Poljakova, M., "Dostoevskij v otraženii sovremennosti," *Literatura i marksizm*, No. 6 (1929), pp. 117-145.
Rozanov, V. V., *Legenda o velikom inkvisitore F. M. Dostoevskogo*. Berlin: Razum, 1924.
Sartre, J.-P., *L'existentialisme est un humanisme*. Paris: Les éditions Nagel, 1946.
Šestov, L., *Dostoevskij i Nitše*. Berlin: Skify, 1922.
——, "Preodolenie samoočevidnostej," in *Na vesakh iova*. Paris: Sovremennye zapiski, 1929, pp. 27-93.
Simmons, Ernest J., *Dostoevski: The Making of a Novelist*. New York: Oxford University Press, 1940.
Skaftymov, A., "'Zapiski iz podpol'ja' sredi publicistiki Dostoevskogo," *Slavia*, VIII (1929-1930), 101-117; 312-339.
Stejnberg, A. Z., *Sistema svobody Dostoevskogo*. Berlin: Skify, 1923.
Struve, Gleb, *25 Years of Soviet Russian Literature (1918-1943)*. London. Routledge, 1946.
——, "Leonid Leonov and his 'Skutarevsky,'" *The Slavonic and East European Review*, XII, No. 34 (1933), pp. 190-195.
——, "Novye varianty šigalovščiny. O romanakh Zamjatina, Khaksli i Orvella." *Novyj žurnal*, No. 30 (New York: 1952), pp. 152-163.
——, "Pisatel' nenužnykh tem: tvorčeskaja sud'ba Jurija Oleši," *Novyj žurnal*, No. 25 (New York: 1951), pp. 139-158.
Taminin, T., "E. I. Zamjatin," *Russkie zapiski*, No. 16 (Paris: 1939), pp. 98-108.
Valéry, Paul, *Variété* [I]. Paris: Gallimard. 1948.
Vengerov, S. A., *Kritiko-biografičeskij slovar' russkikh pisatelej i učenykh* (ot načala russkoj obrazovannosti do našikh dnej). Vol. I. St. Petersburg: I. Efron, 1889.
——, (ed.), *Russkaja literatura XX veka: 1890-1910*. 3 vols. Moscow: Mir, 1914-1916.
Volkov, A., *M. Gor'kij i literaturnoe dviženie konca XIX i načala XX veka*. Moscow: Sovetskij pisatel', 1951.
Volynskij, A. L., *Carstvo karamazovykh. N. S. Leskov*. St. Petersburg: Stasjulevič, 1901.
Voronskij, A., "Literaturnye siluèty. III: E. Zamjatin," *Krasnaja nov'*, No. 6 (1922), pp. 304-322.
——, "Leonid Leonov," *Literaturnye tipy*. Moscow: Krug, 1925, pp. 131-149.
Vorovskij, V., *Literaturno-kritičeskie stat'i*. Moscow: Gosizdat, 1948.
Yarmolinsky, A., *Dostoevsky, a Life*. New York: Harcourt, 1934.
Zakrzewski, A., *Podpol'e: psikhologičeskie paralleli*. Kiev: Iskusstvo i pečatnoe delo, 1911.
Zamjatin, E., *Gerbert Uèlls*. Petersburg: Epokha, 1922.
Zelm, Ellinor, *Studien über Vsevolod Garšin*. Charlottenburg: Hoffmann, 1935.

INDEX